CW00386200

Genetic Data and the Law

Research using genetic data raises various concerns relating to privacy protection. Many of these concerns can also apply to research that uses other personal data, but not with the same implications for failure. The norms of exclusivity associated with a private life go beyond the current legal concept of personal data to include genetic data that relate to multiple identifiable individuals simultaneously and anonymous data that could be associated with any number of individuals in different, but reasonably foreseeable, contexts. It is the possibilities and implications of association that are significant, and these possibilities can only be assessed if one considers the interpretive potential of data. They are missed if one fixates upon its interpretive pedigree or misunderstands the meaning and significance of identification. This book demonstrates how the public interest in research using genetic data might be reconciled with the public interest in proper privacy protection.

MARK TAYLOR is a senior lecturer at the University of Sheffield and Deputy Director of the Sheffield Institute for Biotechnological Law and Ethics. His primary research interest concerns the legal and ethical issues raised by scientific developments in genetic testing and screening technologies.

Cambridge Bioethics and Law

This series of books was founded by Cambridge University Press with Alexander McCall Smith as its first editor in 2003. It focuses on the law's complex and troubled relationship with medicine across both the developed and the developing world. In the past twenty years, we have seen in many countries increasing resort to the courts by dissatisfied patients and a growing use of the courts to attempt to resolve intractable ethical dilemmas. At the same time, legislatures across the world have struggled to address the questions posed by both the successes and the failures of modern medicine, while international organisations such as the WHO and UNESCO now regularly address issues of medical law.

It follows that we would expect ethical and policy questions to be integral to the analysis of the legal issues discussed in this series. The series responds to the high profile of medical law in universities, in legal and medical practice, as well as in public and political affairs. We seek to reflect the evidence that many major health-related policy debates in the UK, Europe and the international community over the past two decades have involved a strong medical law dimension. With that in mind, we seek to address how legal analysis might have a trans-jurisdictional and international relevance. Organ retention, embryonic stem cell research, physician assisted suicide and the allocation of resources to fund health care are but a few examples among many. The emphasis of this series is thus on matters of public concern and/or practical significance. We look for books that could make a difference to the development of medical law and enhance the role of medico-legal debate in policy circles. That is not to say that we lack interest in the important theoretical dimensions of the subject, but we aim to ensure that theoretical debate is grounded in the realities of how the law does and should interact with medicine and health care.

Series editors

Professor Margaret Brazier,
University of Manchester

Professor Graeme Laurie,
University of Edinburgh

Professor Richard Ashcroft,
Queen Mary, University of London

Professor Eric M. Meslin,
Indiana University

Titles in the series

Marcus Radetzki, Marian Radetzki and Niklas Juth
Genes and Insurance: Ethical, Legal and Economic Issues

Ruth Macklin
Double Standards in Medical Research in Developing Countries

Donna Dickenson
Property in the Body: Feminist Perspectives

Matti Häyry, Ruth Chadwick, Vilhjálmur Árnason and
Gardar Árnason
The Ethics and Governance of Human Genetic Databases: European Perspectives

Ken Mason
The Troubled Pregnancy: Legal Wrongs and Rights in Reproduction

Daniel Sperling
Posthumous Interests: Legal and Ethical Perspectives

Keith Syrett
Law, Legitimacy and the Rationing of Health Care

Alastair Maclean
Autonomy, Informed Consent and the Law: A Relational Change

Heather Widdows and Caroline Mullen
The Governance of Genetic Information: Who Decides?

David Price
Human Tissue in Transplantation and Research

Matti Häyry
Rationality and the Genetic Challenge: Making People Better?

Mary Donnelly
Healthcare Decision-Making and the Law: Autonomy, Capacity and the Limits of Liberalism

Anne-Maree Farrell, David Price and Muireann Quigley
Organ Shortage: Ethics, Law and Pragmatism

Sara Fovargue
Xenotransplantation and Risk: Regulating a Developing Biotechnology

John Coggon
What Makes Health Public? A Critical Evaluation of Moral, Legal, and Political Claims in Public Health

Anne-Maree Farrell
The Politics of Blood: Ethics, Innovation and the Regulation of Risk

Mark Taylor
Genetic Data and the Law: A Critical Perspective on Privacy Protection

Genetic Data and the Law

A Critical Perspective on Privacy Protection

Mark Taylor

CAMBRIDGE
UNIVERSITY PRESS

CAMBRIDGE UNIVERSITY PRESS
Cambridge, New York, Melbourne, Madrid, Cape Town,
Singapore, São Paulo, Delhi, Mexico City

Cambridge University Press
The Edinburgh Building, Cambridge CB2 8RU, UK

Published in the United States of America by
Cambridge University Press, New York

www.cambridge.org
Information on this title: www.cambridge.org/9781107007116

First published 2012

Printed in the United Kingdom at the University Press, Cambridge

A catalogue record for this publication is available from the British Library

Library of Congress Cataloguing in Publication Data
Taylor, Mark, 1973 Mar. 26–
   Genetic data and the law : a critical perspective on privacy protection / Mark
Taylor.
      p.   cm. – (Cambridge bioethics and law)
   ISBN 978-1-107-00711-6 (Hardback)
   1. Medical genetics–Law and legislation.   2. Medical records–Access
control.   3. Genetic engineering–Law and legislation.   4. Biotechnology–Law
and legislation.   5. Human chromosome abnormalities–Diagnosis–Law and
legislation.   6. Human genetics–Government policy.   7. Privacy, Right of.
8. Data protection–Law and legislation.   I. Title.
   K3611.R43T39 2012
   344.04′196–dc23

                                                                              2011042621

ISBN 978-1-107-00711-6 Hardback

For Poppy

Contents

Part II   The critique   101

Preface

This book represents a collection of thoughts that date back to the completion of my doctoral studies in 2004. Given its genesis, this seems an appropriate time and place to thank publicly my Ph.D. supervisor, Professor Roger Brownsword, for the extremely generous, illuminating, and supportive, advice he offered me during that period and has continued to offer me since.

Since I wrote my Ph.D. thesis on the subject of genetic discrimination and contractual freedom, I have weaved, or perhaps stumbled, my way towards a broader position on the regulation of genetic data in research. I am especially keen to encourage a critical evaluation of the weight placed upon the idea of 'personal data' in the area of privacy protection. Frankly, I think it is a concept that has been forced to shoulder a disproportionate burden of work and it has made a rather convenient vehicle to transport us from some difficult questions. Rather than continue to pretend that this concept, and the regulatory frameworks that orbit it, are up to the task of fully protecting privacy, and also striking the right balance between the (at times) competing interests engaged by research uses of genetic data, we should recognise both its strengths and its weaknesses, and strengthen weaknesses where we can while, at all times, ensuring that apparent strengths do not undermine our ability to qualify particular protections where appropriate.

The position that I seek to describe in what follows is one that has been reached through linking together thinking stimulated by many different people and involvement in a number of different research projects. Some of the ideas have already found expression, in piecemeal fashion, through a number of articles over the past several years. While it is impossible personally to acknowledge everybody that has progressed my thinking in this area, I sincerely hope that they each realise I appreciate my indebtedness to them and am truly grateful for their support, their insight, and, quite often, their challenge. It would not have been possible to bring together a number of the ideas that have found previous published expression without the generous agreement of the editors of the respective journals. Although most of the ideas have inevitably been developed and revised before inclusion here, there are, at times, particular recidivist paragraphs or sections that have escaped reform. They are reproduced here in their original form and I am grateful for the permission to do so. To some greater or lesser extent, Chapter 5 draws upon an argument first presented in M. J. Taylor, 'Data protection, shared (genetic) data and genetic discrimination', *Medical Law International* 8(1) (2006), 51–77. Chapter 7 draws upon the section I authored for a paper written with Professor Deryck Beyleveld, and published most recently as D. Beyleveld and M. J. Taylor, 'Patents for biotechnology and the data protection of biological samples and shared data', in Jean Herveg (ed.), *The Protection of Medical Data: Challenges of the 21st Century* (Louvain-la-Neuve: Anthemis, 2008), 127–48. A shorter version was earlier published as D. Beyleveld and M. J. Taylor, 'Data protection, genetics and patents for biotechnology', *European Journal of Health Law* 14(2) (2007), 177–87. Chapter 8 draws upon an argument first described in M. J. Taylor, 'Problems of practice and principle if centring law reform on the concept of genetic discrimination', *European Journal of Health Law* 1(4) (2004), 365–80; and Chapters 2 and 9 both contain thoughts first expressed (by me at least) in M. J. Taylor, 'Health research, data protection and the public interest in notification', *Medical Law Review* 19(2) (2011), 267–303. I am also glad to acknowledge that the idea for the cover picture, an anatomical theatre as a metaphor for the public examination of 'internal' aspects of human life occurring when research uses genetic data, was an idea used by Professor Giuseppe Testa in a seminar while visiting the University of Sheffield.

I am particularly grateful to colleagues and students, past and present, who have helped me to clarify and further my thinking on these issues. Specific and heartfelt thanks must be extended to Professor Deryck Beyleveld, Professor Roger Brownsword, Dr Fiona Douglas, Jamie Grace, Dr Richard Kirkham, Dr Ruth Stirton, David Townend and Daniel Wand. Special mention must go to Professor Graeme Laurie who has been typically generous with both his comments and his encouragement. Each of these individuals has, in various ways, been crucial to bringing these ideas forward in their current form. In should be made clear, however, that none of them is responsible for any errors that remain in the final version. Finally, I should thank Dr Natasha Semmens and Mrs Natasha Taylor. For me, together, they represent every reason to do anything.

1   Introduction

The Human Genome Project took approximately fourteen years to complete,[1] involved collaboration between twenty different centres based in six different countries,[2] and cost United States tax payers alone approximately $3 billion.[3] When James Watson's genome was sequenced in 2007 it cost approximately $1 million.[4] In 2009 a company called Complete Genomics announced that it would be able to read entire human genomes for $5,000.[5] Sequencing technology is now within the reach of many researchers and the availability of cheap sequencing is continuing to spread. At least one of the companies currently offering cancer genome analysis for research purposes is now reported to be planning to offer the service to patients and their doctors.[6]

As genetic testing enters primary healthcare there is the potential for large-scale, systematic collection of genetic data.[7] That data will be valuable for research purposes and questions about secondary uses of the data will have to be addressed. This development in the primary healthcare context will be taking place at the same time as there is an unprecedented growth in biobanks and research collections of genetic

---

[1] The project started in 1990 and the finished version of the euchromatic human genome was published in 2004. International Human Genome Sequencing Consortium, 'Finishing the euchromatic sequence of the human genome', *Nature* 431 (21 October 2004), 931–45.

[2] International Human Genome Sequencing Consortium, 'Finishing the euchromatic sequence of the human genome', 931–45.

[3] National Human Genome Research Institute, National Institute for Health, 'The Human Genome Project completion: frequently asked questions' (30 October 2010). www.genome.gov/11006943.

[4] P. Aldhous, 'Genome sequencing falls to $5000', *New Scientist* (6 February 2009).

[5] Aldhous, 'Genome Sequencing falls to $5000', although the question of whether routine genome sequencing can yet be done quite that cheaply may be debated. One laboratory that routinely sequences cancer genomes estimates the cost to be approximately $30,000. See E. Singer, 'Cancer genomics: Deciphering the genetics behind the disease', *Technology Review* (1 June 2011).

[6] Singer, 'Cancer genomics'.

[7] It is predicted that, for one type of cancer sufferer at least, genetic testing will become a routine part of informing patient care. See Singer 'Cancer genomics'.

data. It was estimated in 2009 that there were over 400 biobanks in Europe alone.[8] That was likely to be a conservative estimate even at the time.[9] As research biobanks gather strength, and the prospect of the regular and widespread collection of genetic data within the primary care context edges ever closer, individuals are themselves accessing direct-to-consumer genetic tests and they are beginning to publish the genetic information they discover online. Websites such as 23andme provide a personal genome service, offering a genetic testing service for over 100 different traits and diseases as well as information about ancestry.[10] Other sites, such as the Personal Genome Project, seek to recruit individuals willing to share genetic information openly through public profile pages.[11] All of this data is of potential significance within its original context, and with the possibilities of widespread access, relative permanence and increased future inter-operability between information platforms, the significance of the data shared now is likely only to grow over time.

There are international collaborations, such as P^3G,[12] that have as a core goal the facilitation of collaboration between biobanks. As genetic data research benefits from very large-scale datasets, it will undoubtedly be through such international efforts, and large-scale collaborations, that much of the promise of genetic research and future improvement in healthcare will be delivered. Alongside the hope and optimism there are, of course, concerns. Within the context of informational privacy, these might be divided crudely into two categories: those associated with unwanted access and those associated with unwanted uses of data. Security breach and unauthorised acquisition of genetic data are, of course, always a possibility. Unwanted access can, however, extend beyond the unauthorised.

Whether particular access, to particular data, for particular purposes is considered desirable is often a value judgment and is likely to be subject to a variety of, at times conflicting, views. These views might not even be stable over time, as people's attitudes are affected by personal experiences, the reported experiences of others and other kinds of education (and perhaps even misinformation). In a situation characterised by complex, conflicting and potentially unstable

---

[8] Editorial, 'Biobanks need pharma', *Nature* 461 (24 September 2009), 448.

[9] Over 400 biobanks are currently (June 2011) listed on the Biobanking and Biomolecular Resources Research Infrastructure (BBMRI) catalogue. www.bbmri.eu.

[10] 23andme.com.   [11] www.personalgenomes.org.

[12] Public Population Project in Genomics. www.p3gobservatory.org.

preferences, how does one determine the 'proper' access to genetic data for the purposes of health research?

In recent history, the preferred answer has tended to be that, whatever the potential benefits for others or society more generally, an individual's own preferences on participation in health research should be respected. There are many good reasons for the dominance that the doctrine of informed consent has come to assume in this context. It needs to be expressly recognised, however, that – perhaps particularly in the case of health research using genetic data – there are limits to the ability of 'informed consent' to account adequately for *all* relevant preferences. There will, for example, be occasions when an individual's informed consent cannot be sought for practical reasons. If an individual cannot be asked to express a preference, then 'informed consent' is an inadequate tool by which her preferences might be judged. Alternatively, it might be that, at the time the data is collected, there is no more than the vaguest notion of what, precisely, it might be used for and to whom access might need to be granted. Any consent obtained in such circumstances can only be broad and general, and effectively incapable of expressing any detailed preferences on questions not yet considered. There may also be other occasions where the interests of others are so significantly implicated in the choices concerning access and use of data that to pretend the individual from whom consent is sought would be expressing their preference in a social vacuum would be to betray the interests, and potentially deny the preferences, of others.

These challenges to the adequacy of informed consent to provide a complete answer to the question of how one tackles the difficulties of conflicting preferences, and account for the interests of all implicated by decisions on research use of genetic data, are not posed *exclusively* by research use of genetic data. There is much about genetic data, however, as well as the kind of research that can make effective use of it, which makes these challenges particularly acute.

Genetic data

Genetic data is a difficult term to pin down. Throughout subsequent analysis, I will be relying upon a broad understanding of the idea. In fact, the conception of genetic data that I will be relying upon is broad enough to encompass many different forms of data, each capable of yielding many different kinds of personal information beyond that which might typically be described as 'genetic information'. Given subsequent use of this broad description of genetic data, one might wonder why I persist in maintaining a focus upon *genetic* data at all: why not broaden the analysis to include all personal data, or at least, all personal health information? It will be seen that I do in fact tend to a particular position on the concept of 'personal data' as such. Analysis of the term 'personal data' is, however, best done in a context and genetic data provides a very suitable context in which to study the privacy protection currently provided to personal health data in a research context.

Genetic data's suitability as a case-study depends not only on the fact that decisions about research use can have implications that extend far beyond the individual research participant. The critique of privacy protection that I will advance relies upon recognising a particular relationship between the ideas of 'data' and 'information.' Specifically, I will describe information as a composite concept: the generation of information relies upon a particular interpretive framework being applied to data. Understanding the significance of fluid interpretive frameworks to the relationship between data and information is key to understanding the limitations associated with the law's current protection of privacy. The *distinction* between data and information is a distinction that genetic data is well placed to illustrate.

Genetic data provides an excellent example of data that might often, and plausibly, be placed within multiple, shifting, interpretive frameworks. The same genetic data might, in different contexts, over different periods of time, come to be understood to provide information about many different things, relating to many different persons. It is this *interpretive potential* of genetic data that helps to demonstrate the limitations of the current regulatory system as well as to understanding the multitude of different preferences that might be expressed regarding its access and use. In addition to its suitability as a vehicle to drive a more general critique, there are other reasons why genetic data in particular might provide a particularly suitable case-study.

Genetic science, particularly during the twentieth Century, came to be associated with some very dark moments in human history. The legacy of eugenic programmes, associated in the minds of many primarily with Nazi Germany but supported in less extreme form across Europe and North America, has cast a long shadow over science and the invocation of Science to support public policy agendas. What is more, through some more recent, and quite remarkable, achievements in genetic science – often associated with the hype that can accompany major public investment – research using genetic data has consolidated a contemporary perception that has heightened the significance associated with its access and use.

It is important that genetic data is seen to be subject to appropriate privacy protection. It is important that there is appropriate privacy protection not only for the sake of those individuals whose privacy might otherwise be infringed. It is important that genetic data is *seen to be* subject to appropriate privacy protection for the sake of those who rely upon participants' trust in the security and integrity of the research process. Research using genetic data is often reliant upon voluntary contribution and if participants lose confidence in the ability of the regulatory system to ensure their privacy is suitably assured, then this may have an impact upon their participation. Genetic data, thus, brings into particularly stark focus a number of things about privacy protection, many of which perhaps could be said about other personal data, but not always with the same implications for failure.

The legal protection of genetic privacy

Access to, and use of, genetic data for research purposes is regulated differently across the world. Also, genetic privacy protection *outside* the context of research may have implications for individual attitudes towards participation in research using genetic data. Concerns about the future uses that employers, insurers, government agencies, or one's friends and family might make of genetic data might discourage individuals from genetic testing in *any* context. A concern that individuals not be unduly discouraged from accessing information about their own genetic status, and not be subject to unfair stigmatisation or discrimination as a result of such access, has led a number of regulatory authorities to take steps to ensure that genetic privacy is protected and this protection is often directed at access and use outside of the research context.

The precise nature of the protection found necessary or desirable varies considerably around the world. This is not particularly surprising and might represent an appropriately tailored response to local needs. Countries reliant upon private healthcare insurance to meet citizens' healthcare needs might, for example, take a different position from those that have healthcare systems free at point of care, funded through public taxation. There is no need, nor space, here to undertake a comprehensive survey of different regulatory positions but a couple of relatively recent proposals, both in the United States, might serve to make the point. The state of Massachusetts has recently seen a 'Genetic Bill of Rights' proposed to State legislators. Similarly, the States of California and Vermont are considering introducing legislation that would protect individuals' genetic information in circumstances that go beyond those recognised by the relevant Federal Law. None of these proposals is quite the same as another.[13]

The inconsistency in the approach towards regulating genetic privacy, with some legislators adopting (subtly different) bespoke legislation, and some relying upon more general privacy laws, is creating a situation of bewildering complexity. The complexity alone is creating enormous uncertainty, and no small amount of difficulty, for many researchers, and not least amongst these are those wishing to conduct international research.

When national inconsistencies challenge international co-operation, one might consider the instruments available to international lawyers to move the legal landscape, incrementally, towards a position of some harmony. There are a number of international legal standards that have application to medical research that involves people, or biological material taken from people, in the research process. When standards apply directly to *clinical* research[14] their concern is with research that involves people. They do not have, at the heart of their concern, research that only involves *data* that relates to people. The legal framework with perhaps the most practical significance for international research using 'only' genetic data is currently the law of data protection.

One important example of a relevant international legal standard in the context of data protection law is the EU Data Protection Directive 95/46/EC. The current framework of data protection adopted by a number of countries, across the EU but also beyond, implements the standards represented by this Directive. It represents a binding legal commitment by members of the European Union and is an important standard against which legal frameworks are judged for those wishing to receive data from the European Union.

The Directive relies upon the key concept of 'personal data' to establish its scope and application. This idea, and the associated idea of personal information, is one that is also found within other important international standards concerned with privacy protection. Unfortunately, the idea of 'personal data' is not compatible with appropriate privacy protection – at least, not in the area of research using genetic data. The idea is ill equipped to capture the full range of ways in which

---

[13] D. Vorhaus, 'Is the Genetic Rights Movement Picking Up Steam?', *Genomics Law Report* (16 March 2011). www.genomicslawreport.com/index.php/2011/03/16/is-the-genetic-rights-movement-picking-up-steam/.

[14] Such as that provided by the EU Clinical Trial Directive (2001/20/EC).

privacy might be affected by research using genetic data and the framework of privacy protection built around the idea is incapable of accounting for all relevant interests or preferences.

One of the problems associated with the concept of personal data is that it tends to assume that there will be a single identifiable individual to whom personal data will 'relate' *and* that this individual's privacy is only at risk for as long as they are identifiably associated with that data. These are both assumptions that can be readily challenged within the context of research use of genetic data. They are, however, also assumptions that sit comfortably with the widely adopted mechanisms of 'consent' and 'anonymisation' as ways to protect fundamental rights and freedoms, including the right to privacy. The Data Protection Directive 95/46/EC has effectively consolidated the mechanisms of 'ask' or 'anonymise' as key routes towards lawful processing of personal data. The emphasis placed upon these two mechanisms is unfortunate for privacy protection.

In order to challenge the adequacy of consent and anonymisation as regulatory expectations, while continuing to recognise their importance for the protection of individual privacy in some cases, one might demonstrate the inability of the concept of 'personal data' either to recognise or to protect the full range of privacy preferences on questions of access and use of genetic data in a number of broadly applicable circumstances. Data protection should supplement these traditional mechanisms of protection in those cases where they are inadequate to the task. It should also seek to do so in a way that might bring *increased* certainty, consistency and transparency to the regulatory arena.

Assessing privacy protection

Not only is privacy itself a contested concept but the appropriateness of privacy protection can only be judged when it has been placed alongside other affected interests in a particular scenario. This introduces a number of variables into what is already a complex judgment. The *relative* significance of any privacy infringement can only be assessed according to a particular scheme of values when the practical implications of the infringement are understood: privacy infringement 'X' in situation 'A' might ordinarily be considered impermissible but, if in situation 'B' infringement 'X' is necessary in order to protect more significant interest 'Y', then the prevention of privacy infringement 'X' may be inappropriate. Without constructing a coherent world-view, acceptable by all as representative of the correct values in the correct measure, how might one assess the appropriateness of a legal framework designed to protect certain preferences regarding access to, and use of, genetic data? What is more, how can one embark on this impossible task without first obtaining agreement on the, not undisputed, question of what is meant by privacy?

If one is to maintain confidence in a regulatory framework, then the individuals subject to regulation must be reasonably content that the things that matter to them are *at least* taken into account by the regulatory process. For this reason, I adopt a definition of privacy that places the patterns of behaviour and *preferences* of individuals, relative to access and use of information, at its core. I suggest that the first step towards a realistic assessment of the appropriateness of any legal framework, intended to protect privacy, must be to consider whether it is capable of even accounting for particular patterns and preferences. These patterns and preferences regarding access to genetic data I call 'norms of exclusivity'.

If a legal framework is incapable of bringing particular norms into view, then it is necessarily incapable of appropriately assessing the relative significance of the preferences that they represent. *If* the full range of relevant interests *were* accounted for by a regulatory system, then the next step would be to determine whether the assessment of relative significance was defensible according to a particular normative framework. Next, one might consider whether, if protection was to be *effective*, the protection identified as appropriate could be delivered in practice. In this book, I intend to demonstrate how, in many cases, the existing legal framework can be critiqued according to its inability to take even the first step towards adequate privacy protection: the concept of 'personal data' is incapable of accounting for the norms of exclusivity regarding research use of genetic data.

Public cf. private interest

If the argument is successful, then it has implications beyond demonstrating the inability of the current legal framework to protect the full range of individual privacy preferences. It has implications also for the ability of the existing framework satisfactorily to protect the public interest in research using genetic data. This is not only because a failure to protect privacy may undermine participation in research projects, although that is a distinct possibility. It is because there is a public interest in appropriate privacy protection itself: the public interest is served by the proper protection of privacy.

The suggestion that the public interest might lie in proper privacy protection might strike some as odd. After all, the public interest is often presented as a foil to private interests. While the relationship they share is undoubtedly complex, and at times it may well be fractious, it is perfectly proper to suggest that the public interest is served by the proper protection of privacy. 'Proper' privacy protection is assessed by a value judgment in a way similar to how public interest is assessed: a consistent world-view will reconcile their demands. This is not to suggest that each is simply or inevitably qualified by the other. This may be part of their relationship, but there is more to it than that. *From an individual's perspective*, if there are particular private interests recognised to be worthy of protection, then, all other things being equal, she must prefer a society in which she is protected. From a societal perspective, the public interest will lie in preserving and promoting reasonable accounts of preferred societies. Put crudely, one might respond to the question 'What is in the public interest?' by asking 'What kind of society do you prefer?' *If* agreement could be reached on the latter question, then that agreement would provide an answer to the former.

In the absence of agreement to the latter question, the public interest lies in finding a way to adjudicate legitimately between competing preferences. *Legitimacy* requires, minimally, that these competing preferences be *accounted for* within the regulatory process. The existence and nature of different preferences is a matter of fact to be investigated and their relative significance a matter of value to be debated. The point is, however, that if preferences are to be overridden or trumped in any circumstance, then the *acknowledgment* of those interests is an important precursor to a legitimate decision. If an individual or group is negatively affected by a decision or circumstance, then acceptance of the hardship will be influenced by the perception of whether the process has taken the interests of that individual or group into reasonable account.

Admittedly, legitimacy requires more than simple transparency. Ultimately, people have no reason to accept authority unless they perceive that acceptance to be instrumental to protection of things that they value. If their preferences were to be systematically overridden on a regular basis, then the fact that they were transparently acknowledged by a system before being overridden would provide little comfort or reason for future confidence. Being able to account *reasonably* for the broadest ranges of preferences does, however, first require that regulatory decisions are able to account for interests so that they might satisfy them where they can. Accounting for their interests and preferences also provides people with a way into an argument if they think that their position is not properly being understood. Where it is impossible to reconcile competing demands to everyone's satisfaction, then reasonable account also implies that it is possible to justify the decision to override particular interests in terms that would be acceptable to a reasonable person. For these reasons, there is a *public* interest in the *proper* protection of privacy in research using genetic data. This public interest cannot be fully served by the idea of 'personal data'.

Structure

This book is divided into three sections. Part I, 'The context', attempts to set the scene for subsequent critique. It describes, in Chapter 2, the contested nature of privacy, in Chapter 3, the alternative ways in which the term genetic data might be understood, and, in Chapter 4, the existing legal framework available to protect privacy in research using genetic data. Part II, 'The critique', offers a critical perspective. It focuses upon the legal framework established by the European Data Protection Directive 95/46/EC and challenges its reliance upon the concept of 'personal data'. The limitations of the concept are considered in Chapters 5 and 6. Chapter 5 underlines the limitations that follow from the fact that genetic data is held in common between people. Chapter 6 seeks to underline the significance that genetic data retains, and the preferences regarding access and use that it might attract, even if it is not 'identifiable' (as the term is currently understood by law). Throughout this section, while the European Data Protection Directive is taken as a prime exemplar of a regulatory approach that orbits around the term 'personal data', comments made have significance for privacy protecting frameworks that are based upon similar ideas of 'personal data' or 'personal information'. Part II also includes, in Chapter 7, a critical consideration of the information/sample distinction and, in Chapter 8, a critical consideration of the suggestion that any of the limitations identified to this point should be addressed through bespoke genetic privacy protection. Part III, 'The consequences', seeks in a single chapter to consider the implications for analysis for the future of data protection legislation and for appropriate privacy protection in the context of research using genetic data. The proposals made throughout the book are brought together and certain suggestions made for reforms. These reforms include additional responsibilities to account for a wider range of preferences (including those relating to certain third parties and de-identified data) but within a regulatory environment that ensures that *all* responsibilities are not only much clearer, but also more explicitly *proportionate* to the research in question. The uncertainty surrounding the current framework is unhelpful to research and it is important that research using genetic data is facilitated where it is in the public interest to do so. Protection of the public interest in research is entirely consistent with appropriate privacy protection but not with the current fixation upon the idea of 'personal data'.

Part I

The context

2 Privacy

Within any society there are certain 'rules of engagement' that exist between individuals and between groups. Often implicit, sometimes uncertain, these rules guide social interactions in a similar way that road signs guide traffic: imperfectly and not without a degree of occasional misunderstanding and mistake. Privacy is a word used to describe a host of such patterns and preferences. As with road traffic management, the idea of privacy is (more or less) global, but the local prevalence, penetrance and expression can vary considerably. As a result, privacy is a rather difficult idea to pin down. This chapter begins with a consideration of the idea and an explanation of what I intend to imply through the use of the word. The process of settling upon a particular understanding of privacy, from amongst many possible alternatives, is one that will not involve the consideration of any legal definition; the law is best as a slave and not a master. If it appears later that key terms, such as privacy, are being used in a way that is out of step with a legal definition, then I will consider that a reason as much for reviewing the law as for reconsidering my word-usage.

Having established a working understanding of the term privacy, its relationship with the 'public interest' will be briefly considered. It is suggested that a false dichotomy is sometimes portrayed between the two ideas, and the relationship between them is, while in reality often difficult, ideally mutually supportive. Privacy plays an important part in establishing the conditions that make public life possible. More than this, privacy is part of the infrastructure that enables a *particular kind* of public life to exist. If there is to be a public interest in anything at all, then there must surely be a public interest in preserving the conditions necessary for that life: in maintaining the infrastructure necessary to support the preferred models of relations between persons.

As there is a public interest in proper privacy protection, so also those mechanisms – enshrined within law or adopted as responses to legal requirements – that balance or adjudicate between conflicting preferences in the name of the public interest should take full account of the privacy interests engaged. This is not only so that privacy might be properly protected, but also so that it might be *seen* to be so. As we shall see, different people may see a protection of privacy requiring quite different things. If they are to remain persuaded that the regulatory system is capable of taking *their* privacy into account, then it would be better for any interference to be justified. In other words, accounting for the broadest range of privacy interests, within a public decision-making process, will support the legitimacy of that system and its conception of the public interest.

In the context of voluntary participation in research, the importance of people appreciating that relevant decision-making processes are respectful of their privacy interests goes beyond theoretical questions of legitimacy. If people do not perceive their interests to be duly considered, then they may be discouraged from submitting their interests to those processes in the future. In the case of research using genetic data, this may discourage voluntary participation in research. This chapter finishes with a brief consideration of the range of interests that any relevant system of governance may need to account for within research governance. Failing to account for the range of interests that individuals perceive to be engaged by research using genetic data may undermine not only their privacy, but also the perceived legitimacy of the relevant governance arrangements. It is important that we get privacy protection right, not only for the important sake of privacy itself, but also for the sake of the research using genetic data that is dependent upon its proper protection.

What is privacy?

Capturing an accurate description of privacy seems at times rather like netting fog. Not only is it amongst a class of things, like time or electricity, that is more easily experienced (and lost) than explained; it also extends in many different directions simultaneously. The closer you consider it, the greater the chances of becoming fixated upon some particular aspect of it and losing sight of other possible dimensions. Some commentators, noting the tensions and conflicts inherent within multiple attempts to explicate the meaning of the word, have despaired whether it is an idea that we might usefully address at all.[1]

A survey of literature associated with a wide range of disciplines in 1995 led Newell to conclude that, despite (or perhaps because of) many

---

[1] R. C. Post, 'Three concepts of privacy', *Georgetown Law Journal* 89 (2001), 2087–98 at 2087.

years of academic consideration, disagreements about the concept remained fundamental. Newell noted that we had yet to reach a place where we might even agree on whether 'privacy' is a means, an end, a condition, an attitude or a behaviour.[2] Despite the enduring disagreement, Newell's extensive survey of the literature[3] did reveal one consensus: privacy has a value.[4]

I will not try to defend this particular observation myself. I think the amount written about privacy, the importance that is attributed to privacy within human rights discourse, the shared experiences of anyone who has ever considered their privacy to be violated, support the idea that privacy has a value. I rely upon the work of others, such as Newell, to provide a more robust defence to this intuition. It is remarkable, however, that we appear able to agree that privacy has a value so much more easily than we can agree what that value is, or even, precisely, what it is to which we are attributing that value.[5]

In the face of such uncertainty and controversy we might simply agree to disagree – to recognise that privacy is important to us all and agree to move beyond any differences around how to define the term for the sake of its protection. This may seem a promising strategy if only each of us were then able to retire into our own respective worlds and carry on enjoying our own version of privacy with nothing more to do with each other. The difficulty with this is, of course, we do not lead such isolated lives and interaction can leave individual ideas of privacy vulnerable. What is more, we tend to hope that the vulnerable things of value to us will be protected.[6]

We turn to others, and in particular to those in positions of relative power, to provide protections we are unable to provide for ourselves. If we hope for regulation capable of protecting privacy, then we must also hope for a legal system that will do more than leave it to individuals individually or independently to determine the breadth and depth of valid privacy claims. Successful regulation requires a degree of clarity,

---

[2] P. B. Newell, 'Perspectives on privacy', *Journal of Environmental Psychology* 15 (1995), 87–104 at 87.

[3] *Ibid.*, 98.

[4] In some circumstances, that which privacy facilitates is intensely disliked. This does not mean that it is not valued, it simply means that the value attributed to privacy can be either positive or negative.

[5] For an example of relevant disagreements, see J. Q. Whitman, 'The Two Western Cultures of Privacy: Dignity versus Liberty', *Yale Law Journal* 113 (2004) 1153–1221 at 1153.

[6] This is true whether we regard things as valuable in themselves or valuable as means to ends. I am not then entering the debate here over whether privacy has an intrinsic value or is only valuable instrumentally.

generality, consistency and relative constancy.[7] If privacy is to be regulated in a clear, general and consistent manner, then we must strive to take at least some of the elasticity out of the term.[8] We must also, in turn, seek to agree some understanding of the relationship between privacy and other valued interests, but this is a second-order task; there is a material difference between defining certain conduct outside the scope of a valid privacy claim and, alternatively, considering an otherwise valid privacy claim to be overridden by other interests.[9] Is it possible to identify, within the many, various and at times conflicting accounts of privacy, any kind of consensus to take forward for the purposes of, at least, prima facie legal protection?

In 1977, Stephen Margulis attempted to provide a consensus definition of privacy. After a comprehensive survey of the literature available at the time, Margulis proposed that 'privacy, as a whole or in part, represents control over transactions between person(s) and other(s), the ultimate aim of which is to enhance autonomy and/or to minimize vulnerability'.[10]

In later work, he modified his position when he recognised that his early attempt at a consensus definition 'failed to note that, in the privacy literature, control over transactions usually entailed limits on or regulation of access to self (Allen, 1998), sometimes to groups (e.g., Altman, 1975), and occasionally to larger collectives such as organisations (e.g., Westin, 1967)'.[11] A reworked attempt at a consensus definition might then suggest that, in whole or part, privacy 'represents control over transactions between person(s) and others, limiting or

---

[7] L. Fuller, *The Morality of Law* (New Haven and London: Yale University Press, 1969 [1964]). Lon Fuller suggested that the legal enterprise of subjecting human conduct to the governance of rules depended upon those rules being general, promulgated, prospective, clear, free from contradiction, relatively constant, not requiring the impossible, and administered in practice consistent with the law in the books.

[8] Anita Allen has described privacy as both a 'uniquely' and a 'notoriously' elastic term. A. L. Allen, *Uneasy Access: Privacy for Women in a Free Society* (Totowa, NJ: Rowman and Littlefield, 1988), 5 and 16.

[9] This is an important distinction but it is not as simple as I present it here. There will be times when other interests are actually said to be important to the decision *whether* to classify an action as prima facie 'private'. An example of the problem has been raised in the context of domestic violence. Here, if one understands the activity to be 'private', then one's concept of privacy will inform the conditions under which intervention may be justified. One response is to propose the elimination of the public/private distinction. Another is to reconceptualise privacy itself. K. A. Kelly, *Domestic Violence and the Politics of Privacy* (Ithaca, NY: Cornell University Press, 2003).

[10] S. T. Margulis, 'Conceptions of privacy: current status and next steps', *Journal of Social Issues* 33(3) (1977), 5–21 at 10.

[11] S. T. Margulis, 'Privacy as a social issue and a behavioural concept', *Journal of Social Issues* 9(2) (2003), 243–61 at 245.

regulating access to individuals or groups, with the ultimate aim of enhancing autonomy or minimizing vulnerability'.

Perhaps unsurprisingly, the ideas put forward by Margulis have attracted strong criticism. It would be possible to challenge this 'consensus' definition on a number of grounds. For example, the definition not only assumes that there *is* 'an ultimate aim' of privacy, but actually dares to identify it. If the former is contestable, then the latter is hugely contentious. Also, the definition states that privacy is about 'control'. This idea has itself been disputed. It is, however, an idea of privacy that I intend to pursue – albeit with a particular idea of what is implied by the idea of control – and so it will be necessary to consider some of the objections to it.

Privacy as control

One of the most significant monographs concerned with genetic privacy is Graeme Laurie's book *Genetic Privacy*. Laurie rejects 'control-based' concepts of privacy for at least two important reasons. Owing to the importance of the book, and the strength of its conclusions more generally, it is important to spend a little time addressing the concept of privacy that it advocates and its rejection of the kind of concept that I will come to propose. It is also important to note that the discussion of privacy under consideration here is largely focused upon what has been described as 'informational privacy'. Privacy claims can, of course, apply to more than just information.[12] What is more, the comments that I wish to make about privacy do, I believe, have application to more than just informational privacy. However, when considering research uses of genetic data, it will be informational privacy that is our primary concern. Also, if I am wrong to suggest that informational privacy may be defined in terms of control over access to information, then I will be wrong when I come to extend my preferred concept of privacy to other aspects of research use of genetic data.

First, Laurie cites with approval an objection made by Parent to control-based theories in general:

Parent has argued that such theories fail because they are both conceptually and empirically too broad: 'To define privacy as the control over (all) information about oneself implies that every time I walk or eat in public my privacy is compromised.'[13]

---

[12] I discuss the different dimensions of privacy more fully later in this chapter in the section titled 'Norms and the transactional variable'.
[13] G. Laurie, *Genetic Privacy: A Challenge to Medico-Legal Norms* (Cambridge: Cambridge University Press, 2002), 53.

A second, and particularly significant, objection to control-based theories, cited by Laurie, is that,

> [i]f someone cannot exercise control, control-based theories offer us no option but to conclude that privacy has been compromised, yet this might not be the case.[14]

Taking these two criticisms in turn: even if we were to concede, for the sake of argument, that a control-based concept of privacy *must* hold that control is to be exercised over *all* information about oneself, then it is not clear why this would be too broad either conceptually or empirically to be successful. Certainly, *if* one were to assume that control must be understood to be a general and overriding right exercised by individuals determining access to any and all information about themselves, then that would be hugely problematic. But control can take many forms and it can be exercised in many different ways. If we look a little closer at the example of walking or eating in public, then we might point out that *relevant* control in such circumstances might only extend to preventing the recording of such activities through concealed equipment. I am not actually seeking to establish this as the relevant standard; I am only seeking to illustrate that the criticism itself assumes a rather narrow idea of control. Control *could* be exercised, surrendered, suspended or delegated in many different ways *by* many different people. What is more, this criticism seems to imply that privacy has an absolute value. Even if privacy did demand (a relatively narrow kind of) control over *all* information about an individual, then it does not follow that others' interests and freedoms might not trump that control in certain circumstances, for example when in a public space. This particular criticism seems to assume rather too much both about how a theory of privacy tied to ideas of control would play out in a particular social context, and about how any entitlement to control information would be understood to engage with other interests.

Moving on to consider the second criticism of 'control-based' theories, one might initially note that the criticism appears simply to beg the question against any theory that does not accord privacy to someone incapable of exercising any control. It is assumed, for example, that a comatose patient *does* have a privacy that might be infringed and, therefore, any failure to recognise this is a failing in a theory of privacy. Why, however, should such an assumption be made? It might be that any intuition that accords the comatose patient privacy is not representative of the most coherent reading of a complicated and contested

---

[14] *Ibid.*, 54.

concept. Even if, again for the sake of argument, we might accept that comatose patients (or others lacking capacity to control) do possess a privacy capable of compromise, then a similar response to the criticism might be made to the one offered above: it seems to assume a relatively narrow idea of control. Within Margulis' definition he seeks to assert only that privacy 'represents control over transactions between person(s) and other(s)'. There is no statement about who exercises that control, or how or when it might be exercised. Do control-based theories necessarily deny the possibility that comatose individuals possess a privacy that should be respected? Perhaps unsurprisingly, I would answer that they do not.

If privacy is (at least in part) about regulating transactions between persons (including information flows), then it might be that control is exercised by an individual, a group or a larger collective, who may, or may not, be the object of the (potential) privacy infringement. It might be exercised at the time of the interaction, or it might be expressed at an earlier point in time. So, to return to the example of the comatose patients, there is nothing incoherent about the claim that their privacy may be infringed through a lack of respect for preferences expressed either by themselves when conscious or by others (at any time).

While I am not currently attempting to defend Margulis' claims about the *aims* of privacy, it should perhaps be conceded that the fact that he asserts both 'autonomy enhancement' and 'minimising vulnerability' to be aims of privacy *does* suggest that control would ideally be exercised by individuals themselves. Even this would, however, be conditional upon particular circumstance: it is consistent with the enhancement of autonomy, and the minimising of vulnerability, that transactions between persons are controlled by others when individuals are not in a position to exercise such control themselves. It may be that others have a responsibility to regulate transactions on behalf of a comatose patient in ways that promote, wherever possible, opportunities to exercise control in the future.

There are two further criticisms of control-based theories that should be addressed before considering the merits of operating with a definition of privacy that is 'control-based'. The first is that all such theories 'confuse the two distinct values of privacy and liberty and freedom'.[15] To some extent, it is understandable why, at least within a Western literature, there might be confusion between these different values. In Western liberal democracies there is a close association between the idea

---

[15] *Ibid.*, 54.

of privacy and the ideas of autonomy, liberty and individual freedom. This is evidenced, for example, by the close connection between 'privacy' and 'consent' and this relationship can perhaps be seen reflected in Margulis' own attribution of privacy with the 'ultimate aims' of enhancing autonomy or minimising vulnerability. It can certainly be seen in the widespread public acceptance of the idea that people can shift reasonable expectations of access to their own personal space and personal information through voluntary agreement, i.e. an exercise of free choice can shift what privacy demands: permission can change a privacy-invading act into a privacy-respecting one.[16] These are not, in fact, ideas that I would support. I would suggest that respecting the autonomy or individual liberty of an individual – allowing that individual to choose what information is given access to under what circumstances – is no guarantee of privacy. In this respect, I would support maintaining a distinction between privacy, liberty and autonomy.[17] To get caught up in this argument, at this time, would, however, be to lose sight of the point that is being made. There appears to be no real reason to conceive of privacy as something necessarily associated with individual liberty or freedom simply *because* one associates it with the idea of control, any more than there is a need to associate it necessarily with individual control simply because one associates it with autonomy or the protection of vulnerability.[18] To assert that control-based theories of privacy confuse the values of privacy and liberty and freedom is to make certain assumptions about the content of any such theory.

The only aspect of Margulis' control-based theory that I am currently supporting is that, at root, privacy represents some kind of 'control over transactions between person(s) and other(s), that usually entailed limits on or regulation of access to self, sometimes to groups, and occasionally to larger collectives such as organisations'. It will be remembered that Margulis' definition was itself an attempt to identify a consensus within the literature. Although this exercise may have swept up privacy theories

---

[16] This can be seen in the widespread phenomenon of 'privacy policies' on websites. Once you have 'agreed' to a privacy policy, then use of your private information consistent with that policy will not constitute a privacy violation.

[17] And, in this respect, I am in complete agreement with one of Laurie's central themes (*Genetic Privacy*, 80–85).

[18] When surveyed on the use of 'sealed envelopes' on the electronic health record, 'Around a quarter of patients (22%) and the public (26%) thought anonymised data from "sealed envelopes" should never be used.' That meant, not even with consent. Research Capability Programme Consultation Team, 'Summary of responses to the consultation on the additional uses of patient data', NHS Connecting for Health (27 November 2009), 6. www.dh.gov.uk/prod_consum_dh/groups/dh_digitalassets/documents/digitalasset/dh_110715.pdf.

that are susceptible to the criticisms described, the criticisms considered do not convincingly rebut the idea that privacy is grounded in the fact of, or the preference for, control over transactions between persons that typically concern access to persons.

The final criticism of control-based theories of privacy that I will consider is put forward by Neil Manson and Onora O'Neill. They reject the view that (informational) privacy may ground a claim to control personal information about oneself 'given the range of different communicative acts in which information can be used'.[19] While they accept that certain persons might be entitled to refrain from disclosure of information, they assert that there are so many different ways in which people might attain information, that it would be too problematic to consider there to be a right to control each of them. For example, '[w]e *can't* control what people think, or the conclusions they may draw from public evidence'.[20] Again, this is a criticism that appears to me to be perfectly sound *if* applied to particular kinds of control-based theory: namely, any theory that would seek to assert that privacy justifies a claim by an individual to absolute control over all information about her. I do not seek to defend such a control-based theory of privacy.

Manson and O'Neill's criticism runs deeper *if* control-based theories of privacy are necessarily aligned with the idea that information is a 'thing' that can be controlled. They are keen to discourage what they describe as the container/conduit view of information and instead encourage a focus upon the act of communication itself. A control-based theory of privacy is not, however, committed to the idea that information is a 'thing' that can be controlled. Control must be exercised, but not necessarily over information itself.

If privacy is understood to represent control over *transactions* between person(s) and other(s) (rather than control over information per se), and relevant control (exercised in many different ways) can be evidenced through the norms of patterns and preferences in social interaction (rather than being understood to reside within the exercise of individual discretion), then I believe that particular species of control-based theories of privacy can avoid the criticisms that Manson and O'Neill appear to level against the genus.

Of course, even if the criticisms of control-based theories considered here can be rebutted, that itself offers no positive reason for accepting

---

[19] N. C. Manson and O. O'Neill, *Rethinking Informed Consent in Bioethics* (Cambridge: Cambridge University Press, 2007), 106.

[20] *Ibid.*

any such theory. I suggest that a reason for preferring a control-based notion of privacy might be found by aligning a simple observation with the commonplace already noted: privacy has a value.

Value and control

It is a relatively simple observation that, if privacy is to be understood to attach to discreet conditions or behaviour within a particular community, then there must be some means of distinguishing those conditions, or that behaviour, from alternates. If privacy is valued, then value will be attached to such distinctions: particular conditions, or behaviours, will be preferred to alternatives. Preferences may be expressed by persons either in support of, or in objection to, particular patterns of behaviour within a society. If particular preferences are given effect within social relations, i.e. if people act in accordance with them, then they will further embed associated patterns of behaviour, which will in turn effectively establish the expectations for particular kinds of interaction. The prevailing patterns may kaleidoscope over time, as the dominance of different preferences rises and falls, but for as long as value is attached to the idea of privacy, then there will always be a motive to normalise particular patterns or preferences for certain conditions or behaviours. If these are normalised within a society, then the normalisation itself will exert a form of control as it gives rise to expectations. Before expanding upon this point, the observation that privacy attaches *only* to certain kinds of behaviour needs to be a little further unpacked. As the observation informs my justification for a control-based theory of privacy, the fact that it is an observation applicable to *more than* control-based theories of privacy is important.

The suggestion that one must be able to distinguish between conditions, or behaviours, that are capable of engaging an individual's privacy and those that are not is important because it implies the need for some *method* for determining the range of interactions that might be privacy affecting. The need for such a method is not restricted to those theories described as 'control-based'. I have already suggested that Laurie prefers to use an idea of privacy that is expressly not associated with a control-based theory. He prefers to strip back the idea of privacy to the simpler idea of a state or condition per se.

First, [privacy] can be viewed as a state of non-access to the individual's physical or psychological self – what can be called *spatial privacy*. Second, privacy can be seen as a state in which personal information about an individual is in a state of non-access from others – *informational privacy.* One unifying definition can be deduced from these two concepts: privacy is a state of separatedness from others.[21]

However, not even this approach can avoid the need to find a way to distinguish between different kinds of states. While there is much to commend Laurie's approach generally, if one operates with this unifying definition of privacy, then how does one determine the relevant range of states that might engage privacy? What are the material facts in any description of separation? For example, 'If a family home is burgled, then is the privacy of a child at boarding school invaded?' 'Can there be private funds in a joint bank account?' Even the simple description of a state presupposes a judgment about the properties by which separation is to be judged. For any concept, there must be some way of determining its boundaries. I would readily accept that Laurie is correct to underscore the significance of the state of separateness *from others* within any discussion of privacy. However, *relevant* separation from others can only be assessed against a particular yardstick: *relevant separation can only be determined if claims about privacy are grounded in particular norms.* As soon as you accept the idea that privacy is grounded in norms, and you accept that those norms are valued, then it is hard to escape a control-based theory of privacy.

The idea of a norm itself means only either (a) typical, usual or expected patterns of behaviour[22] or (b) a required standard (which is a matter of obligation). Norms are, therefore, always established by particular patterns or preferences regarding behaviour. If established by preferences, then those preferences may be rooted in more general normative frameworks, which seek to justify the nature of any obligation. These may, in turn, be informed by particular philosophical, political, economic or moral theories that may have their own ideas about the proper relation between persons within a society. It is also possible, however, that people *perceive* a required standard, understanding action in accordance with that standard to be something which others 'ought to do', without being able to articulate or defend that preference with reference to a broader moral or political philosophy. Typical, usual or expected patterns of behaviour may arise as a result of cultural practice, religious belief, specific (or even non-specific) promises, or any number of other things. They may also, therefore, be highly varied, variable,

---

[21] Laurie, *Genetic Privacy*, 6.

[22] Which may itself be tied to factual circumstance; for example, facts of efficiency and efficacy support the social norm that people walk rather than crawl, at least after the first few months of life.

difficult to delineate clearly within a particular society, and entirely context dependent. They will, however, for as long as they are associated with *privacy*, always be valued.

Whether rooted theoretically, or simply arising through patterns of behaviour, we then return to the idea that privacy establishes certain 'ground rules' for engagement between person(s) and group(s). The norms provide a justification for distinguishing between different behaviours: preferring *relevant* states of separation. *If* privacy is valued (and that is the one constant that we have allowed ourselves to assume), then *maintaining* relevant separations will also be valued. If patterns are to be maintained, or preferences expressed, then some form of control has to be in operation.

At the very least, one might expect that patterns and preferences will give rise to certain *expectations* regarding relevant separation. Even in its most attenuated form, this will affect the transactions involving those who hold and value those norms. If such preferences establish patterns of behaviour within a society more broadly, then such expectations may come to affect more than those who hold or have reason to value them. As individuals observe others acting in particular ways, then such behaviour may be normalised. This will typically create an environment that exerts an additional, albeit imprecise and uncertain, kind of control. In time, particular kinds of expectation of behaviour may become socially sanctioned and non-compliance can be experienced as harm by an individual and met with censure by the community.[23]

One might question whether the kind of control required to preserve particular norms within a society fits the idea of a control-based theory of privacy. I would concede that it seems at times that 'control' may be too strong a word. But the key point is that value is being attached to particular kinds of access – or separation – and that states of (non)access cannot be maintained without some form of control being exercised. Certainly, some patterns of behaviour (and perhaps also preferences) can arise without any kind of deliberative judgment or voluntary nature. Examples might be observed within the animal world where interactions can be consistently observed to respect certain states of separation. Even in these examples, however, the norms that enable one to identify *relevant* states of separation are apparently imbued with some kind of value by the animals acting consistently with them. It is the fact that the norms are valued that lead to behaviour being modified to conform with them, and norms of

---

[23] Post, 'Three concepts of privacy', at 2092.

separation or states of (non)access cannot be valued without instrumental value also being attached to that which supports them:
control.

Privacy as a norm of exclusivity

It is possible to draw some of these ideas together and to summarise the
point that I think has now been reached in our consideration of the
concept of privacy. Privacy is established by norms regulating access to
individuals or groups of individuals: it represents a relevant state of
separation defined and mediated by particular standards. In order to
capture more fully the idea that *relevant* separation can only be assessed
according to particular norms, I suggest that privacy concerns 'norms of
exclusivity'.[24]

I favour the term 'exclusivity' over simple 'separation' for two reasons.
First of all, it clearly implies exclusion: a private conversation is private
because others are excluded from it; a private house likewise. This can
be contrasted with a public conversation (cf. a conversation in public) or
a public house where there is not the same kind of exclusivity. In this
way, exclusivity can imply that a particular expectation of separation is
considered to be justified: I may not be able to prevent anyone from
listening to my conversation, or from gathering particular information
about me, but I might have views about whether they are entitled to do
so. This suggests the second reason for preferring the term 'exclusivity':
it more explicitly captures the normative dimension of the relevant
separation: the term exclusivity implies a standard by which *relevant*
separateness may be judged. Although I may be standing as close to
my friend as the stranger in the train carriage, my friend and I still
consider the stranger to be separate from our conversation. This can
only be because we are relying upon norms that judge *relevant* separation, in this context at least, by particular criteria and not others. Also,
it is important to recognise that 'norms of exclusivity' can also give rise
to certain expectations regarding a *lack of separation*: it can be expected

---

[24] This idea is very close to the norms of information flow that are described by Helen
Nissenbaum as part of her concept of 'privacy as contextual integrity' (H. Nissembaum,
'Privacy as contextual integrity', *Washington Law Review* 79(1) (2004), 119–58).
Indeed, I believe norms of information flow may be one component of relevant norms
of exclusivity. The notion of norms of exclusivity is, however, broader than norms of
information flow alone and is not only applicable to information relating to particular
identifiable individuals. In fact, although Nissenbaum only applies her idea of 'norms of
information flow' in relation to individual, identifiable persons, I think the idea has
important application outside of this context.

for access to be granted. Members of a private club might expect to be granted entrance because they are relying upon a particular norm of exclusivity.

In so far as norms are related to typical patterns of behaviour, they may be largely explainable by reference to factual circumstance. Social norms reliant upon a theoretical framework will also often be cognisant of the practical realities (ought does, after all, imply can). There is then a relationship between factual circumstance and normative standard, and exclusivity itself may then (1) exist as a matter of fact or may (2) relate to a particular social norm. The fact that there is such a tremendous variation in both factual circumstances and potentially relevant norms has clear implications for the range of transactions that might be brought within the scope of a privacy claim. In other words, variation in the underlying norms, as well as variation in the material circumstances in which they are unpacked, will play directly into determining the range of transactions considered to be potentially privacy infringing.

Norms and the transactional variable

If one imagines all the different ways that individuals might interact with each other, both as individuals and as members of groups, then you have the full range of ways in which access to persons, and particular kinds of separation, might conceivably be assessed. As already indicated, any particular concept of privacy must clarify that part of the possible spectrum of transaction that does in fact, or should in theory, actually attract privacy expectations. Crucially, the range will be determined by the nature of the underlying norms being worked out in particular factual circumstances: different patterns and preferences will establish a different range of transactions between persons capable of engaging norms of exclusivity.

Although I have been preoccupied with what has been described as 'informational privacy', I have already noted that privacy as a concept extends far beyond the control of information alone. When seeking to elucidate the different dimensions of privacy evident within recent academic writing on genetic privacy in particular, Anita Allen distinguished between four dimensions: 'informational, decisional, physical and proprietary dimensions of privacy'.[25]

---

[25] A. L. Allen, 'Genetic privacy: emerging concepts and values', in M. A. Rothstein (ed.), *Genetic Secrets: Protecting Privacy and Confidentiality in the Genetic Era* (New Haven, CT: Yale University Press, 1997), 31.

(1) Informational privacy concerns access to personal information; (2) physical privacy concerns about access to persons and personal spaces; (3) decisional privacy concerns about governmental and other third-party interference with personal choices; and (4) proprietary privacy concerns about the appropriation and ownership of interests in human personality.[26]

It is interesting not only to note the breadth of human interaction potentially covered by this list but also to consider the ambiguity regarding the penetrance of privacy along each dimension. That is to say, it is not clear from this list whether informational privacy is, for example, supposed to cover *all* personal information or just a sub-set – an issue we have already seen to be the matter of some debate. Similarly, it is not clear whether physical privacy is supposed to concern any or all access to persons and personal spaces or just some, etc. The accuracy of the list with regards to not only its breadth, but also the extent to which any or all instances of behaviour across these dimensions might raise a privacy concern, is entirely dependent upon how underlying norms unpack in particular circumstances.

Within the variation, one can imagine different kinds of interaction and transaction being given different labels. This does in fact happen in practice. For example, in English, the term 'confidential' may be reserved to describe the exclusive nature of certain information, whereas privacy would be something that only persons (and perhaps animals) can enjoy (but not information).[27] For now, I am going to ignore such differences. The point is that there are alternative norms and normative standards, and therefore alternative transactions captured within the scope of 'privacy' as I have described it, even if some of these may develop specific terminology.[28]

Recognising inconsistency in the *language* of privacy does, of course, open up the possibility that the word 'private' may be used inconsistently to apply to a particular range of transactions. We will see, within Chapter 4, that the law represents a particular concept of privacy within the activities that it protects and that this does not necessarily represent an effective protection of 'privacy' from the perspective of alternative norms. What is more, there is nothing to suggest that norms of

---

[26] *Ibid.*, 33.

[27] Not only are there other kinds of distinction that can be drawn within the English language, there are lots of other interesting distinctions that are drawn within other languages. See K. Hoeyer, 'The role of privacy and informed consent in Danish and Swedish biobank practices: exploring donor perspectives', *Medical Law International* 10 (2010), 269–85.

[28] Hoeyer, 'The role of privacy and informed consent in Danish and Swedish biobank practices'.

exclusivity might not apply to information about groups and communities as well as individuals. Just as particular examples of the language of privacy might represent choices regarding the range of transactions that might be privacy infringing, so also might they represent choices regarding the range of social units, from individuals to entire communities, that could have their privacy infringed. Variation along this particular dimension might be described as variation according to the 'relational variable'.

Norms, transactions and the relational variable

Some transactions – including particular information flows – within society might affect only particular, identifiable individuals. Others might affect families, groups, organisations, or wider communities or societies, etc. If privacy may relate to limits on or regulation of access to self, to groups, and occasionally to larger collectives such as organisations, then each of these represents an alternative relational unit (i.e. a social unit representative of different kinds of relations) that might be the object or the subject of privacy claims. The possibility of any, each or all of these social units (and others) being associated with some kind of normative expectation regarding particular kinds of transaction concerning genetic data is dependent entirely upon the underlying norm being unpacked in a particular context. The possibility of privacy claims extending beyond the individual is an important one to recognise and it might manifest in a number of different ways.[29]

One can imagine circumstances, and particular examples will be considered later, where members of a family or a wider community might consider themselves to have a justified expectation to control access to information originally gathered about a third party. This expectation might relate to their access or it might relate to the access of another. Invariably, however, such concerns will relate to the possibilities that access to genetic data in one circumstance will also enable access to information that could be associated with them in some (typically unwanted) way. This (unwanted) association might be at the level of an identifiable individual, or it might be at the level of a family, group or community, but access to data originally obtained from another might nevertheless be associated with them with a wide range of possible consequences. For this reason, and given the concerns that exist regarding *potential* associations, the identifiability – or anonymity – of

---

[29] This is an issue taken up more fully within Chapter 6.

data in one circumstance is not as relevant as the possibility of future associations with that data in foreseeable circumstances.

Up to this point, I have sought simply to present privacy as representative of particular norms of exclusivity, to recognise the various ways in which such norms may be grounded, and to clarify the ways in which they might unpack according to both transactional and relational variables. This has been an important exercise. It has, I hope, helped to provide a way of representing some of the variation between different conceptions of privacy – as they vary according to the normative, transactional and relational aspects – and has also helped to underline the significance of 'control' from an individual or group perspective, as privacy is valued.

However, it is important now to emphasise that the way in which such preferences are managed is a matter of some significance for society as a whole. As privacy helps to define the expectations of interaction between different social units, its protection will contribute towards shaping the broader relations between persons. A number of commentators have remarked upon this constitutive aspect of privacy;[30] and recognising that the protection of privacy is a defining quality for any society highlights what is at stake. Not only is there an important relationship between privacy and the public interest, but there is also an important relationship between the protection of privacy and the legitimacy of those mechanisms that seek to protect the public interest.

Privacy, public interest and legitimacy

Similarly to 'privacy', the 'public interest' is a notoriously uncertain idea. When Frank Sorauf attempted to summarise and catalogue different uses of the term in 1957 he described four connotations which were abundant in the literature at the time: public interest as 'commonly-held values'; as the wise or superior interest; as moral imperative; or as a balance of interests.[31] This non-exhaustive classificatory scheme still accommodated sufficient variety to cause Sorauf to doubt whether the term could serve any useful function as an analytical tool 'simply because of the conflicting definitions with which it is fraught'.[32] Even if one focuses upon the meaning that Sorauf considered may have the greatest support, the idea that the public interest resides in interests commonly held by members of the public, so that a decision in the public interest 'serves the ends of the whole public rather than those of

---

[30] See for a very useful summary of a number of commentaries, D. J. Solove, 'A taxonomy of privacy', *University of Pennsylvania Law Review* 154(3) (2006), 477–560 at 487.

[31] F. J. Sorauf, 'The public interest reconsidered', *Journal of Politics* 19(4) (1957), 616–39.

[32] *Ibid.*, 637–8.

some sector of the public',[33] then there is still considerable room for disagreement about what are common interests and ends.

The possibilities for convergence and divergence will vary depending (amongst other things) upon your view of publics. It would matter, for example, whether you hold a 'communitarian' view and consider publics to have their own emergent interests and functions, or whether you prefer a more 'libertarian' view (which sees 'a public' rather more as an aggregate of individual interests). Whichever view you take, one of these alternatives or some other entirely, there is still room for disagreement about precisely how common a particular interest needs to be to qualify as a 'commonly held' *public* interest. Were it possible to agree the relevant threshold for a public interest, then one would still be left to debate how to resolve any conflicts that might arise between different public interests or between public interests and interests of other kinds. In fact, the more one considers the idea of 'the public interest', the clearer it becomes that it is not straightforward and, whatever approach one takes towards defining it, some difficult questions are going to have to be answered.

However, it is not necessary to engage with all of these difficult questions to make a relatively simple, but nevertheless important, point about public interest *decision-making* and *legitimacy*. Admittedly, legitimacy, like privacy and public interest, is a term that permits many different interpretations. At this point, I cannot hope to do more than be clear about how I intend to use the word. I am here working with the idea that legitimacy can be defined as 'the capacity of the system to engender and maintain the belief that the existing political institutions are the most appropriate ones for the society'.[34]

I rely upon this idea of legitimacy to make a simple proposal as regards the 'public interest': if you tie the idea of the public interest to the idea of common interests, then the legitimacy of public interest decision-making is dependent upon the ability of the system to *account for common interests* within the decision-making processes. The capacity of a system to engender and maintain a belief in its *appropriateness* will be determined (in part) by its *perceived* capacity to take such individually (or jointly) valued interests into account within its operation. This idea of legitimacy shares similarities with what has been described as social (empirical) legitimacy[35] and

---

[33] M. Meyerson and E. C. Banfield, *Politics, Planning, and the Public Interest* (New York: Free Press, 1955) at 322 cited in Sorauf, 'Public interest reconsidered', 619.

[34] S. M. Lipset, *Political Man: The Social Bases of Politics* (Baltimore, MD: Johns Hopkins University Press, 1981 [1959]) at 64.

[35] '[S]ocial legitimacy refers to the affective loyalty of those who are bound by it, on the basis of deep common interest and/or strong sense of shared identity.' D. Curtin and

represents only a slight shift from a view of legitimacy associated particularly with liberal philosophy.

The liberal principle of legitimacy states that the exercise of political power is justifiable only when it is exercised in accordance with constitutional essentials that all citizens may reasonably be expected to endorse in the light of principles and ideals acceptable to them as reasonable and rational.[36]

Whatever the merits of the system (whether liberal, libertarian, communitarian or supportive of some other principle entirely), if one intends to justify the exercise of political power, and through it the promotion of an idea of the public interest, then one should hope to be able to demonstrate that any decision is taken 'in the light of principles and ideals' that those affected might find 'acceptable to them as reasonable and rational'. Of course, this does not imply that the legitimacy of a system depends upon everyone perceiving the public interest to align with their own contingent interests. It certainly does not imply that *privacy* interests would be privileged within this calculation. Public interest decision-making should, however, ensure that when the interests of others displace any individual's interests, those individuals affected should have confidence that *their* interests were taken into reasonable account when the decision was made. If privacy interests are common within a society, then they will be part of this calculation. This requires some level of transparency within the decision-making process regarding privacy interests.

Of course, very much more could be said about precisely which interests are common between people in a particular community, about which limitations upon individual interests ought to be accepted as 'reasonable', etc. It is, however, just at this point that the differences in one's world-view begin to bite. There are many different ideas of what it is reasonable for 'the system' to strive to achieve. In fact, one might note that the concept of public interest is susceptible to just as much variation as the normative bases of privacy previously considered. It might also be noted, however, that a consistent world-view would reconcile these concepts from a particular normative perspective. In this way, although privacy

A. J. Meijer, 'Does transparency strengthen legitimacy?', *Information Polity* 2 (2006), 109–22 at 112. It may also be associated with what has been called, in the EU context, input legitimacy: 'Input legitimacy … means that social acceptance of the structure in question derives from a belief that citizens have a fair chance (however understood) to influence decision-making and scrutinise the results.' *Ibid.*, 112. I am here focusing on 'social' or 'input' legitimacy because I am concerned with the perception of those affected by decision-making processes. People might perceive their interests to be appropriately taken into account even if they have not actively participated in the decision-making process itself.

[36] L. B. Solum, 'Public legal reason', *Virginia Law Review* 92 (2006), 1449–1501 at 1472.

and the public interest are sometimes presented as antithetical ideas that must be brought into balance,[37] they can, and often do, share a very close relationship. Proper privacy protection is not simply *consistent* with the public interest – it is crucial to it. If privacy is a common interest, valued within a society, then it is one of the interests that public interest decision-making must be seen to take into account if decision-making processes intended to advance 'the public interest' are to retain legitimacy.

The point thus far has been to argue that accounting for privacy interests is a necessary element of any general theory of *public interest* for so long as privacy interests are commonly valued in a particular society. What is more, it has been intended to establish that this principle is so firmly embedded in legitimate public interest decision-making that it transcends more particular theories of the public interest: it extends, as a principle, to alternative views of the public, and so it remains a valid observation whatever substantive concept of public interest is preferred. It should be emphasised, however, that the relationship between legitimacy and the public interest is not based upon a simplistic notion of transparency.[38] There is no suggestion that simply giving reasons for a decision will alone *necessarily* strengthen legitimacy.[39] Simply providing more information about decision-making processes, or including more people within those processes, will not automatically reassure anyone that their interests have been *appropriately* taken into account. Indeed at times it might even be counterproductive.[40] It is not *just* transparency that is here advocated as supportive of legitimacy but rather transparency that individual (or group) conceptions of privacy have been taken into reasonable account within a decision-making process.

I believe that this idea of legitimate public interest decision-making is consistent with the 'modest conception' of public interest that Sorauf himself proposed: 'we expect only that this political organisation will settle in an orderly, equitable way the differences that divide us'.[41] It is

---

[37] See, for example Editorial, 'Striking the right balance between privacy and public good', *The Lancet* 367 (9507) (2006), 275; Human Genetics Commission, *Inside Information* (London: HGC, May 2002), esp. 4; J. E. Cooper, 'Balancing the scales of public interest: medical research and privacy', *Medical Journal of Australia* 155(8) (21 October 1991), 556–60. See also National Health and Medical Research Council, 'Guidelines approved under Section 95A of the Privacy Act 1998' (Canberra: AusInfo, December 2001), A.1.1.

[38] The complexities of the relationship between legitimacy and transparency has frequently been considered in the context of debate over the legitimacy of EU law and legal institutions. See generally G. de Búrca, 'The quest for legitimacy in the European Union', *Modern Law Review* 59 (1996), 3.

[39] Curtin and Meijer 'Does transparency strengthen legitimacy?', 112.

[40] *Ibid.* See also J. Lodge, 'Transparency and democratic legitimacy', *Journal of Common Market Studies* 32(3) (1994), 343–68.

[41] Sorauf, 'Public interest reconsidered', 633.

difficult for differences to be seen to be equitably resolved if it is not clear that valued interests were taken into account within the resolution. Legitimacy is dependent upon this accommodation of individual interests both taking place and being apparent to the people (negatively) affected. This analysis supports a few more specific observations about the particular kind of transparency that is minimally required.

The first observation is that it should be possible for reasons to be offered for any interference with the privacy preferences of individuals and groups. What is more, it can also be said that, ideally at least, these 'reasons' should take the form described by Rawls as 'public reasons':

Public reasons ... are limited to premises and modes of reasoning that are accessible to the public at large.[42]

This not only supports the idea that the decision-making process itself should clearly take particular interests into account, it also supports the idea that the decision-making process needs to understand the assumptions and presumptions of the public it affects. Relevant transparency cannot be effected by a one-way mirror; it is not enough for the regulated to have confidence in the ability of the regulators to take their interests into account; if that confidence is to endure challenge, then regulators actually need to know what those interests are and need to be able to frame their decisions in ways that can be seen to account for them. For this reason, public attitudes and expectations offer important contributions towards an understanding of what is at stake.[43]

Secondly, this idea of public interest decision-making supports the idea that the impact of any measure taken in the public interest needs, again at least ideally, to be acceptable to any reasonable person: legitimacy 'mirrors public perceptions as the rightness of authority'.[44] It is easier for individuals to be assured that decisions taken are 'right', if they are confident that their interests have been taken into account. If a decision affects them negatively, and they do not consider that impact to have even been taken into account within the calculation, this may undermine confidence in the rightness of the authority. This itself suggests a third substantive idea: any interference with an individual's interests should be justifiable as necessary and proportionate (with the proportionality of any interference, itself, to be demonstrable in terms of common interests). Together, these ideas may be summarised as

---

[42] Solum, 'Public legal reason', 1468.

[43] While 'expectations' are not synonymous with 'interests', positively valued expectations may provide evidence of perceived interests: one does not tend to value things that one considers to be inconsistent with one's interests.

[44] Lodge, 'Transparency and democratic legitimacy', 365.

transparency, acceptability and proportionality. While different ideas of society might flesh these ideas out in different ways (according to a different idea of what is 'reasonable'), for as long as the legitimacy of the system is a concern, they will not be ignored.

To clear even the relatively low threshold set by the requirement of 'transparency' outlined here, it is necessary to *know* what public expectations *are* with regard to research using genetic data. It is not at all clear that the law does currently *know* what these expectations are; references to popular novels within court judgments do not encourage confidence that at least case law is operating with the most reliable indicators of public attitude.[45] Not only does this leave any determination about the public interest without important information, but it exposes the vulnerability of the legitimacy of the decision-making process. What is more, in the context of research using genetic data, it is not even enough for the law to recognise the prevalent 'common interests' across society as a whole. The expression of particular patterns or preferences within particular communities may be important if they are the very communities that research is seeking to engage with. Maintaining the legitimacy of the decision-making process, for the maximum range of people, involves at least demonstrating that the process is capable of taking the maximum range of privacy interests into account. Even if these interests are not ultimately found to hold sway, they should at least be accounted for and, ideally, good (public) reasons should be available if they are ever overridden. When considering the range of possible interests it is important that particular preconceptions about relevant normative variables, or specific spectra within the transactional and relational variable, are set aside. From the perspective of legitimacy and pursuit of the public interest, the public expectations of access to genetic data are more important than the existing legal standards recognise.

Public expectations and genetic research

I have sought to emphasise the significance of norms to a plausible theory of privacy because, as privacy is valued, if those norms are violated, then harm may be caused. If individuals expect others to meet, or police, their expectations, and they fail to do so, then those individuals may modify their behaviour in the future. Trust, evidenced through a reliance upon an expectation, will be lost if people no longer expect their

---

[45] See references made by Lord Woolf to the public appreciation of Aldous Huxley's *Brave New World* and George Orwell's *1984*. *R (S and Marper)* v. *Chief Constable of the South Yorkshire Police* [2002] EWCA Civ 1275; [2002] 1 W.L.R. 3223 at 3234.

values to be protected.[46] If decisions are taken 'in the public interest' that fail even to account for the values at stake, then the legitimacy of the decision-making process is also at stake.

Genetic research relies upon the participation of individuals. Certain kinds of important genetic research rely upon mass participation. If a regulatory system loses people's trust in its ability to protect the privacy preferences that are important to them, then it jeopardises not only its legitimacy but also, and importantly, their willing participation in the activity of genetic research. It is, therefore, important that we do at least know what people expect and what 'norms' might inform *their* understanding of the relationship between different kinds of genetic research, the 'public interest' and privacy.

Unfortunately, there have only been limited systematic, Europe-wide studies asking citizens to identify the range of public attitudes towards privacy (and other interests) in information relevant to genetic research.[47] While there is a need for much more research into public attitudes towards both privacy and public interest (and their relationship) in the area of genetic research, some degree of consistency, and diversity, can be inferred from the work that has already been done. For example, public attitude surveys have demonstrated high levels of support for medical research.[48] Research has also consistently shown that people typically expect to be asked before their personal health information is used for research purposes,[49] although their informed

---

[46] The term 'trust' is being used here only to refer to reliance upon an expectation. Leith has suggested that trust involves knowing how one can behave with another, and how that other will view oneself. P. Leith, 'The socio-legal context of privacy', *International Journal of Law in Context* 2(2) (2006), 105–36. In this sense, building an expectation of others, and testing it, is a social process that requires access to information and can be in competition with privacy. Here I am suggesting that access to certain information, through transparency in a decision-making process, may be crucial to the legitimacy of the decision-making process (as it enables trust to be built). I do not think this access needs to be in competition with privacy norms as those norms themselves expect the access in question.

[47] D. Townend, M. J. Taylor, J. Wright and D. Wickins-Drazilova, 'Privacy interests in biobanking: a preliminary view on a European perspective', in J. Kaye and M. Stranger (eds.), *Principles and Practice in Biobank Governance* (Aldershot: Ashgate, 2009), 141.

[48] See, for example, S. Butt, E. Clery, V. Abeywardana and M. Phillips, 'Wellcome Trust Monitor 1: tracking public views on medical research', Survey Report (Wellcome Trust, September 2009), 101.

[49] See V. Armstrong, J. Barnett, H. Cooper, M. Monkman, J. Moran-Ellis and R. Shepherd, *Public Perspectives on the Governance of Biomedical Research: A Qualitative Study in a Deliberative Context* (London: Wellcome Trust, 2007), 59, 87; IPSOS MORI/MRC, *The Use of Personal Health Information in Medical Research* (London: Medical Research Council, 26 June 2007), 9; G. Gaskell, S. Stares, A. Allansdottir, N. Allum, P. Castro, Y. Esmer, C. Fischler, J. Jackson, N. Kronberger, J. Hampel, N. Mejlgaard, A. Quintanilha, A. Rammer, G. Revuelta, P. Stoneman, H. Torgersen and

consent is not necessarily their only, or even their primary, concern.[50] Some studies have identified a willingness to delegate decision-making in some circumstances[51] although this picture is not entirely consistent across different studies.[52] This is perhaps not surprising as attitudes are likely to vary according to a range of criteria.

We might confidently assert that people will inevitably prefer that their information is not used in a way that they would consider contrary to their best interests. While there may be differences of opinion as to how best to achieve the desired protection, the fact that there is concern about (perceived) misuse of the information that genetic research might yield is itself beyond doubt. This concern extends to information that has been effectively de-identified (see Chapter 6 for a fuller discussion of identifiability), and some information is so sensitive that the public do not expect it to be used even if it is not in personally identifiable form.[53]

A Eurobarometer survey, in 2005, asked approximately 1,000 respondents in each EU Member State a number of questions about

W. Wagner, *Europeans and Biotechnology in 2010: Winds of Change?*, Special Barometer 341 (European Union, October 2010), 64: The majority of Europeans asked (67%) felt that researchers should ask for permission for every new piece of research conducted using data in a biobank. Almost one in five (18%) felt that permission should be asked only once, while only 6% felt that there was no need to ask permission at all.

[50] K. Hoeyer, B. O. Olofsson, T. Mjorndal and N. Lynoe, 'The ethics of research using biobanks: reasons to question the importance attributed to informed consent'. *Archives of Internal Medicine* 165 (2005), 97–100.

[51] Å. Kettis-Lindblad, L. Ring, E. Viberth and M. G. Hansson, 'Perceptions of potential donors in the Swedish public towards information and consent procedures in relation to use of human tissue samples in biobanks: a population based study', *Scandinavian Journal of Public Health* 35 (2007), 148; K. Hoeyer, B. O. Olofsson, T. Mjorndal and N. Lynoe, 'Informed consent and biobanks: a population-based study of attitudes towards tissue donation for genetic research', *Scandinavian Journal of Public Health* 32 (2004), 224–9.

[52] While the majority (95%) of those participating in the Estonian Genome Project are reported to consider it important to be informed about what kind of research will be done using their data, a majority (81%) also support the idea that fresh consent should be required before new research is conducted on existing samples. K. Korts, 'Estonia', in M. Häyry, R. Chadwick, V. Árnason and G. Árnason, *The Ethics and Governance of Human Genetic Databases* (Cambridge: Cambridge University Press, 2007), 51. A similar proportion indicated a preference for fresh consent before new research is conducted upon a biological sample in the study conducted for the UK Human Genetics Commission: Human Genetic Commission, 'Public attitudes to human genetic information – People's Panel Quantitative Study conducted for the Human Genetics Commission' (London: HGC, March 2001), 42. This is not dissimilar to the results reported in Castro *et al.*, *Europeans and Biotechnology in 2010*, 64.

[53] Research Capability Programme Consultation Team, 'Summary of responses to the consultation on the additional uses of patient data', NHS Connecting for Health (27 November 2009), 6. www.dh.gov.uk/prod_consum_dh/groups/dh_digitalassets/documents/digitalasset/dh_110715.pdf.

the acceptability of different uses of genetic data.[54] The results indicated that the European public is broadly willing to support research into the origins of disease (58% willing; 36% unwilling) and to support police access (59% willing; 35% unwilling) but are broadly opposed to other societal uses of the data. Only 25% would be willing to give government access to genetic information (with 69% unwilling) and only 14% would be willing to allow private insurance companies access (with 81% unwilling).[55] It is clear that there is a concern about who can access genetic data for what, and, that substantial numbers of people are concerned with both commercial access and also government and police access to genetic data.

While different studies may not be directly comparable, and may not enable us to gauge levels of particular concern across Europe or beyond, they do allow us to see the broad range of interests that individuals have perceived to be engaged by research using genetic data.[56] This sweep of interests includes those that relate to consent, in being told what the data are used for, and by whom, and certain kinds of access being prevented, in knowing whether a resource is to be commercialised and if it is privately or publicly owned, in data being held securely and confidentially, in the ability to withdraw from a study, in receiving general feedback on research and in being told if research uncovers information of relevance to the individual or the family.[57] For at least one individual, this has stretched to include an interest in determining whether a relative's contribution is withdrawn from a research database.[58]

---

[54] G. Gaskell, A. Allansdottir, N. Allum, C. Corchero, C. Fischler, J. Hampel, J. Jackson, N. Kronberger, N. Mejlgaard, G. Revuelta, C. Schreiner, S. Stares, H. Torgersen and W. Wagner, 'Europeans and biotechnology in 2005: patterns and trends', Eurobarometer 64.3, Report to the European Commission's Directorate-General for Research (May 2006). http://ec.europa.eu/research/press/2006/pdf/pr1906_eb_64_3_final_report-may2006_en.pdf.

[55] *Ibid.*, 52–6.

[56] For a country-by-country summary of selected research into public attitudes towards research using genetic data see www.privileged.group.shef.ac.uk/projstages/stage1/bycountry/.

[57] G. Haddow, S. Cunningham-Burley, A. Bruce and S. Parry, 'Generation Scotland, Preliminary Consultation Exercise 2003–2004, public and stakeholder views from focus groups and interviews', Innogen Working Paper No. 20 (November 2004); R. Hapgood, C. McCabe and D. Shickle, 'Public preferences for participation in a large DNA cohort study: a discrete choice experiment', Sheffield Health Economics Series Discussion Paper, Ref. 04/5, The University of Sheffield (2004); Human Genetics Commission, 'Public attitudes to human genetic information'; Craig Ross Dawson, 'Public perceptions of the collection of human biological samples' (London: Wellcome Trust, 2000); Korts, 'Estonia', in Häyry *et al.*, 51–2.

[58] *Ragnhildur Guðmundsdóttir* v. *The State of Iceland*, No. 151/2003, Icelandic Supreme Court.

A Eurobarometer report on biotechnology has confirmed people's general concern with access to genetic data across Europe.[59] The special Eurobarometer asked questions about biotechnology in general but also about attitudes towards biobanks[60] in particular. The Eurobarometer found that 46% of those questioned would be willing to provide personal information to a biobank while 44% would not.[61] Amongst concerns expressed about biobanks were the issues of ownership of samples and whether there are sufficient laws in place to prevent misuse of the samples and information.[62] People were concerned with leaving it to governments to determine which uses of biobanks were in the public interest.[63]

These public attitude surveys are not cited to provide definitive evidence of particular reasonable expectations of privacy. They may not be evidence of particular privacy expectations, or *norms* of exclusivity, at all. What such surveys can effectively illustrate, however, is the spectrum of possibility when it comes to the range of transactions that *could* be captured within a concept of privacy. In many areas involving new technologies, or technologies that most people have little awareness or understanding of, there are not currently established 'patterns of behaviour'. There may not even be considered preferences for many people. It is in just such areas that the responsibility to determine the appropriate norms of exclusivity falls upon those with the ability to regulate access: the rule-makers must fill in the gaps in social norms. If they are to do so in a way that will retain public confidence in, and a belief in the legitimacy of, that decision-making power, then they should attempt to do so aware of how the conditions of access that they determine may be received as and when the conditions are brought to public light. They also have a responsibility to attempt to *constitute* society, through the rules that they create, in a way that appreciates the impact that particular rules will have upon people (whether those people understand that impact themselves or not) and the relations between people.

Reflection

Privacy is a phenomenon that can be understood to extend along different dimensions. Some of this variation can be captured within a description of different transactional and relational variables. Such variation will

---

[59] TNS Opinion and Social, 'Biotechnology', Special Eurobarometer 341/ Wave 73.1, Report for European Commission (October 2010).

[60] Biobanks are described in the report as taking several forms including depositories of DNA material. We are concerned here, of course, with the informational content of biobanks but the concerns expressed in the report relate to both the biological material and the genetic data. For more on the distinction between these two things see Chapter 7.

[61] TNS Opinion and Social, 'Biotechology', 147.   [62] *Ibid.*, 137.   [63] *Ibid.*, 144.

be traceable, at root, to variation in the norms that ground expectations regarding access to, and exclusivity of, different aspects of people's lives. For this reason, it might be said to be difficult to adopt *a* critical perspective on privacy protection. Research using genetic data might be more, or less, adequately regulated when judged from a number of privacy perspectives.

To address the difficulty of alternative privacy perspectives, a legal critique may take one of three forms. First, it might seek to demonstrate that the law, in its attempts to protect privacy, reflects a particular view of the privacy concept. Locating this particular conception of privacy amongst the alternatives will highlight the choices that the law represents. Secondly, a critique might seek to demonstrate how legal protection engages with particular expectations regarding access to, and use of, genetic data in research as expressed by those with an interest in such research. If privacy concerns norms of exclusivity, then such expectations might inform a view on the adequacy of the law when it comes to protecting the exclusivity of genetic data from the perspective of those interested in research using genetic data. Thirdly, a critique might demonstrate that the legal framework is currently arbitrary with regard to the privacy protection that *it* recognises as important. More an internal critique, it may be possible to determine whether a legal framework represents an inconsistent and arbitrary protection of *the same privacy interests* if held by different people.

It will be suggested in this book that the current legal framework inadequately protects privacy if assessed according to *each* of these different forms of critique. It is not argued here that the law fails to protect a particular normative framework. It is suggested instead that the current framework fails even to account for particular interests in its regulation of genetic research. This is not only a failure to protect privacy. Owing to the relationship between privacy and the public interest, the current framework also fails adequately to recognise the public interest or to recognise the importance of protecting the legitimacy of any public interest decision-making process. What is more, the protection that is offered is available to an unjustifiably narrow range of persons. A distinction is currently drawn within the law between different persons, which is arbitrary from the perspective of the underlying norms that the law seeks to protect, and that only provides protection to the narrowest range of alternatives under the relational variable.

It is, of course, absolutely correct that individuals within a society have responsibilities as well as rights and there should be no automatic assumption that an individual, or a group, would have absolute control over any social interaction. Nor should we assume that privacy would be the dominant value in any society even if people should express a wish that it be so.[64] However, we must hope for a regulatory system that is capable of, at least, consistently *accounting* for the broadest range of privacy preferences. It is important to account for them, even if we do not accede to them, because ignoring the patterns or preferences that shape the public's expectations of privacy risks the legitimacy of the regulatory process and the perception that privacy is properly protected in research. As we shall see in the next chapter, data might be associated with people even if it is not associated with them, in current context, as particular identifiable individuals. We might, therefore, hope that regulation is capable of accounting for preferences as they may be expressed in relation to access to such data. As we shall also see, however, such hope would currently be rather forlorn.

---

[64] B. Moore, *Privacy: Studies in Social and Cultural History* (Armonk, NY: M. E. Sharpe, 1984), 274, cited in Leith, 'The socio-legal context of privacy', 105.

3   Genetic data

If one is concerned with genetic privacy, then one should be concerned with the flow of any genetic data that has the interpretive potential to yield genetic information in relevant circumstances. Relevant circumstances will be determined by the normative basis to the privacy claims, but to understand the significance of the claim that any genetic data might possibly engage such claims, we must first consider the relationship between *data* and *information*.

Data and information

There is a dependent relationship between data and information. Data represents material for analysis. Information is what follows from that analysis. The significance of the data that we perceive is understood only so far as it is interpreted: we are informed only by our interpretation of perceived data, and data are rarely perceived in a disinterested way.[1] As Liebenau and Blackhouse put it, *information* 'cannot exist independently of the receiving person who gives it meaning and somehow acts upon it'.[2]

It is possible to recognise the *potential* for interpretation *before* interpretation takes place. For example, it is possible that we might recognise a recipe book to contain culinary information even if it is written in a language that we do not (yet) understand. In this way we might recognise data to have the potential to yield information of a particular kind before we have interpreted the data to do so: we recognise the data's *interpretive potential*. Once data has been perceived and interpreted, and information has been gathered, then the results of that

---

[1] Richard Jenkins makes the point that *classification* is rarely disinterested: R. Jenkins, *Social Identity* (London: Routledge, 3rd edition, 2008), 7. *Classification* is, however, an inevitable and integral part of understanding that which we perceive.

[2] J. Liebenau and J. Blackhouse, *Understanding Information: An Introduction* (London: Macmillan, 1990), 3.

interpretation can be recorded. If set down in physical (or digital) form, then the act of recording information effectively recasts it as data. However, those (recast) data now have a particular *interpretive pedigree*.

Before information can be gathered from data with a particular interpretive pedigree, the data must be reinterpreted by someone capable of applying a fresh interpretive framework to the data in question. The result of that fresh interpretation might itself be recorded – recast once again as data – for future reference. This can lead to a regular, and at times frequent, interaction between the experience of 'data' and 'information' and the words can, in our everyday experience of them, be used in an overlapping way.

It is important to retain the distinction, or at least to remain aware that a distinction can be drawn, because it underlines the significance of *interpretation* to the generation of information. Put simply then, the relationship between data and information might be presented thus: information = data + *interpretation*. This itself highlights the importance of context for an understanding of the informational content of any given data. The same data, placed in different contexts, may yield information of wildly differing kinds and potentially also massively varying significance: it can mean different things, to different people, with different consequences, as contexts shift.

The significance of interpretation, and the potential fluidity of contexts, complicates the question of whose interests ought to be taken into account when regulating the access to, and use of, any particular genetic data. In later chapters, it will be suggested that much genetic data is held in increasingly fluid interpretive contexts. Maximising the research utility of that data often relies upon those contexts becoming *more* fluid over time. This presents certain challenges for privacy protection in a number of related ways. First of all, it undermines the idea that it might only be a particular individual's privacy that is potentially put at risk through the use of any given data. The interpretive potential of data to yield information of significance to identifiable individuals other than the individual from (and/or about) whom data was originally gathered is more fully considered later (in Chapter 5). Also, and somewhat ironically given what we will see is the law's preoccupation with particular identifiable individuals, it tends not to be their identity per se that individuals are concerned about. It is *other* information, regarded as significant in particular contexts, that they prefer not to be associated with, and such associations can be made using data that would not be regarded as identifiable, e.g. 'larger waist size increases health risks' (which may be true) and 'blondes have more fun' (which may not be). As well as explaining why the fluidity of interpretive contexts can undermine the protection associated with anonymisation (in Chapter 6) it is an idea that will also be used to explain (in Chapter 7) why the distinction between sample and data may also prove to be an arbitrary distinction in some cases. As such, regulatory differences founded upon the distinction may fail to provide necessary protections. Finally (in Chapter 8), the idea of fluid contexts will also be relied upon to demonstrate why genetic discrimination legislation is not the answer and to point the way towards a more context-specific response. The significance of interpretive context, and the fluidity of the same, cannot then be overestimated for the arguments to come. It is, therefore, important that we clear the way for such arguments by first further clarifying the significance of *interpretation* for the relationship specifically between *genetic* data and *genetic* information.

Genetic data cf. genetic information

Somewhat confusingly, within the English language, the move from (1) describing data according to the nature of its perceived characteristics, to (2) describing interpret*able* data according to the potentialities associated with it, and (3) describing interpret*ed* data according to what has been learnt from it is not clearly marked. The confusion that this can cause can be clearly demonstrated through the example of genetic data.

(1) Data might be described as 'genetic'[3] owing to the physical form in which that data is held. If we are directly interrogating 'genetic material', such as an extraction of DNA sequence from tissue, then the data observed might be described as 'genetic data' owing to its physicality or at least its physical biography. The move from describing 'genetic material' to 'genetic data' is marked in this case by the *preparation* of material for analysis.[4] It is only prepared for analysis, however, because its potential to inform has been realised. Therefore, (2) data might be described as 'genetic data' because it is recognised as *susceptible* to a genetic interpretation: it is interpret*able* in a particular way. Alternatively, (3) data might be described as 'genetic' because it represents the record of a *prior* genetic interpretation: it represents the record of an interpretation that has previously yielded genetic information. An example here might be a family history taken orally and recorded in a family tree for the purposes of identifying patterns of inheritance.

'Genetic data' can thus be understood most broadly to include *any data* prepared in a way that it might yield genetic information if subject

---

[3] That is to say, relating to genes or hereditary.

[4] See L. A. Bygrave, 'The body as data? Biobank regulation via the "back door" of data protection law', *Law, Innovation and Technology* 2(1) (2010), 1–27 at 14.

to genetic interpretation. By 'subject to genetic interpretation' I mean only subject to an interpretive framework that perceives the data to be susceptible to an interpretation capable of yielding genetic information. It is the preparation itself that marks *data* out from other observable matter: data is specifically represented for analysis.[5] If one is to retain the distinction between (genetic or other) material and *genetic* data, then one might insist that it has been prepared *specifically* to yield genetic information. The difficulty with such an insistence from a regulatory perspective, or from a perspective that is concerned with what people *might* do with data at their disposal, is that it focuses upon a historic fact (i.e. the interpretive pedigree of the data) rather than the future possibilities (i.e. its interpretive potential). If we are, for now at least, concerned with a broad understanding of 'genetic data' (only to be refined and narrowed for good reason), then we should begin at least with any *data* that is represented in such a way that it is possible for genetic information to be interpreted from it as genetic data.

If genetic data is understood to be any data capable of being interpreted to provide genetic information, then one is left with an extremely broad reading of genetic data. Just how broad, and the implications that this would have for the practicalities of regulating access to it, will be considered later (in Chapter 8). It should be noted at this point, however, that although extremely broad, this definition of genetic data would exclude biological material in an unprepared state. The plausibility, and desirability, of maintaining even this distinction between samples and information is taken up later (in Chapter 7). For now, I will focus upon the implications of this understanding of the relationship between genetic data and genetic information for our understanding of genetic information itself.

What is genetic information?

A gene is the basic physical and functional unit of heredity.[6] Genes are responsible for coding the proteins that are essential to the construction and functioning of an organism. Genetic information can broadly be

---

[5] See *ibid.*, 14.

[6] http://ghr.nlm.nih.gov/handbook/basics/gene (last accessed 5 January 2011). The term 'gene' wasn't coined until 1909 when Wilhelm Johannsen used it to denote a hypothetical medium of inheritable traits. For the next forty-four years there was a great deal of controversy over the medium through which these hypothetical 'genes' might be transmitted. It was not until Watson and Crick finally elucidated its double helical structure in 1953 that it was accepted that DNA (deoxyribonucleic acid) was capable of carrying a code of the complexity necessary to convey all the information needed to construct an organism.

understood to include any information relating to genes: information about what genes are, their number, variety, sequence or arrangement in a particular context, their function, the impact of that function (or non-function) upon the organism itself, and, relatedly, information about how gene expression affects the phenotype. This potentially huge range of information can be divided into two basic categories: information about the genetic architecture – what it '*is*', and what it '*means*'.

Information about what the architecture is might be information about the number, type, sequence, arrangement (either nucleotide sequence, combination of alleles or arrangement of alleles within chromosomes), etc. Information of this sort will inevitably begin as information about some aspect or detail of the physical architecture of a specific sample, e.g. 'this genome has gene LRRTM1 on chromosome 2p12', or 'there are 23 pairs of chromosomes in this cell'. The information gathered through the examination may then be generalised. It may be generalised to a particular family, community or entire species, e.g. 'in humans, each cell typically contains 23 pairs of chromosomes'. This kind of statement does not, of course, have the same kind of certainty as the first kind: with generalisation comes the possibility of inaccuracy at the individual level. While human cells do *typically* contain 23 pairs of chromosomes it is not an accurate statement about *all* human cells,[7] nor indeed *any* human cells in *some* humans.[8] When particular aspects of architecture are discovered through direct examination, it will never be known exactly how prevalent those characteristics are within a particular population. The more examinations that are conducted, the greater the certainty with which prevalence can be assessed, but, unless every aspect of genetic architecture were directly examined, there will always be the possibility of inaccuracies due to the inherent limitations of inductive reasoning. Interpretive frameworks are often imprecise.

On the other hand, specific architectural features will rarely be unique to a particular individual and, for as long as genetic architecture is associated with significance, information about what the genetic code *is* for one individual will have implications for (blood) relatives. The relevance of what information about architecture *means*, therefore, will rarely be confined to a particular individual. Information relating to the significance of architecture may be presented in general

---

[7] Sex cells (sperms and eggs) and enucleated red blood cells are both haploid rather than diploid: each contains only one set of chromosomes.

[8] Aneuploidy is the term used for an abnormal number of chromosomes. Monosomy is a condition where there is only one copy of a particular chromosome. Trisomy is a condition where there are three copies of a particular chromosome.

statements, e.g. inheritance of LRRTM1 affects handedness[9] (whether an individual is left or right handed) or this information may be joined with information about architecture and applied to a specific individual, e.g. this genome, Bob's genome, has gene LRRTM1 on chromosome 2p12 and, therefore, Bob is likely to be left handed. It is important to remember, however, that even if presented in the latter form, any information about the *significance* of the variation for Bob may be relevant to others *both* because information about what Bob's architecture *is* may be generalised to them (e.g. as blood relatives) and the *significance* of possession of that architecture even if they are not related to Bob. Of course, *significance* of a variation will go beyond the significance for the observable characteristics; it will extend to include those things that are associated with the observable characteristics. In the example of 'handedness', this would include the consequences of any social stereotyping of sinister left-handers. Of course, the accuracy of any generalisation as to *significance* may be just as fallible as the accuracy of any generalisation as to *architecture* itself. This is because the information about what the genetic code *is* is invariably only probabilistic when it comes to the manifestation of observable characteristics: not all individuals with LRRTM1 on chromosome 2p12 will be left handed. Its significance for social reasons is, of course, also highly variable. This does not prevent the attribution of qualities associated with a particular individual that has certain architectural features being applied more broadly: information about individuals will inform the interpretive frameworks applied to others.

This makes it difficult to know, when data is (initially) attributed with significance for one individual, what significance this will have, or come to have, for others. The uncertainty is compounded by the fact that, not only do the two types of genetic information not always travel together, but they may be generated at quite different times. In the past the *significance* of architecture tended always to be known before the architecture itself could be identified: it was possible to know what it meant before it was possible to know what it was. The significance of particular genetic variations was evident in phenotypic traits before we had the wherewithal to identify the detail of the associated architecture. For example, that haemophilia is an inherited condition was known long before even the pattern of inheritance was worked out (by 'the Eugenics

[9] C. Francks, S. Maegawa, J. Laurén, B. S. Abrahams *et al.*, 'LRRTM1 on chromosome 2p12 is a maternally suppressed gene that is associated paternally with handedness and schizophrenia', *Molecular Psychiatry* 12(12) (2007), 1129–39, (Epub. 31 July 2007). www.ncbi.nlm.nih.gov/pubmed/17667961.

Society' in 1911).[10] Once the pattern of inheritance had been worked out, then the *risk* of haemophilia could be calculated before an individual displayed symptoms by gathering information about their relatives. The significance of the architecture was, therefore, known before a particular (presymptomatic) individual's architecture could even be estimated. As the probabilistic data about architecture for particular individuals was gathered from information about their relatives, individuals subject to particular interpretations by others would at least, typically, have had warning that their own data might be interpreted in particular ways. This is no longer the case.

It is increasingly likely that details of architecture will be known before the significance of this architecture *for anyone* can be assessed. This further undermines an ability to know what others might (come to) conclude from any architectural information they perceive about us (now). Our inability to know what information others gather about genetic architecture, as well as the significance they attribute to that information, is exacerbated by the fact that it will often not be considered important to know precisely *what* our individual architectures are – only (the chances of) *whether* we possess relevant features. Information indicative of *whether* particular architectural features (which are, or which become, associated with significance) may be perceived by others without us appreciating that genetic information about either architecture or significance is being gathered at all.

What cf. whether

People are generally only interested in knowing what genetic architecture is because they want to know *whether* an individual possesses a variation associated with some *other* trait[11] to which they attribute significance.[12] Knowing whether an architectural variation associated with a particular meaning is possessed will typically be more valuable information than knowing what is the precise nature of that variation. This kind of genetic information – information about *whether* a particular architecture is possessed – would be particularly hard to regulate if the interpretive potential of data were neglected. This is because it is just the kind of

---

[10] S. Jones, *In the Blood: God, Genes and Destiny* (London: HarperCollins, 1996), 252.

[11] Or a characteristic, e.g. consanguinity, not easily described as a trait per se.

[12] If we return to the example of haemophilia, then even now the value of knowing precisely which genetic variation is responsible for an individual's haemophilia lies only in the significance of that information for other decisions, e.g. the particular kind of treatment received, or the eligibility for particular trials. www.ptcbio.com/6.1.3_HAB_Genetic_Testing.aspx.

information that can be *inferred* from many things other than data recognised as *genetic* because of its interpretive pedigree.

Genetic information as an indicator

Possession of a genetic variation (variation 'a') associated with a particular valued trait (trait 'z') might be inferred through display of the trait (such as with haemophilia) or knowledge and understanding of the details of the architecture of the variation itself *if* that detail can itself be presented for analysis. These two ways of gathering genetic information might be put at opposite ends of a spectrum. They are so distinct, it is even possible that a party could fail to make the connection between them, e.g. one might observe phenotype without understanding the genetic significance or one might observe genotype without understanding the phenotypic significance. It may, however, also be possible to identify a relationship between the variation ('a'), the trait ('z') and some other characteristics ('b', 'c', 'd', etc.). These 'indicative' characteristics might not (otherwise) possess any particular significance but they might be located at any point along that spectrum described and sometimes more closely associated with one end (i.e. genotype) or the other (i.e. phenotype).

A 'test' for a genetic variation ('a', and, in turn, the significant trait 'z' associated with it) might then assume the nature of a test for an 'indicative characteristic' (such as 'b', 'c' or 'd'). It is quite possible that the association between the indicative characteristic and either genetic variation or significant trait may be due to a simple correlation rather than any causal relationship. If the correlation is taken to be sufficiently reliable, then the observation of the indicative characteristic may nevertheless serve as a proxy test for either architecture or significant trait.

Such proxy tests can be hugely variable with regard to both sensitivity and specificity.[13] Indicative characteristics can yield genetic information even though they may, scientifically speaking, have no genetic basis. For example, it was once thought that males with an extra Y chromosome

---

[13] An example of where there is a variation in the accuracy of a test is provided by Down's syndrome. An individual with Down's syndrome will possess a chromosomal anomaly of three chromosome no. 21. Information about this aspect of the child's genetic architecture is almost equally available to one capable of interpreting the phenotypic characteristics as to one capable of accessing and understanding a karyotype of the child's genome. Assuming no procedural errors, a karyotype will be 100% accurate. Phenotypic observation will, however, be accurate in 95% of cases. While the vast majority of children with Down's syndrome (approximately 95%) have an extra 21 chromosome, this is not true in all cases. www.thearc.org/faqs/down.html.

would be predisposed to violent criminal behaviour.[14] If violent criminality ran in a family, then one might have hypothesised that the male
members of that family were more likely than most to be carrying an
extra Y chromosome. Although the link is now discredited, it is the
perception that informs an interpretive framework. While one would
hope that the instances of such mistake were rare in clinical testing, they
may occur rather more regularly in the public consciousness (perhaps
driven by the media reporting of the results of particular studies as there
being a 'gene for ...'[15]). What is more, unfortunately, even systematic
and hugely important decisions by public authorities have not been
immune to erroneous associations in the past.[16] The point is that the
reliability of indirect tests yielding accurate genetic information can be
hugely variable. What is more, perceptions can change and shifts in
interpretive frameworks can dramatically alter the nature and quality
of the information gathered from 'indicative characteristics'.

In all cases, the motivation for interpretation is always towards the
trait 'z'. As with genetic architecture, indicative characteristics are valued
because of their ability to inform of other things. At times, however, the
nature of those other things does turn upon the *genetic* interpretation of
the data perceived, and the significance of that interpretation may
change over time. An example here might be colour blindness. Colour
blindness is (most often) due to genetic architecture. A test for colour
blindness can, therefore, reveal something about the genetic architecture
of the person tested: an inability to distinguish between certain colours is
itself an indicative characteristic. Of course, the genetic qualities of the

---

[14] For discussion of the limitations of studies, including the study that sought to link an
extra Y chromosome to criminal behaviour, see an editorial in the *BMJ*: 'Biological
influences on criminal behaviour: how good is the evidence?', *BMJ* 310 (1995), 272.

[15] It would be easy to read an article such as Andy Coghlan's 'Elite athletes are born to
run', *New Scientist* (30 August 2003), 2410 and draw conclusions about the probable
genetic architecture of Usain Bolt. However, it is true that if someone were looking to
have an athletic child, then they might have considered Bolt a suitable partner (or sperm
donor) regardless of whether they had read an article on ACTN3. This is because, as
already noted, it is whether genetic variation attributed significance is perceived that
matters and not what that architectural variation is perceived to be. However, such
articles do promote a particular kind of genetic information, i.e. more detailed
information about architecture, and this might have significance if that detail comes to
be associated with other things. What is more, it might link genetics to characteristics
not previously considered to be related to genetic architecture at all, e.g. perhaps
possession of a 'beer belly': BBC, 'Beer belly "gene" found' (8th January 2003).
http://news.bbc.co.uk/1/hi/health/2636509.stm.

[16] See, for example, the association between 'feeble-mindedness' and genetics
found within Eugenic sterilisation laws passed in many countries in the early twentieth
century and infamously upheld in the US Supreme Court case of *Buck* v. *Bell*, 274 U.S.
200 (1927).

test will, as with *any* genetic information, only be revealed if the appropriate genetic interpretation is applied to the test data. For most purposes, it will be largely irrelevant that the condition is inherited (as it is the phenotypic trait that matters to people). However, in the past, *heritable* colour blindness has been controversially associated with manic-depressive illness.[17] For an individual making *that* association, it *will* matter whether colour blindness was due to genetic factors or caused by accident or illness.

Some definitions of 'genetic tests' acknowledge that their purpose is typically to indicate significant traits rather than to reveal genetic architecture for its own sake. For example, the US Task Force on Genetic Testing stated that, broadly defined, genetic tests include,

The analysis of human DNA, RNA, chromosomes, proteins, and certain metabolites in order to detect heritable disease-related genotypes, mutations, phenotypes, or karyotypes for clinical purposes. Such purposes include predicting risk of disease, identifying carriers, establishing prenatal and clinical diagnosis or prognosis. Prenatal, newborn, and carrier screening, as well as testing in high risk families, are included. Tests for metabolites are covered only when they are undertaken with high probability that an excess or deficiency of the metabolite indicates the presence of heritable mutations in single genes. Tests conducted purely for research are excluded from the definition, as are tests for somatic (as opposed to heritable) mutations, and testing for forensic purposes.[18]

In the UK, the Human Genetics Advisory Committee (HGAC) described genetic testing as,

testing to detect the presence or absence of, or alteration in, a particular gene sequence, chromosome or a gene product, in relation to a genetic disorder.[19]

Each of these definitions is consistent with the idea of genetic testing for indicative characteristics for particular purposes: in these examples,

---

[17] M. Baron, 'Linkage between an X-chromosome marker (deutan color blindness) and bipolar affective illness occurrence in the family of a lithium carbonate-responsive schizo-affective proband', *Archives of General Psychiatry* 34(6) (1977), 721–5; J. Mendlewicz, P. Linkowski, J. J. Guroff and H. M. Van Praag, 'Color blindness linkage to bipolar manic-depressive illness', *Archives of General Psychiatry* 36(13) (1979), 1442–7. However, see also E. S. Gershon, S. D. Targum, S. Matthysse and W. E. Bunney, Jr, 'Color blindness not closely linked to bipolar illness', *Archives of General Psychiatry* 36(13) (1979), 1423–30.

[18] Task Force on Genetic Testing of the NIH-DOE Working Group on Ethical, Legal and Social Implications of Human Genome Research, 'Final Report of the Task Force on Genetic Testing: promoting safe and effective genetic testing in the United States' (Baltimore, MD: NIH, 1997), Introduction. www.genome.gov/10001733.

[19] Human Genetic Advisory Committee (HGAC), 'The implications of genetic testing for employment' (London: Department of Trade and Industry, June 1999).

indirect genetic testing for clinical purposes in connection with a genetic disorder. The purpose and method of genetic testing in such circumstances may render *detail* of genetic architecture of little significance. If a particular genetic disorder is associated with the presence of specific product 'b', then a test for 'b' may be just as effective and reliable a test for that variation as direct analysis of the genetic architecture. If a particular phenotype, 'z', is strongly associated with possession of the allele, then observation of the phenotype itself will again indicate possession of the relevant architecture.

There will be circumstances where indirect tests yield information of equivalent certainty or reliability as direct examination of the architecture of 'a'. However, there will probably be many more occasions where there is a variation in the specificity and sensitivity of an 'indirect' test, at least when it comes to revealing details of architecture. Given the methodological differences between direct and indirect genetic tests it might, therefore, be tempting to add a third category of genetic information to the two previously described. In addition to recognising information about genetic architecture and genetic significance as categories of genetic information we might add genetic indicators: information from which possession of a specific genetic variation may be deduced or inferred. To add this category would, however, be to suggest a distinction without a substantive difference.

It has already been emphasised that it is information about *significance* that is important, and it is information about significance that will inform the relevant interpretive framework. It cannot be assumed that direct analysis of the architecture of DNA will necessarily lead to more reliable *significant* information or a more accurate interpretation of the perceived data. Not only need it not necessarily lead to more reliable information about an individual's architecture (this will depend, at least in part, upon the reliability and integrity of *particular* methods of testing) but, more importantly, even if detail of architecture could *always* be known with greater certainty through direct testing, the attribution of that architecture *with significance* relies upon an association made through other evidence. The association between *significant* characteristic and test result might even be stronger through an 'indirect test' than a 'direct test'. For example, the fact that Bob has gene LRRTM1 on chromosome 2p12 might be known with relative certainty if we directly interrogate chromosome 2p12, but the 'significant' information that Bob is, therefore, more likely to be left handed, or suffer social discrimination as a result, relies upon other information which has a completely different evidence base (and may be more or less reliable than the information about architecture itself).

One might conclude, therefore, that information about *whether* a trait attributed with significance is possessed, through genetic interpretation, will *always* be obtained *through* a proxy for the significant trait itself. Even a direct genetic test will only reveal information about genetic architecture associated (or not) with the characteristic associated with significance. If the characteristic has yet to be observed in the individual, and its manifestation is expected to be observable, then, until the trait manifests, the proxy will continue to stand as an indicator of uncertain reliability. What is more, it uncertainly indicates something that the individual may be wholly unaware of themselves. It is this uncertainty, coupled with the predictive quality of much genetic data[20] – potentially revealing things that the individual is unaware of, and may not want to be aware of – that fuels some of the disquiet surrounding the acquisition and use of genetic information.

In the case of *R* v. *Chief Constable of South Yorkshire ex parte S and Marper*[21] Baroness Hale quoted the Canadian Privacy Commissioner in his report on *Genetic Testing and Privacy*:[22]

Modern explorers have set sail on voyages into the genetic microcosm, seeking a medically powerful but potentially dangerous treasure: information about how our genes make us tick. Today, we can ask who among us is likely to have healthy babies or fall ill with a genetic disease. In the future, we may be able to use genetic testing to tell us who will be smart, be anti-social, work hard, be athletic or conform to prevailing standards of beauty.[23]

While the Privacy Commissioner's fears may have as much to do with science fiction as with any realistic science future, it is the fear itself that is real: it is the perception that informs the interpretation. In this future, it is *whether* you are perceived to possess a particular genetic variation *that is attributed with significance* that will count. This is why a composite understanding of genetic information is so important to understanding the perceived privacy risks associated with access to genetic information at large. These risks cannot be adequately addressed by an understanding of genetic information that associates it simply with a particular *interpretive pedigree*.

---

[20] The idea of a 'future diary' has been used to describe this particular quality. See e.g. G. L. Annas and S. Elias (eds.), *Gene Mapping: Using Law and Ethics as Guides* (New York: Oxford University Press, 1992), 9 or G. J. Annas, 'Privacy rules for DNA databanks – protecting coded "Future Diaries"', *Journal of the American Medical Association* 270 (1993) 2346–50.

[21] [2004] UKHL 39.   [22] Para. 74.

[23] Privacy Commissioner of Canada, 'Genetic testing and privacy' (Ottawa, Ontario: The Privacy Commissioner of Canada, 1995), 2.

A composite understanding of genetic information

If it is correct to suggest that information is a composite of data and interpretation, then there is a significant implication for our understanding of both the character and the acquisition of genetic information. If information can only be described as being of a certain character when it is placed within an interpretive framework that recognises it as such, then it follows that, by changing the interpretive framework, you can change the character and status of information.[24] Whether a particular piece of data is correctly described as genetic information will depend as much upon the nature of the interpretation as upon the physical characteristics or source of the data itself. A karyotype is an example of data that has been extracted and presented in such a way that it is difficult for one receiving it to deny acquisition of genetic information. A modern example of data that indicates its potential for 'genetic' interpretation through its form of presentation may be represented by a series of the four characters A, C, G and T. Not all genetic information will be gathered from data presented for analysis in a way deliberately to indicate its potential for genetic interpretation. If it is the *acquisition and use* of genetic information that threatens particular expectations of exclusivity, then emphasis should be shifted from the physical characteristics of the data that is interpreted, to the nature of the information that is extracted from it: it is the possibility of interpretation that is significant. More than this, it is the possibility of *association* with information that is significant. Neither historic[25] nor prophetic[26] examples of unfair uses of genetic information have been exclusively associated with specific kinds of genetic data.

Concern with genetic discrimination in the employment context, for example, has described those at risk as including not only (a) those individuals currently asymptomatic or presymptomatic who possess a particular genetic predisposition to future disease but also (b) those

---

[24] It also forces recognition of the fact that data may correctly be described as non-genetic information in one context but also correctly described as genetic information in another. If the data, in the context, informs of something about genetic status then it is genetic information; if it does not, it is not.

[25] P. R. Billings, M. A. Kohn, M. de Cuevas, J. Beckwith, J. S. Alper and M. R. Natowicz, 'Discrimination as a consequence of genetic testing', *American Journal of Human Genetics* 50 (1992), 476–82; L. N. Geller, J. S. Alper, P. R. Billings, C. I. Barash, J. Beckwith and M. R. Natowicz, 'Individual, family, and societal dimensions of genetic discrimination: a case study analysis', *Science and Engineering Ethics* 2 (1996), 71–88.

[26] W. Allen and H. Ostrer, 'Anticipating unfair uses of genetic information', *American Journal of Human Genetics* 53 (1993), 16–21.

individuals who are carriers of a recessive deleterious gene and who are mistakenly *perceived* to be at increased risk of developing a disorder, and (c) relatives of those individuals who have, or are presumed to have, genetic conditions.[27] Individuals have reported genetic discrimination in the insurance context as a result of family history as well as genetic test results.[28] The uncertainty associated with the genetic information gathered following a presumption made about an individual's relative does not undermine the description of the information as genetic information. Rather it confirms the need to recognise any data susceptible to a genetic interpretation as capable of yielding relevant genetic information.

The difficulty with this analysis is the fact that interpretive frameworks themselves may be hard to predict, control or at times even recognise. The diversity and fluidity of interpretive frameworks could render the category of 'genetic information' hopelessly uncertain. This may raise some practical difficulties if an attempt is made to distinguish genetic information from other types of 'data' for the purposes of regulation. It is, however, an inevitable conclusion once the composite nature of genetic information has been realised and it does not prevent regulation targeting of the relationships in which genetic data exposes particular vulnerabilities. A very broad concept of genetic information appears to be the one preferred by some respectable bodies that have considered the issue. For example, the Human Genetics Commission (HGC) stated, in their report *Inside Information*,

We consider personal genetic information to be information about the genetic make-up of an identifiable person, whether derived directly from DNA (or other biochemical) testing methods or indirectly from any other source.[29]

Nevertheless, perhaps in an attempt to avoid some of the problems inherent in recognising such a broad definition of genetic information there have been attempts to break down this broad concept in particular ways. For example, the HGC themselves go on in their report to distinguish between three different types of *personal* genetic information:

the genotype provides details, at the fundamental level of DNA or protein, of precise variations inherited from both parents;

---

[27] J. D. Gardner-Hopkins, 'Unemployable genes: genetic discrimination in the workplace', *Auckland University Law Review* 9(2) (2001), 435–68 at 438–9.
[28] Y. Bombard, G. Veenstra, J. M. Friedman, S. Creighton, L. Currie, J. S. Paulsen, J. L. Bottorff and M. R. Hayden, 'Perceptions of genetic discrimination among people at risk for Huntington's disease: a cross sectional survey', *BMJ* 338 (2009), b2175.
[29] HGC, 'Inside information' (London: HGC, 2002), 13.

the phenotype is the observable outcome in terms of physical (e.g. eye colour) or physiological (e.g. blood pressure) characteristics, and;

family information, showing the pattern of inheritance of different phenotypes, is another way of presenting genetic detail.[30]

Consistent with the previous analysis, I suggest that the attempt to subdivide genetic information into different types defined *according to source* alone would be flawed as a regulatory strategy with any ambition to protect privacy. The categorisation unjustifiably privileges one aspect of the information-gathering process and fails to pay sufficient heed to the composite nature of genetic information. If genetic information is to be subdivided into 'types' at all, then these 'types' must surely be derived from differences in the information perceived (and the treatment of that data by norms of exclusivity) rather than due to a feature of its interpretive pedigree. Otherwise, we are in danger of attempting to distinguish between types of egg by naming the hens laying them.

The HGC do in fact offer an alternative breakdown of genetic information according to differences in the information that is perceived. Again, however, I think there would be problems with the categorisation if one is concerned with ensuring that a regulatory system conceptualised genetic information in ways that were consistent with privacy protection. In fact, the problems with a classification of genetic information that divided it into the categories of 'observable' versus 'private' genetic information might be particularly acute.

Private vs. observable cf. sensitive vs. non-sensitive

The HGC subdivide the class of information that they describe as 'personal genetic information' in a way that is significant if one is trying to understand the privacy implications of access to genetic information. They represent the relationship between the different categories through the use of a diagram that uses four circles each to represent a different category of genetic information: 'non-sensitive genetic information', 'private genetic information', 'sensitive genetic information' and 'observable genetic information'.[31] Through the use of the diagram they attempt to demonstrate the ways in which these different categories of genetic information might overlap and the distinctions which are maintained. In particular, they claim that a distinction may be drawn between personal genetic information which is private and that which is

---

[30] *Ibid.*, 26.   [31] *Ibid.*, 28.

observable, and that a further distinction can be drawn between that which is sensitive and that which is not.[32]

It is by suggesting that a distinction may be maintained between 'private' and 'observable' genetic information that I think the HGC categorisation proves most problematic. While, in the last chapter, I supported Laurie's contention that privacy relates to a state of separateness from others, I also claimed that relevant separation could *not* be assessed unless one took stock of particular norms of exclusivity. Exclusivity may be demanded irrespective of whether information is observable. Indeed, I previously relied upon the example of a conversation on a crowded train to make the point. While not separate from others in a geographical sense, we might nevertheless expect them to avoid particular kinds of transaction with us: e.g. to avoid intruding upon a private conversation. That is to say, a conversation may be 'private' in one sense even though it is 'observable' in another. What is a reasonable expectation of separation from others will be determined by the operative norm of exclusivity.

When this is put into the context of genetic information, it can be shown to be a mistake to concede – from a perspective concerned with privacy protection – that the fact that genetic information is 'observable' means that it is not private. I place the word observable in inverted commas because, of course, it should be clear by now that genetic information is not observable per se. The necessity of an interpretive framework, which may be more or less widely shared, can help to illustrate that what is 'observable' genetic information to one individual might most definitely be considered 'private' information by another. This can perhaps be seen most clearly when the interpretive framework is not so common. The fact that information has been interpreted from observable characteristics does not automatically entitle the individual who has interpreted those characteristics to disclose the findings. For example, a missing piece of chromosome 22 is associated with not only a one in ten chance of developing schizophrenia but also a characteristic face.[33] Anyone with such a characteristic face, but unaware of its significance, will be unwittingly displaying genetic information to all who possess a suitably informed interpretive framework. The public display

---

[32] This approach can be contrasted with one that considers all genetic information to be private information. For example, David Keays claims that 'genetic information is by its very nature extremely private'. D. Keays, 'The legal implications of genetic testing: insurance, employment and privacy', *Journal of Law and Medicine* 6 (1999), 357–72 at 361.

[33] Jones, *In the Blood*, 235.

of the interpretable data does not entitle an individual who perceives the risk of schizophrenia to deny automatically that it is private information.

One more possible distinction needs to be considered before I revert to my insistence that it is really only information about *whether a genetic variation associated with significance* is possessed that is important. This is the distinction between personal genetic information and human genetic information.

Personal genetic information vs. human genetic information

The HGC draw a distinction between 'personal genetic information' which is 'information about a person's genetic characteristics'[34] and 'human genetic information' which is information about the genetic characteristics of the human race more generally. As already implied, however, it is worth explicitly recognising that it is no more meaningful to talk of 'the' human genome in the abstract than it would be to talk of 'the' human. *Every* complete human genome is, by definition, that of an individual. There are, of course, remarkable consistencies between human genomes and vast amounts of the detail of sequence and arrangement are held in common. One might describe those things that human genomes have in common, as one may describe those things that people have in common. This means that information about an individual's genetic architecture will also, most likely, be information about the genetic architecture of others. This is a truism that genetic research relies upon for much of its value. Exactly how likely we are to share architecture will depend, in large part, upon how closely related we are, but each of our individual genetic differences will (most likely) be held in common with others whether related or not. We just will not know which differences are shared with others (unless we can observe characteristics which we interpret to yield common data). Which others share precisely which similarities and differences *in architecture* will only be definitively determined through testing more than one individual and comparing the results. We will only ever be sure exactly how common, and how different, our genomes are by determining the architecture of each of them.

The more genomes that are compared, the more certainly the frequency and pattern with which particular sequences and arrangements are common between persons can be predicted, and the more tests that can be developed for specific (combinations of) variations. As the

---

[34] Human Genetics Commission, *Inside Information: Balancing Interests in the Use of Personal Genetic Data* (London: HGC, 2002), 7.

individuals that are tested vary in various phenotypic ways, links will be drawn between the possession of specific genetic characteristics and the possession of, predispositions towards or susceptibilities to certain other observable characteristics and traits.[35] Eventually, such associations may form the basis of tests for genetic variations themselves: the phenotypic trait may be the 'non-genetic data' that is interpreted to inform of the genetic characteristic. As genetic research continues, one can expect such associations to be made with increasing regularity and reported. As this happens, the availability and content of the interpretive frameworks yielding 'personal genetic information' are directly related to the research designed to yield information about 'human genetic information'.

There is no clear-cut distinction between 'personal' and 'human' genetic information. This means all research using human genetic information has potential privacy implications for the accessibility and content of personal genetic information. If relevant 'human' interpretive frameworks proliferate, then access to 'personal' genetic information will change.

Changing access to genetic information

Access to genetic information is undoubtedly becoming easier for a number of reasons. Tests which directly interrogate samples of DNA for specific variations are becoming cheaper and technically easier to perform. A sample of genetic data is relatively easy to come by (hair or bodily fluid may be obtained surreptitiously), and genetic testing kits are becoming available 'over-the-counter' and genetic testing services are increasingly available through the Internet and via mail-order.

Miniaturised testing platforms using micro-chip array technology and known as 'gene chips' have been developed which enable the almost instant testing of a single DNA sample for hundreds of known genetic variations. In 2002 the journal *Nature: Biotechnology* published a supplement[36] (the second in fact) on the subject of DNA chips. Titled 'The Chipping Forecast II', it described not only how the use of micro-array technology has become widespread but also how it continues to

---

[35] For an example of research reliant upon this principle see the International HapMap Project. The project's goal is to compare the genetic sequences of different individuals to identify chromosomal regions where genetic variants are shared. The hope is that this information will allow researchers to associate particular shared variations with particular diseases. http://hapmap.ncbi.nlm.nih.gov/.

[36] 'The Chipping Forecast II', *Nature Genetics* 32(4) (2002), Supplement, 461–552.

transform the study of gene expression.[37] Technological advances are then undoubtedly making it increasingly easy to retrieve genetic data about an individual from a (non-intimate) body sample.

It should be emphasised, however, that the utilisation of such technology to facilitate the delivery of tests to consumers is unlikely to generate information (for that consumer) about (detailed) genetic architecture. The consumers of such testing services and products will probably only be concerned about *whether* they possess a variation associated with some significance. In the same way as a pregnancy test can give an individual information about whether she is pregnant without her understanding (or having much interest in) how the test works, a genetic test may enable an individual to discover whether she possesses a genetic variation associated with some significant characteristic, without her knowing (or caring) what genetic architecture is actually associated with that variation. As information about whether a genetic variation is possessed is still genetic information, however, so long as the individual is aware that the test implies something of her genetic architecture she will gather genetic information (although it will not be of any superfluous detail).

Access to genetic information through such genetic tests is only likely to continue to improve, as there is a clear financial incentive for companies to continue to identify genes associated with particular traits and then market tests which indicate whether an individual possesses a particular gene (variant). As companies have invested in identifying particular associations, there will be a strong financial incentive for them to attempt to recoup those investment costs through the aggressive marketing of diagnostic and prognostic tests.[38] It should not be thought, however, that access to genetic information will increase solely due to private sector activity. Genetic research, and the identification of genetic characteristics that may be associated with phenotypic traits, has also been heavily funded by the public sector. Large international research projects continue to be funded by the public purse.

---

[37] For commentary, specifically on some of the problems that remain with the use of the technology, see J. Knight, 'When the chips are down', *Nature* 410 (2001), 860–1. See also A. Brazma, A. Robinson, G. Cameron and M. Ashburner, 'One-stop shop for microarray data', *Nature* 403 (2000), 699–700, for the problems and the promise associated with a public DNA-microarray database.

[38] This may be related to what has been described as market-driven manufacturing, or, as described by Professor Heidi Li Feldman in a presentation at the Ahrens Tort Symposium, as 'markufacturing'. For comment on the concerns associated with the practice see R. Brownsword, 'Causes for concern and causes of action: a comment on "pushing drugs"', *Washburn Law Journal* 42(3) (2003), 601–14.

Reflection

As the interpretive frameworks capable of generating genetic information flourish, so access to genetic information will continue to increase. As specific genetic variations come to be associated with phenotypic characteristics within the popular consciousness, e.g. breast cancer and BRCA1 and BRCA2, then people will *perceive* genetic information more readily. The combined effect of technological progress coupled with the shift in popular consciousness (and the dissemination of 'genetic' interpretive frameworks) is that, as well as it becoming easier to access genetic information, the volume of genetic information available for access is actually increasing.

The quality of the information gathered is likely to vary dramatically, but the more that data is (correctly or incorrectly) perceived to have a genetic dimension, the more that people will have access to genetic information. That information will take one of two forms: information about what a genetic code *is* or information about what it *means* to possess a particular kind of genetic architecture. Because the direction of travel is always towards an understanding of the significance of any genetic variation, indicative characteristics may be considered as important as detailed information about architecture: information about *whether* a particular variation may be possessed, and the significance of it, may be perceived without a detailed (or even accurate) understanding of the underlying genetic architecture of the variation, and indirect tests for genetic variation may be relied upon in preference to direct genetic tests. One reason for such preference might, in some cases, be the relative accessibility of data, such as observable characteristics, even if the genetic information generated was a less reliable indicator of genetic architecture than any direct genetic tests.

The range of potential data sources renders it unlikely that it will often be useful, and indeed at times it may even be potentially counterproductive, to define types of genetic information according to the data source. In so far as source has an impact upon the information gathered, then there may be circumstances in which it would be relevant to take it into account, but, ultimately, it will be the significance *given* to data that will have an impact upon people's lives.

The relevance of the interpretive frameworks to the generation of significant data should not, therefore, be underestimated. As interpretive frameworks change in their quality and character it may become increasingly unhelpful (and perhaps even less meaningful) to attempt to limit 'genetic information' to information derived from a particular data source. Also, the significance of the perception of what is understood to be an indicator of a particular genetic architecture is not dependent simply upon the perception of *that* data. The significance attached to the perception will be informed by an interpretive framework informed by other genetic information, often gathered from a range of sources, many of which will typically have had no previous association with that individual. The links that are drawn between what the code is and what it means will have implications for many more individuals than those involved in the original association. What is more, the relevant indicator itself may not even be associated with an individual as a particular identifiable individual. It is possible that the indicator perceived to have some kind of significance is associated with membership of a particular family, group, organisation or broader community.

Any regulatory regime concerned with access to information of a particular kind should, therefore, be concerned with *any* data that has a particular interpretive potential and not fixate upon interpretive pedigree. What is more, if *privacy* is concerned with respecting particular norms of exclusivity, then regulatory regimes should recognise that the *associative potential* of data is determined by many things other than whether data is *currently* associated with a particular identifiable individual. Research using genetic data is seeking to uncover what possession of particular genetic variations *means* for particular individuals. That which is learnt will have significance for many more than those individuals or groups currently involved.

4   The law

Privacy was described in Chapter 2 as concerning norms of exclusivity. It was recognised that norms might be established in patterns of behaviour or particular preferences and that any shift in the underlying basis of such norms could have an impact on the transactional and the relational aspects of privacy. Normative shifts might occur over time and it is clearly possible to imagine these changes affecting the scope and nature of privacy expectations either dominant within a particular society or claimed by particular individuals or groups. Also, the same norms might unpack quite differently in different social and environmental circumstances. So, even if the normative base were to remain static (which may itself be unlikely), one would still expect to see privacy expectations shift as social and technological environments changed. For example, the development of photography and of the printing press dramatically affected the range of transactions considered caught within reasonable privacy claims.[1] Communities are currently grappling with determining reasonable expectations in relation to the use of mobile phones, covert cameras and the diverse possibilities of social media – including the use of Facebook and Twitter and the posting of photographs and information relating to others on globally accessible platforms.[2] Changes in the information technology associated with access to genetic information may also come to affect changes in privacy patterns, preferences and social norms of exclusivity. Changes in the underlying norms that ground privacy expectations might simply be a reflection of changing factual circumstances (changing patterns) or they might also reflect more deep-seated shifts in normative framework (changing preferences).

[1] S. D. Warren and L. D. Brandeis, 'The right to privacy', *Harvard Law Review* 4 (1890), 193. www.law.louisville.edu/library/collections/brandeis/node/225.
[2] B. Johnson, 'Privacy no longer a social norm, says Facebook founder', *The Guardian* (11 January 2010). www.guardian.co.uk/technology/2010/jan/11/facebook-privacy.

Philip Leith has suggested that, primarily because of technological and cultural changes, privacy is becoming less prevalent in society.[3] Despite this, he would agree that the juridification of privacy is most certainly not on the wane.[4] In fact, within his work Leith describes this as a paradox, with privacy rights growing apace, just at the same time as the reality of privacy recedes.[5] While it is perhaps not surprising that the relationship between the idea of privacy understood by the law and the idea of privacy extant – or perhaps even extinct – within society more generally may be indirect, the relationship between those two ideas is nevertheless important. Not least of all for the reasons pointed to earlier: there has to be some perceived coincidence between the privacy valued by people and the privacy accounted for by law, if the protection of privacy by law is to be viewed as legitimate (see Chapter 2). The relationship is also important because legal expectations are themselves likely to contribute towards the factual circumstances that help to shape the norms themselves. The norms surrounding research use of genetic data are not yet fully formed. The law plays an important part in providing the 'net drive'[6] within a society, and this is an important opportunity to help constitute a particular conception of reasonable expectations in the area.

However, this chapter does not seek to trace an idealised form of legal regulation. Rather it is concerned with trying to describe the idea of privacy that the law currently reflects. If the law is encouraging particular privacy expectations, then what are the transactional and relational aspects of the concept of privacy that it reflects? This inquiry is divided into two parts. Section I is concerned with the legal protection of privacy in general terms. It seeks to build a picture that describes the approach to privacy taken by some foundational legal instruments. Particular attention will be paid to Directive 95/46/EC of the European Union (24 October 1995) on the protection of individuals with regard to the processing of personal data and on the free movement of such data. This European Directive establishes the legal framework for data protection that is applicable across much of Europe. The requirements of the Directive are relevant to any individual or organisation, including researchers, wishing to exchange personal data with an individual or organisation that is subject to European law. It also relies upon the key term 'personal data' that has analogues in privacy law around the world. Similarity in legal protection is not particularly surprising. Not only are many countries under a responsibility to protect the right to privacy

---

[3] Leith, 'The socio-legal context of privacy', 105.   [4] *Ibid.*   [5] *Ibid.*
[6] K. Llewellyn, 'The normative, the legal, and the law-jobs: the problem of juristic method', *Yale Law Journal* 49(8) (1940), 1355–1400 at 1387.

contained within the foundational instruments discussed in Section I, but the pressures of international trade are likely to see privacy laws becoming increasingly harmonised internationally. Nevertheless, if the background right to information privacy continues to be articulated through a protection for 'personal data', then this raises some important questions for the legal protection of genetic data in research – not least of all because the Directive fails to articulate clearly for the full range of interests engaged by research using genetic data. For this reason, it does not clearly represent a sufficient protection of the public interest in proper privacy protection.

Section II is concerned with exploring some of those legal instruments that are aimed more specifically at guiding access to genetic data or to personal information in the research context. We will see the extent to which they might resolve some ambiguities or difficulties in the framework of privacy protection described in Section I. In particular, they point to some ways in which the focus upon 'personal data', and the expectations of an individual data subject, might be tempered. These more specific instruments should be consistent against the more general, background obligations considered in Section I and provide an insight into how the concept of privacy contained within those instruments might be more precisely specified in the context of research uses of genetic data.

SECTION I   A LEGAL CONCEPT OF PRIVACY

How are the normative, the transactional and the relational variables of privacy reflected in law? Given that the focus here is upon how the law establishes expectations of access to genetic *data*, only those legal standards that apply to either data or information will be considered. Those concerned specifically with norms surrounding access to human biological material, especially human tissue, are considered in Chapter 7. Having said that, *the distinction* between data, information and tissue is not explicitly recognised by a number of important legal instruments.

Universal Declaration of Human Rights

The Universal Declaration of Human Rights was adopted by the General Assembly of the United Nations on 10 December 1948. Article 12 of the Declaration proclaims that:

No one shall be subjected to arbitrary interference with his privacy, family, home or correspondence, nor to attacks upon his honour and reputation. Everyone has the right to the protection of the law against such interference or attacks.

The Universal Declaration represented a landmark in the international recognition of a right to enjoy privacy without unjustified interference. It did not, however, explain what was meant by the term 'privacy', nor did it indicate how the idea should be understood to relate to family, home, correspondence, honour or reputation. It also failed to indicate how any interference with privacy (or the other things listed) was to be judged arbitrary; important questions about what is non-arbitrary interference are unaddressed by Article 12. Later, specifically within Article 29(2), it is recognised by the Declaration that:

In the exercise of his rights and freedoms, everyone shall be subject only to such limitations as are determined by law solely for the purpose of securing due recognition and respect for the rights and freedoms of others and of meeting the just requirements of morality, public order and the general welfare in a democratic society.

Thus, Article 29(2) does go some way to explaining what might constitute a justified interference with privacy, but its conditions are still not clear. When precisely would it be permissible for law to allow interference for the purposes of securing either the rights and freedoms of others or the just requirements of morality, public order and the general welfare in a democratic society? If the conditions of qualification were to be entirely at the discretion of national law, then the right to privacy recognised by the Declaration would be seriously compromised. If there are limits to the extent that national law might encroach upon the right to privacy in the name of, for example, 'the general welfare', then how are those limits to be determined?

The language of the Universal Declaration does not itself provide clear answers to these questions. It does, however, take us an important step towards recognising that privacy must, at least, be accounted for by a regulatory system and justification must be provided for any failure to prevent an interference with it. Because of the norms enshrined within the Universal Declaration, it is also implicit that the justification must be consistent with the idea of fundamental rights and freedoms. The Declaration's recognition of such fundamental rights and freedoms only in relation to *the individual* does, however, indicate a relatively narrow range of social units that might have their privacy infringed. Society as a whole is specifically mentioned only when describing the conditions that might justify a restriction of privacy and not within the positive expression of the right itself. The indication is not, of course, conclusive. It is possible to construct a reading of the Declaration that holds individuals as members of groups to be entitled to enjoy privacy as well as if they were identifiable as particular persons.

Language that is open to interpretation tends to be clarified only through application. However, as the Universal Declaration does not establish binding legal obligations, there is no mechanism whereby a definitive application of the rights it recognises may be judged and there is no clarifying jurisprudence to which we might turn to aid our understanding.[7] Despite its ambiguity, the countries that have signed up to the Universal Declaration have, nevertheless, undertaken to strive to ensure that the laws for which they are responsible are consistent with its requirements. In Europe, the requirements of the Universal Declaration are now represented (admittedly in filtered form) within a regional commitment of some considerable significance. While cast, like the Universal Declaration, at a relatively high level of abstraction, this commitment itself provides useful insight into how the rights and freedoms identified by the Universal Declaration have been more specifically understood.

The European Convention for the Protection of Human Rights and Fundamental Freedoms

In 1950, members of the Council of Europe resolved:

as the governments of European countries which are like-minded and have a common heritage of political traditions, ideals, freedom and the rule of law to take the first steps for the collective enforcement of certain of the rights stated in the Universal Declaration.[8]

It was agreed that the obligation to secure the rights defined within the European Convention on Human Rights (the 'Convention') was to be legally binding. Through Article 19 of the Convention, the members created the European Court of Human Rights (the 'Court'). Since its inception the Court has been responsible for determining the precise nature and scope of the rights that, although originally stated in the

---

[7] The rights have been carried forward into two international covenants that are legally binding: the International Covenant on Civil and Political Rights (www2.ohchr.org/english/law/ccpr.htm) and the International Covenant on Economic, Social and Cultural Rights (www2.ohchr.org/english/law/cescr.htm). To some extent their importance for many countries, including for members of the Council of Europe, has been overtaken by other human rights developments. Certainly, in Europe, the European Convention for the Protection of Human Rights and Fundamental Freedoms (ECHR) represents a more significant undertaking by Member States and I will not further consider the relevance of these two international covenants here. The interested reader may, however, refer to J. H. Gerards, A. W. Heringa and H. L. Janssen, *Genetic Discrimination and Genetic Privacy in a Comparative Perspective* (Antwerp, Oxford and New York: Intersentia, 2005), 28–30.

[8] Preamble.

Universal Declaration, have been subsequently enshrined within the Convention. The most important of these for the protection of privacy is Article 8 of the Convention. Article 8 states:

1 Everyone has the right to respect for his private and family life, his home and his correspondence.
2 There shall be no interference by a public authority with the exercise of this right except such as is in accordance with the law and is necessary in a democratic society in the interests of national security, public safety or the economic well-being of the country, for the prevention of disorder or crime, for the protection of health or morals, or for the protection of the rights and freedoms of others.

Although Article 8 refers to 'private life' rather than 'privacy', it carries forward the commitment within the Universal Declaration to protect privacy, and the Article 8 right has long been understood to require that privacy is properly protected by national law.[9] The qualification on the right established in 8(1), found in 8(2), can also be seen to mirror imperfectly the more general qualification found within Article 29(2) of the Universal Declaration. The change in the relative placement of the qualification need not itself signify any more substantive change in the scope or nature of the right, but small variations in wording between Article 8 of the Convention and Article 12 of the Declaration, as well as within their respective qualifications, are more interesting.

Article 8 of the Convention appears, prima facie, to be more limited than Article 12 of the Universal Declaration because it does not explicitly include within its scope attacks upon honour or reputation. In fact, the Court has interpreted the two terms 'private and family life' in particularly broad fashion, and this inclusive approach taken towards defining the scope of each of the 'four areas of personal autonomy – private life, family life, the home and one's own correspondence' – has almost certainly brought both honour and reputation within the scope of the Convention. Indeed, the Court has suggested that there should be 'no exhaustive definition of the notion of private life' and so has expressly avoided excluding anything from the scope of activity that might potentially be privacy infringing.[10]

---

[9] For example, in 1970, the Parliamentary Assembly of the Council of Europe adopted Resolution 428 (23 January), containing a declaration on mass communication media and human rights. The Resolution noted that the right to freedom of expression is fundamental to a democratic society but also that this right could come into conflict with the right to privacy protected by Article 8. This Resolution, and the fact that an interference with privacy constitutes an interference with an individual's private life, was recently supported by the Court in *Mosley v. The United Kingdom* [2011] ECHR 774 (10 May 2011).
[10] *Niemietz v. Germany*, no. 13710/88 (1992) 16 EHRR 97.

The breadth of things that have already been recognised by the Court as engaging one's Article 8 right to a private life is described in a briefing note issued by the Council of Europe. The concepts of 'private and family life' are described as encompassing at least the following areas: the physical and psychological integrity of a person including medical treatment, psychiatric examinations, mental health and information on risks to one's health; aspects of an individual's physical and social identity, including one's name, picture, reputation, gender, sexual orientation; sexual life; the right to personal development and to establish and develop relationships with other human beings and the outside world; the right to self-determination and personal autonomy; certain activities of a professional or business nature as well as restrictions on entering professions or earning a living; files or data gathered by security services or other organs of the state; searches and seizures; surveillance of communications and telephone conversations.[11]

What is striking about this list is perhaps not only the breadth of the transactional variables implied – for it barely seems that there is an area of an individual's life that could not conceivably be subject to a privacy claim – but rather the narrowness of the relevant 'social unit' engaged in such activities. The list of activities already found by the Court to be potentially privacy infringing seems to confirm the suspicion that the relational aspect of the legal concept of privacy (at least as recognised through Article 8) is to be drawn extremely narrowly. Even the right to develop relationships with others is tied to 'personal development'. There is nothing to suggest that family, group or community interests might fall within the scope of the concept of privacy protected by the Convention.

On a more positive note, *for as long as we restrict ourselves to the perspective of the individual*, this inclusive approach to determining the scope of relevant transactions gives us every reason to suppose that access to genetic data *could* fall within the scope of Article 8 of the Convention (and presumably also Article 12 of the Declaration). I say 'could' rather than 'would' because, even though we might be confident that there will be circumstances in which an individual's genetic data would fall within the scope of Article 8, it is not entirely clear exactly *when* this will be the case. This is not only true of activities involving

[11] European Court of Human Rights, 'The concepts of "private and family life"', key case law issues, European Court of Human Rights, 24th January 2007. www.echr.coe.int/NR/rdonlyres/F6DC7D2E-1668–491E-817A-D0E29F094E14/0/COURT_n1883413_v1_Key_caselaw_issues__Art_8__The_Concepts_of_Private_ and_Family_Life.pdf.

'genetic data'. For example, although the taking and distribution of one's photograph *can* engage Article 8, it is equally clear that the taking of an individual's photograph will not *always* engage Article 8.[12] Similarly, even if we were to be confident that the acquisition of genetic data could engage Article 8, it is certainly not clear that it would *always* do so. Would there be any interference with an individual's private life if during a conversation, observing somebody to be male, I remarked that that he is likely to possess a single Y chromosome? Here the notion of 'norms of exclusivity' might be usefully invoked to explain the discrepancy but, without certainty as to the underlying norms informing the contextual judgment, it remains unclear exactly when the Court would consider research using genetic data to engage Article 8(1). Despite this background uncertainty, there are a number of relatively specific circumstances in which we can anticipate that the Court would find Article 8 engaged because of similarities with other circumstances.

Not all research using genetic data has the improvement of human health as its purpose[13] but much of it does.[14] For this reason health research will, unsurprisingly, often require access to personal information relating to an individual's health or physical condition. Acquisition of this kind of information has been found by the Court to constitute an interference with the right to a private life.

In *M.S. v. Sweden* (1997), the court noted that,

respecting the confidentiality of health data is a vital principle in the legal systems of all the Contracting Parties to the Convention. It is crucial not only to respect the sense of privacy of a patient but also to preserve his or her confidence in the medical profession and in the health services in general.[15]

---

[12] When seeking to determine the scope of the protection afforded by Article 8 in the context of photographs, the European Commission of Human Rights had regard to whether the photographs related to private or public matters and whether the material thus obtained was envisaged for a limited use or was likely to be made available to the general public. See *Von Hannover v. Germany*, no. 59320/00 (2005) 40 EHRR 1 [52].

[13] There are significant research programmes that use genetic data to consider Genetic Anthropology, Ancestry, and Ancient Human Migration. See, for example, The Genographic Project, which is seeking to discover new information about the migratory history of the human species (https://genographic.nationalgeographic.com/genographic/index.html). See also a special supplement of *Nature Genetics*: 'Genetics for the human race', *Nature Genetics* (Supplement) 36(11) (November 2004).

[14] Perhaps the most significant research project so far conducted was the Human Genome Project (HGP). One of the explicit motivations for the project, and the justifications for the huge sums of public money committed to it, was the belief that increased knowledge about the effects of DNA variations might lead to revolutionary new ways to diagnose, treat and potentially even prevent thousands of medical disorders (www.ornl.gov/sci/techresources/Human_Genome/project/about.shtml)

[15] Case 74/1996/693/885 [41].

There are numerous other examples where the court has found information relating to an individual's medical treatment or psychiatric examination to fall within the scope of Article 8(1).[16] While genetic data and health data are not synonymous (particularly given a broad reading of genetic data), they may often be closely linked and, in such cases, genetic data will engage Article 8(1).

Even if genetic data is not acquired because of its significance for health, there are still indications that it can engage Article 8 in some circumstances. In S. and Marper v. The United Kingdom [2008] ECHR 1581 (4 December), the Court found that the retention of both biological material and DNA profiles might engage an individual's right to a private life. The retention of biological material was considered significant, in part, because of the potential future uses of that material.[17] Similarly, it was the interpretive potential of DNA profiles, in this case the capacity to provide a means of identifying genetic relationships between individuals, and the possibility that DNA profiles may create inferences to be drawn on ethnic origin, that was considered significant.[18] Although the courts have shown an appreciation of the sensitivity of genetic data for individuals owing to its (not fully determined) significance beyond the details of architecture itself, what remains elusive is a clear explication of why the acquisition or retention of certain genetic data might only engage Article 8(1) in certain circumstances but not in others. Not all genetic data will have the same interpretive potential.

When S. and Marper was heard in the domestic courts, Lord Woolf stated in the Court of Appeal that it was his view that DNA material was 'regarded as being personal to the individual from whom it is taken' and it was for this reason that its retention required legal justification.[19] There must be some doubt, however, whether the simple fact that (genetic) data is 'personal to the individual' is enough for retention of data to infringe an individual's privacy. For example, as noted above, the taking of a photograph will not always be understood to engage an individual's privacy even when a photograph might be described as 'personal to the individual'.[20]

---

[16] See, for example, Z v. Finland, no. 22009/93 (1997) 25 EHRR 371 [95].

[17] Z v. Finland [69–71]. See also the comments of Baroness Hale in R. (S. and Marper) v. Chief Constable of the South Yorkshire Police [2004] UKHL 39; [2004] 1 W.L.R. 2196 at 3234.

[18] Z v. Finland, [75–6].

[19] R. (S. and Marper) v. Chief Constable of the South Yorkshire Police [2002] EWCA Civ 1275; [2002] 1 W.L.R. 3223, 3233 [32].

[20] The European Commission for Human Rights had considered it an open question whether the retention of fingerprints, photographs and records of such information amounted to an interference with the right to respect for private life under Article 8(1). McVeigh, O'Neill and Evans v. UK (1981) 5 EHRR 71 [227].

In *S. and Marper*, it appears that Lord Woolf was in part swayed by his perception of the public attitude towards the state retaining information personal to the individual.[21] Although cultural attitudes would certainly represent one normative foundation for any privacy claims, it is one that may lead to Article 8 being engaged differentially across Europe.[22] This was an implication that Lord Steyn in the House of Lords was not prepared to accept.[23] The question of retention of DNA material by the state, under conditions materially similar to those of this case, was one that he considered should receive uniform answer throughout states party to the Convention. He does not, however, explain *how* this question is to be answered if it is *not* with reference to the cultural traditions of those affected other than by reference to the jurisprudence of the European Court of Human Rights itself. While this might answer the question for UK courts, it simply pushes the question up to the Court and back to an interpretation of the Convention itself. As we have already seen, the Convention text does not provide a clear answer, and the Court has been reluctant to attempt to draw precise distinctions between those activities that can and those that cannot engage Article 8(1).[24]

When the case of *S. and Marper* did reach the European Court of Human Rights, the Court agreed that the retention of DNA samples constituted an interference with an individual's right to a private life. The explanation for this rested in large part upon the fact that the information which *could* be gathered from data owing to its interpretive potential (e.g. information relating to health) had *previously* been considered by the Court to be capable of engaging Article 8(1).[25] Again, however, such reasoning by analogy does not reveal the underlying

---

[21] He claimed that 'at least for a substantial proportion of the public there is a strong objection to the state storing information relating to an individual unless there is some objective justification for this happening'. [2002] EWCA Civ 1275; [2002] 1 W.L.R. 3223, 3234.

[22] The authors of the Special Eurobarometer on data protection introduced their findings with the observation that '[t]hroughout this survey, it will become increasingly apparent that fundamental variations in attitude are usually based upon a country-by-country view rather than on a particularly socio-demographic characteristic such as gender, age, education or occupation' (Special Eurobarometer 196, 'Data Protection', Wave 60.0, (2003), p. 5).

[23] Although he did suggest cultural differences might have a part to play in determining when an interference with Article 8(1) could be justified by reference to Article 8(2). *R. (S. and Marper)* v. *Chief Constable of the South Yorkshire Police* [2004] UKHL 39; [2004] 1 W.L.R. 2196, 2208 [27].

[24] *Niemietz* v. *Germany*, no. 13710/88 (1992) 16 EHRR 97 [29–30].

[25] *S. and Marper* v. *The United Kingdom*, no. 30562/04 [2008] ECHR 1581 [71–2].

principle. What is more, there was no indication in the context of this case that the genetic data held would, in fact, be interpreted to yield that kind of information.

Elsewhere within the Court judgment there were references to the effect that (potential) processing of genetic data might have upon individuals. For example, the Court considered that the fact that DNA profiles could be used for familial searching, with a view to identifying a possible genetic relationship between individuals, was in itself sufficient to conclude that the retention of genetic data (at least in the form of a sample) interfered with the right to a private life. Again, therefore, it would appear to be a particular interpretive potential of data that was considered key. In this case, there was more reason to suspect that the data in question might actually be subject to such analysis. Familial searching is a technique used, on occasion, by the police in the UK. In such cases, the interpretive potential is also for associations to be made between the data *and other persons*. If data possesses this kind of associative potential, then this might provide a justification for claiming Article 8(1) to be engaged. If this is the case, then it should be emphasised that it is the interpretive (and associative) potential of the data that is important and not its genetic pedigree.

Even if we were to establish that Article 8 would be engaged, in certain contexts, by the processing of genetic data, it does not follow that the interference would be proscribed by the Convention. As already noted, there are circumstances in which a prima facie interference with fundamental rights and freedoms can be considered justified. Indeed, in the case of *M.S.* v. *Sweden* already mentioned, the Court found the disclosure to be justified even though they accepted that the access to the health records did interfere with the claimant's Article 8(1) right to private life. To be justified, the interference must be in pursuit of a legitimate aim,[26] in accordance with the law, and satisfy the test of necessity 'in a democratic society'.[27] Interference will be considered necessary in a democratic society in pursuit of a legitimate aim only if it answers a 'pressing social need' and if it is proportionate to the legitimate aim pursued.

---

[26] In the case of *MS* v. *Sweden* the disclosure was considered to be in pursuit of the aim of protecting the economic well-being of the country. Arguably, this could be said to show how low the threshold of 'legitimate aim' can be if the courts consider the interference to be justified in the broader context of a case.

[27] Article 8(2).

Research and proportionate interference

It must be remembered that it is the contracting States that have the responsibility to secure, within their respective jurisdictions, the rights and freedoms described by the European Convention on Human Rights. Individuals are not, therefore, directly responsible for an interference with Article 8 of the Convention *unless* domestic law provides for that responsibility. However, if an interference with Article 8 were to be perceived, and domestic law did not provide an effective remedy, there is then the possibility of a claim against the State for its failure to provide that remedy. To the best of my knowledge, the Court has not yet heard *any* case where an interference with an individual's private life has been defended on the grounds that it was a necessary, and proportionate, interference on the grounds of research. One can, however, imagine that an argument could be made that research is a legitimate aim to be pursued within a democratic society. It is crucial to the progress of knowledge and the advance of society, and, in the field of healthcare at least, it is instrumental to the delivery of safe, effective and sustainable care and treatment. I would suggest that, if the Court were ever to reject such a claim, then it would most likely be on the grounds of proportionality in the circumstances of a particular case: not all research is equally valuable and some methods of acquiring research data are more intrusive than others.

However, the lack of case law, and the absence of any precise formula for evaluating proportionality, does leave some doubt about when an interference with an individual's right to a private life would be justified in the case of research access to genetic data. Certainly we might acknowledge rather vaguely that the research in question must answer a 'pressing social need' and that this, in turn, is likely to be assessed in part by the nature of the question that the research seeks to address: how much of a problem is it, and, how likely is it that the research will contribute towards resolving that problem? It is not even clear, however, whether the magnitude of the problem (against which the proportionality of any interference will be judged) would be assessed qualitatively, quantitatively or through some combination of both – nor the relevant time frame within which either the problem itself, or the possibility of resolution, would be judged.

We do know that the reasons offered to justify the invasion must be considered by the Court to be both relevant and sufficient. While there is a 'margin of appreciation' left to national authorities to determine such matters, the final assessment remains subject to review by the Court. The breadth of the margin of appreciation will vary according to a number of factors, but the sensitivity of genetic data that the Court has hitherto assumed would probably lead the Court to pay close attention to any national measure seeking to retain and use genetic data in interference with privacy.[28] However, the same level of scrutiny may not apply to *all* genetic data. If the courts were to recognise the kind of variation in interpretive potential that I have described, then not only might the processing of genetic data not always breach the Article 8 right to privacy, but the threshold for a justifiable breach would also vary. The significance of the context does mean that it is unlikely that any blanket policy, permitting the use of any genetic data without consent for research purposes, would ever be considered proportionate,[29] not least of all because it would be hard to demonstrate that it was *necessary* to interfere within individual's private lives in this way. If certain kinds of research could proceed on a voluntary, consented basis, then there is no need for the interference.

A consideration of the European Convention helps us to appreciate the range of circumstances in which privacy might be engaged by the acquisition, use and retention of genetic data. It does not, however, yield clear answers to the questions of precisely when, or why, Article 8(1) will be engaged through the acquisition and use of genetic data. Certainly, it does not indicate when any such interference will be considered justifiable other than to indicate the hurdles that it has been established such justifications would need to overcome. It *is* clear that genetic data, at least that which is *personal to the individual*, will, at times, engage an individual's right to a private life. It is also likely that a non-arbitrary interference with this right will have to be reliant upon context specific justifications rather than upon any kind of blanket policy. Certainly, if Article 8(1) is engaged, then any particular use of that data for research purposes would need to be considered both necessary and proportionate to any interference with privacy.

Research and data protection

Although the European Convention has unpacked and given particular interpretation to certain rights contained within the Universal Declaration, until the Court considers a case dealing with genetic data and its

---

[28] The intrinsically private character of this information calls for the Court to exercise careful scrutiny of any state measure authorising its retention and use by the authorities without the consent of the person concerned'. *S. and Marper* v. *The United Kingdom*, no. 30562/04 [2008] ECHR 1581 [104].

[29] *S. and Marper* v. *UK* (30562/04) [89].

acquisition and use for research purposes we are left to draw imprecise analogies and perform some educated guesswork about when data will be 'personal to the individual' and where the line of 'proportionate' interference would be drawn. These questions would, of course, need to be adjudicated if a citizen of a country that was a member of the Council of Europe alleged that the Article 8 right to privacy had been arbitrarily infringed. The Member States are, through ratification of the Convention, committed to protect those rights through law. Rather than waiting for someone to claim that her rights have been violated and seeing how the arguments play out in Court, we might alternatively look to see how the members of the Council of Europe have sought to protect those rights, especially the Article 8 right to a private life, within more specific regulation. How have the issues of conflicting interests, e.g. both in protecting privacy and also in permitting research access to data, been resolved within applicable law?

There are two regional instruments that should be mentioned, although I will consider only one in full. The first is an instrument of the Council of Europe (CoE) itself: the Data Protection Convention (DPC).[30] The purpose of the DPC is to secure respect for the rights and fundamental freedoms of each individual, in particular the right to privacy, with regard to the automatic processing of personal data (Article 1). The second represents an attempt by the European Union to ensure that the transfer of information between Member States meets the minimum standards of protection for fundamental rights and freedoms set out in the European Convention of Human Rights (and, more specifically, the CoE DPC). The European Directive is supposed to 'give substance to and amplify' the principles of the protection of the rights and freedoms of individuals, notably the right to privacy, which are contained in both CoE Treaties, and it will be this instrument that I will take as an exemplar of how the right to privacy recognised by the European Convention (and the Universal Declaration before it) has been unpacked more precisely into law. It should be mentioned also that, since the Treaty of Lisbon, the Charter of the Fundamental Rights of the European Union[31] has placed the whole range of civil, political, economic and social rights of European citizens on a discrete legal

---

[30] The full title is the Convention for the Protection of Individuals with regard to Automatic Processing of Personal Data (Strasbourg, 28.I.1981). See also the Additional Protocol to the Convention for the Protection of Individuals with regard to Automatic Processing of Personal Data regarding supervisory authorities and transborder data flows (Strasbourg, 8.XI.2001).

[31] 2000/C 364/01.

footing. Article 7 of the Charter recognises that everyone is entitled to 'respect for private and family life' and Article 8 recognises that everyone is entitled to 'the protection of personal data concerning him or her'. These rights are, however, also cast at a relatively high level of abstraction and it is within the European Data Protection Directive that they are currently most explicitly protected.

The Data Protection Directive (95/46/EC)

The European Data Protection Directive establishes the minimum requirements for the processing of 'personal data' within the Member States of the European Union. It also has relevance beyond the twenty-seven members of the European Union and the three additional members of the European Economic Area.[32] The importance of being able to effectively exchange personal information with Europe has led organisations, and countries, to put in place measures to demonstrate relevant equivalence in privacy protection. A good example of this is the arrangement for 'Safe Harbour' with the United States. American organisations wishing to rely upon the 'Safe Harbour' arrangements need to be able to demonstrate that they provide protections equivalent to those demanded by the European Directive.

What is more, key principles contained within the Directive, most notably the idea of 'personal data', have analogues in privacy law around the world. Remaining with the example of America, the Fair Information Practice Principles refer to 'personal information',[33] the Privacy Act 1974 applies to records 'about an individual' (that are maintained by an agency),[34] and the Health Insurance, Portability and Accountability Act (HIPAA) refers only to 'individually identifiable health information'.[35] In Canada, the Personal Information Protection and Electronic Documents Act (PIPEDA) defines personal information as 'information about an identifiable individual that is recorded in any form'. In Australia, the Privacy Act 1988 restricts its definition of

---

[32] The agreement creating the European Economic Area allows the European Free Trade Association (EFTA) members Iceland, Liechtenstein and Norway to participate in the internal market of the EU on the basis of their application of relevant Community acquis: the accumulated body of EU Law.

[33] Federal Trade Commission, 'Fair Information Practice Principles'. www.ftc.gov/reports/privacy3/fairinfo.shtm.

[34] Section 552a(4) Privacy Act of 1974, 5 U.S.C, Public Law no. 93–579.

[35] Section 1171(6), Health Insurance Portability and Accountability Act of 1996, Public Law 104–191, 104th Congress. http://origin.www.gpo.gov/fdsys/pkg/PLAW-104publ191/html/PLAW-104publ191.htm.

personal information to identifiable individuals.[36] The Organisation for Economic Co-Operation and Development (OECD) privacy principles also use the language of 'personal data', and these principles, in particular, tie closely to European data protection legislation and use.[37]

One can expect the pressure of international trade to continue to exert a harmonising influence upon international privacy law. Indeed, one of the primary objectives of the Directive, as with all EC Directives, was precisely the furtherance of European integration. Failure to ensure an acceptable minimum level of protection for fundamental rights and freedoms in the processing of personal data throughout Member States could act as an impediment to the flow of personal information around the European Union.[38] Accordingly, the Directive aimed to create 'a European zone of free information flow' in relation to personal information.[39] Adequate protection was sought by ensuring that any automatic processing[40] of personal data, or the processing of data that while not automatic nevertheless forms part of a relevant 'filing system',[41] took place according to a series of data protection principles.[42]

The idea of 'personal information' or 'personal data' is a key concept emerging as a gateway to the application of data protection principles across the world. The idea of 'personal data' might be seen as an attempt to articulate more clearly when data will be 'personal to the individual' and, therefore, capable of engaging the individual's right to privacy as recognised by the European Convention (and the Universal Declaration before it)

'Personal data', as defined by the Directive, is,

---

[36] S.6, Part II – Interpretation, Privacy Act 1988, Act No.19 of 1988 as amended. Although, interestingly for discussion of the data/information distinction, it extends to include information 'whether recorded in a material form or not'.

[37] http://oecdprivacy.org/.

[38] Recital 3: 'Whereas the establishment and functioning of an internal market in which, in accordance with Article 7a of the Treaty, the free movement of goods, persons, services and capital is ensured require not only that personal data should be able to flow freely from one Member State to another, but also that the fundamental rights of individuals should be safeguarded.'

[39] G. Greenleaf, 'The European privacy Directive – completed', *Privacy Law and Policy Reporter* 2 (1995), 81. http://austlii.edu.au/~graham/PLPR_EU_1.html#RTFToC2.

[40] '[P]rocessing' is defined in an inclusive sense to capture not only the collection, recording, organization, use and disclosure of data but also, inter alia, its storage, alteration, combination, blocking, erasure and destruction (Article 2(b)).

[41] Article 3; Recital 27. '[F]iling system' is defined as 'any structured set of personal data which are accessible according to specific criteria, whether centralized, decentralized or dispersed on a functional or geographical basis' (Article 2(c)).

[42] A useful commentary to the Data Protection Directive 95/46/EC is provided by Deryck Beyleveld at www.privireal.org/content/dp/directivecommentary.php.

any information relating to an identified or identifiable natural person ('data subject'); An identifiable person is one who can be identified, directly or indirectly, in particular by reference to an identification number or to one or more factors specific to his physical, physiological, mental, economic, cultural or social identity (Article 2(a)).

It can be said with certainty that when genetic data satisfies this definition it falls within the scope of the Directive and is protected as 'personal data'. Unfortunately, the more this definition is studied, the less clear it becomes exactly when *any* data will fall within it.[43]

What is personal data?

Directive 95/46/EC established, through Article 29, a working party to provide independent advice on its application and interpretation.[44] Known as the Article 29 Working Party (WP29), this group regularly issues statements on matters relevant to the consistent and effective implementation of the Directive across the EU.

WP29 issued an opinion on the concept of personal data that sought to examine in detail the four elements of the definition that were considered essential to determining its scope: 'any information', 'relating to', 'identified or identifiable' and 'natural person'. As the opinion illustrates, some considerable time could be spent examining each of these elements. For the purposes of illustrating some of the difficulties in establishing the overlap between 'genetic data' and 'personal data' it is sufficient to consider only the first of them: the term 'relating to'.

Before genetic data could be considered to be 'personal data', it must 'relate to' an identifiable individual. WP29 stated that information could be considered to 'relate' to an individual in a number of different ways. There will be certain situations where data is clearly 'about that individual' and the fact that the information 'relates to' that individual is self-evident, e.g. 'the results of medical analysis clearly relate to the patient'.[45] Even this first variant, when data can be said to possess a particular 'content element', can be problematic. The group noted that whether data possesses the relevant 'content element', and *obviously*

---

[43] S. Booth, R. Jenkins, D. Moxon, N. Semmens, C. Spencer, M. Taylor and D. Townend, 'What are personal data?', Study conducted for the UK Information Commissioner (2004). www.ico.gov.uk/upload/documents/library/corporate/research_and_reports/final_report_21_06_04.pdf.

[44] An independent European advisory body on data protection and privacy, its tasks are described in Article 30 of Directive 95/46/EC and Article 15 of Directive 2002/58/EC.

[45] Article 29 Data Protection Working Party, 'Opinion No. 4/2007 on the concept of personal data', WP 136, 20 June 2007, 10.

'relates to' an individual, can be context dependent.[46] They gave, as an example of a more difficult case, the value of a house. In some circumstances, information about the value of a house might be considered only to be 'about' the house. In other circumstances, the same data might provide information that 'relates to' the occupier, e.g. in relation to an obligation to pay certain taxes. We might ourselves note the corollary with genetic data. In one situation, information about the significance of a particular architecture might be only 'about' that architecture. When that architecture is associated with a particular person, the same data may then possess a particular 'content element' and *obviously* 'relate to' them in a way capable of infringing their privacy.

WP29 identified other ways in which data might 'relate to' a person, other than 'obviously being about them'. They also considered that data, as well as possessing a particular 'content' element, might relate to an individual if a relevant 'purpose' element, or a 'result' element, could be demonstrated.[47] They suggested that the relevant 'purpose' element might be present when, taking all of the circumstances into account, it appears that the purpose of processing the data was to inform behaviour directed towards a particular individual.[48] They suggested that the relevant 'result' element might exist if use of the data were likely to have a particular impact upon a particular person's fundamental rights and freedoms. They noted that this need not be a major impact; it would be enough if it could be shown that the processing of the data had led to an individual being treated differently from others.[49]

Given that WP29 suggest that data need only possess a relevant 'content', 'purpose' *or* 'result' element, it is clear just how difficult it is to limit the potential scope of the term 'personal data'. The difficulty does not significantly decrease if we focus only upon genetic data. There are a broad range of circumstances in which genetic data could 'relate to' an individual in terms of 'content', 'purpose' or 'result'. Any processing of genetic data satisfying *any one* of these elements, in relation to a particular (living) identifiable individual, would be subject to the regulatory framework established by the Directive according to the concept 'personal data' preferred by WP29.

---

[46] *Ibid.*, 9.
[47] *Ibid.*, 10. It is important to recognise that the group themselves emphasised that these are mutually exclusive alternatives. This conclusion is at odds with the conclusion reached by Booth *et al.*, 'What are Personal Data?'
[48] Article 29 Data Protection Working Party, 'Opinion 4/2007 on the concept of personal data', 10.
[49] *Ibid.*, 11.

Given that *one* of the ways that data might 'relate to' a particular person is by impacting upon their fundamental rights and freedoms (set out in the European Convention on Human Rights and Freedoms, and the Universal Declaration before it, in particular the right to privacy) this single variant of the phrase 'relates to' manages alone to import successfully all of the additional uncertainty that has previously been considered in relation to the requirements of the right to privacy contained within the European Convention and the Universal Declaration.

However, *if* data *is* considered to be 'personal data', then the detail of the Directive *does* provide an important opportunity to understand how the right to privacy might be unpacked. The Directive articulates a number of specific expectations that attach to the processing of personal data, including genetic data. Before going on to consider these expectations in more detail, it is worth pausing to remark briefly upon two things further about the relationship between the ideas of 'genetic data' and 'personal data'.

Multiple data subjects and biological samples

It is almost certainly the case that, in some circumstances, genetic data will possess the 'content' element in relation to one individual, i.e. it might be 'obviously about' X, and yet simultaneously possess the relevant 'purpose' or 'result' element in relation to Y or Z. This appears to open the door to the possibility that data might relate to more than one individual at the same time, and, simultaneously, to the prospect that they might *both* be data subjects in relation to it.[50] In other words, it might seem to represent a step away from the idea that personal data relates exclusively to *a particular* identifiable individual. Is this a sign that the concept of privacy represented with the Declaration and the Convention, at least as represented through the Directive, might not be as individualistic as it first appears? Might there be multiple data subjects? Might individuals even be understood to be data subjects owing to membership of particular groups?

---

[50] This is indeed a possibility that the Article 29 Working Party (WP29) considered plausible in a working document on genetic data, although they noted that it would probably give rise to a number of conflicts between different persons, either to have access to information or to keep it confidential, which would need to be considered. WP29 did, however, point favourably to an Italian case where the Garante per la protezione dei dati peronali had granted a woman the right to access her father's genetic data, although her father had dissented to such access, for reasons of her psychological and physical well-being. Article 29 Working Party, 'Working Document on Genetic Data', WP91, 17 March 2004, 8–9.

Unfortunately, there is no indication that any country has implemented the Data Protection Directive in a way that expressly extends the interpretation of 'personal data' to include the possibility of multiple data subjects: not even in the more limited sense that there may be more than one particular identifiable individual to whom data relates at the same time. This is an issue taken up more fully later (in Chapter 5) but it is worth noting here that there is some evidence, presented by the actions of the UK courts at least, that the judiciary are inclined to emphasise the 'content' element, over the alternatives described by WP29, with the result that data tends only to be understood to be 'about' one person at any one time: the individual that the data identifies in the occurrent context.

The second thing that will only be briefly mentioned here, again because it is more fully considered later (this time in Chapter 7), is the question of whether human biological material might satisfy the definition of personal data. Human biological material, especially human tissue, might possess a 'content' that relates to identifiable individuals, be processed for a 'purpose' that relates to them, or yield 'results' capable of significantly affecting them. On the question of the relevance of the medium in which information is contained, WP29 state that,

[c]onsidering the format or the medium on which that information is contained, the concept of personal data includes information available in whatever form, be it alphabetical, numerical, graphical, photographical or acoustic, for example. It includes information kept on paper, as well as information stored in a computer memory by means of binary code, or on a videotape, for instance.[51]

This view is entirely consistent with the position that I have sought to develop that places considerably more emphasis upon the interpretive *potential* of data than upon its interpretive pedigree. It might also be thought to be consistent with holding biological material, in certain contexts at least, to be personal data. However, despite the opinion expressed by the Working Group on the concept of personal data generally, they expressly rejected the idea that tissue samples might fall within the scope of personal data,[52]

---

[51] Article 29 Data Protection Working Party, 'Opinion 4/2007 on the concept of personal data', 7.

[52] It should be noted that in an earlier opinion expressed specifically about genetic data, WP29 were much more ambivalent about whether biological material might itself constitute personal data, specifically stating: 'in regulating genetic data, consideration should also be given to the legal status of DNA samples' (Article 29 Working Party, 'Working Document on Genetic Data', p. 5). It must be assumed, however, that the most recent opinion represents their current thinking.

Human tissue samples (like a blood sample) are themselves sources out of which biometric data are extracted, but they are not biometric data themselves (as for instance a pattern for fingerprints is biometric data, but the finger itself is not). Therefore the extraction of information from the samples is collection of personal data, to which the rules of the Directive apply. The collection, storage and use of tissue samples themselves may be subject to separate sets of rules.[53]

It would seem then that potential is important, but a particular pedigree is also necessary. Data that is the product of a prior interpretation (that represents 'recorded information') may be captured by the definition of 'personal data' but not otherwise.

Personal data and norms of exclusivity

If genetic data is considered to be 'personal data', then what are the consequences? In general terms, the data protection principles require that a data controller (i.e. anybody who determines the purposes for which data are processed) ensure that personal data are,[54]

1 processed legitimately: fairly and lawfully
2 processed only in a way that is compatible with specified, explicit and legitimate purposes[55]
3 adequate, relevant and not excessive in relation to the purposes for which they are processed
4 accurate and, where necessary, kept complete and up to date, and
5 not kept in personal form for longer than necessary.[56]

The most relevant of these, when determining the conditions under which genetic data may be processed for research purposes, are principles 1 (legitimate processing), 2 (compatible processing) and 5 (minimally identifiable processing). Unpacking these principles in the context of research use of genetic data will help to illustrate the expectations of the Directive in the research context.

---

[53] Article 29 Data Protection Working Party, 'Opinion 4/2007 on the concept of personal data', p. 9.
[54] Article 6; Recital 28.
[55] The Directive states that the further processing of personal data for historical, statistical or scientific purposes shall not be deemed to be incompatible with the original specified purposes provided that Member States provide appropriate safeguards.
[56] The principles are set out in Article 6 of the Directive.

Legitimate data processing

In order for processing to be legitimate under the terms of the Directive, the processing must satisfy one of a number of alternate conditions set out within Article 7.[57] The first alternate listed is that the data subject has 'unambiguously' given consent to the processing. The last alternate condition listed[58] is that processing is necessary 'for the legitimate interests of the data controller', except 'where such interests are overridden by the interests for fundamental rights and freedoms of the data subject'. There are other alternates listed, but these two in particular are most likely to be relevant to a researcher processing genetic data.

If genetic data reveals 'racial or ethnic origin, political opinions, religious or philosophical beliefs, trade-union membership' or concerns 'health or sex life', then it will fall within the category of personal data that is deemed sensitive and subject to additional conditions of 'fair processing'. The Directive establishes a rebuttable presumption against the processing of any sensitive personal data. The presumption can, however, be rebutted according to a series of specified circumstances. The first of these detailed is that the data subject has given 'explicit consent' to the processing of the sensitive data. Additional justifications for the processing of sensitive personal data, without consent, are set out in the Directive and may only be added to by Member States when implementing the Directive into domestic law 'for reasons of substantial public interest' and if they ensure the provision of 'suitable safeguards'.[59] Research is *not* specifically mentioned as a justification for processing sensitive personal data. However, the Directive does expressly indicate

---

[57] Member States shall provide that personal data may be processed only if:

(a) the data subject has unambiguously given his consent; or
(b) processing is necessary for the performance of a contract to which the data subject is party or in order to take steps at the request of the data subject prior to entering into a contract; or
(c) processing is necessary for compliance with a legal obligation to which the controller is subject; or
(d) processing is necessary in order to protect the vital interests of the data subject; or
(e) processing is necessary for the performance of a task carried out in the public interest or in the exercise of official authority vested in the controller or in a third party to whom the data are disclosed; or
(f) processing is necessary for the purposes of the legitimate interests pursued by the controller or by the third party or parties to whom the data are disclosed, except where such interests are overridden by the interests for fundamental rights and freedoms of the data subject which require protection under Article 1 (1).

[58] Article 7(f).
[59] Article 8(4). The establishment of additional conditions for the processing of sensitive personal data should be notified to the Commission (Article 8(6)).

that one of the reasons 'of substantial public interest' that might motivate Member States to exercise the option of adding to the list of justifications is in the circumstance of 'scientific research'.[60]

Each of the alternates listed in Article 7, and each of the conditions justifying processing of sensitive personal data under Article 8, may be subject to the same question: are they only applicable when there is a valid reason *not* to seek (explicit) consent? In other words, is consent, as a route to satisfaction of the first data protection principle, preferable *in law* to the alternatives? This is an important question when considering the legitimacy of research use of genetic data (if provided for by national law) as it determines the conditions under which it is lawful to turn to alternatives to consent to justify the processing of genetic data for research purposes *without* consent and remain consistent with the requirements of the Directive.

There is no explicit ordering by priority within Article 7, or Article 8, specified by the Directive. It must be remembered, however, that it is an express object of the Directive that data processing should respect fundamental rights and freedoms, notably the right to privacy recognised by the European Convention (and the Universal Declaration).[61] The countries implementing the Directive, each of which is a member of both the European Union and the Council of Europe, are also under an independent obligation to ensure that their laws respect and promote the fundamental rights and freedoms recognised by the Convention.

If the processing of personal data *without* consent represents a prima facie interference with an individual's Article 8 right to a private and family life, then the Directive *must* be read to permit reliance upon an alternative to consent *only* if it can be demonstrated that such interference satisfies the conditions set out in Article 8(2) of the European Convention and described earlier. Namely, the interference must be in accordance with the law and both *necessary* and *proportionate* in pursuit of a legitimate aim.

Although there is no explicit ordering by priority within the Directive, this would suggest that parties may only move beyond the first alternate under Article 7 or Article 8 (and the requirement to obtain 'unambiguous' or 'explicit' consent) where there is good (necessary and proportionate) reason to do so. The question of when it will be considered 'necessary and proportionate' to process (sensitive) personal data without consent is not addressed by the Directive. As this is a question raised by the responsibilities that a country owes under the European

---

[60] Recital 34.   [61] Established by the Directive's second recital.

Convention on Human Rights (and the Council of Europe Data Protection Convention), it must be answered with reference to the text of these
Treaties and to the relevant European Court of Human Rights
jurisprudence on their interpretation. Unfortunately, as we have already
discovered, neither the text nor the jurisprudence specifically addresses
the question of when research without consent might be justified as a
non-arbitrary interference with an individual's right to privacy.

Supplementary material?

In the context of research using personal data, there are ways to supplement an understanding of the concept of privacy that might be embedded within the international legal standards, and which might help to
demonstrate how norms might be modified by particular contexts. To
illustrate this point, I continue with the example of research use of
genetic data without consent. There are a number of international
standards that seek to articulate the reasonable expectations of patients
and research participants and which deal expressly with non-consented
research. Amongst the most respected of them is the Declaration of
Helsinki.

The Declaration of Helsinki (2008) is a statement of ethical principle
made by the World Medical Association (WMA). First made in 1945,
the Declaration has been reviewed, reformulated and restated a number
of times since, most recently in 2008. While the WMA has no legal
powers, its Declarations have carried significant weight in national and
international debate.

The Declaration of Helsinki (2008) establishes that *physicians* must
normally seek (preferably written)[62] 'consent for the collection, analysis,
storage and/or reuse' of identifiable human material or data.[63] Significant here is that the Declaration of Helsinki does recognise that there
may be reasons for departing from this norm. Unlike the Data Protection Directive, however, it not only provides an indication of *when* it
might be appropriate to depart from the necessity of informed consent,
but also indicates what kind of safeguard might be suitable in the context
of research:

25. There may be situations where consent would be impossible or impractical to
obtain for such research or would pose a threat to the validity of the research. In
such situations the research may be done only after consideration and approval of
a research ethics committee.

[62] Para. 24.   [63] Para. 25.

The Declaration thus makes clear that if it is 'impossible or impractical' to gain consent, or if seeking consent would 'pose a threat to the validity of the research', *then* it is permissible to seek proxy permission from a research ethics committee (REC). In this way it provides specific guidance as to what might constitute 'good reasons' for not seeking consent in the research context and, if consent is not sought, one indication of a potentially appropriate alternative safeguard: REC approval.

There is, of course, no legal requirement to read the Data Protection Directive in a way that is consistent with the Helsinki Declaration and, as emphasised above, it is itself anyway drafted to apply specifically only to physicians. However, when it comes to reviewing the alternative criteria for making data processing legitimate within the Directive, consent must – if the Directive is to be read consistent with the European Convention – be given priority. Reading the Helsinki Declaration and the *European Convention* together would introduce a particular subtlety to an understanding of when an infringement of Article 8(1) might be described as 'necessary' and 'proportionate' in terms of Article 8(2).

It could be usefully clarified that research *can* be a justification for processing personal data, without consent, within the framework of privacy protection established by the Directive, but only where it would be impossible or impracticable to gain consent due to logistical impediments, *or* where seeking consent would be practicable but would 'pose a threat to the validity of the research', *and* appropriate REC approval for the research had been given. This *might* represent a proper reading of the concept of privacy already embedded within the Directive, but unfortunately it is not a reading that the Directive itself provides.

Such clarification would represent a significant development in our understanding of the application of the European Convention right to privacy in this context and the associated interpretation of the first data protection principle of the Directive. There are, for example, epidemiological studies that involve large numbers of persons and which would be seriously compromised if it were necessary to obtain the informed consent of every participant, because of either the administrative cost or the bias that active or passive dissent would introduce into the research data.[64] It is not currently certain when, or even if, the issues of either cost or bias would tip the balance with regards to a justification for relying upon an alternate to consent as a justification for legitimate processing. Researchers are reliant upon Member States exercising the

---

[64] An example of such epidemiological research is the work of the cancer registries.

option to enable the processing of sensitive personal data for research purposes in their own way and with their own safeguards. Even the use of such supplementary material as the Helsinki Declaration would not answer all questions. It would, however, represent a step towards framing some relevant questions.

At this point, however, it is perhaps important to underline that – despite some uncertainties – it is possible to establish at least one aspect of the privacy norms that the Directive reflects: if processing personal genetic data, then there should be a good reason *not* to gain the consent of the data subject. We may not be able to say *exactly* what those good reasons are but we can begin to suggest some more precise expectations through the use of supplementary material. Before turning to consider any other supplementary material, we should consider the other principles of good data processing established by the Directive.

Other principles of data protection

The second data protection principle, the principle of 'compatible processing', requires that personal data are only processed in a way that is compatible with specified, explicit and legitimate purposes.[65] Running alongside this principle, as a key feature of the data protection framework, is the requirement that data subjects are notified of the purposes of processing personal data.

Articles 10 and 11 of the Directive provide detail about the information that must be notified to a data subject by a data controller. Article 10 deals with the circumstance where the data controller has received the data directly from a data subject and Article 11 deals with the circumstance where the data has been received through a third party. In both cases, a data controller is required to provide a data subject (unless they already have it) with information about the identity of the data controller, the purposes of the processing, and any further information necessary in the specific circumstances of the processing, to guarantee that the processing is 'fair' to the data subject.

This responsibility to notify is independent of the responsibility to gain consent and it continues to apply even if it is not necessary to obtain consent in the circumstances (as determined by Article 7 and Article 8 discussed above). Of course, the notion of what it is necessary to provide in order to be 'fair' may be contested, but the Directive is clear that

---

[65] The Directive states that the further processing of personal data for historical, statistical or scientific purposes shall not be deemed to be incompatible with the original specified purposes provided that Member States provide appropriate safeguards.

certain information must minimally be provided: information about the categories of the data processed, the identity of any recipients of the data, the existence of the right of access, and the existence of the right to rectify any inaccurate data held.[66] Article 11 also makes clear that this responsibility to provide information to the data subject does not apply, *in cases where the data has been received from a third party*, where provision of the information would involve a disproportionate effort.

The relationship between the responsibility to notify a data subject of, inter alia, the purposes for which personal data will be processed and the principle of 'compatible processing' can be seen clearly in the context of research uses of personal data.

Having stated in Article 6(1)(b) that personal data must not be further processed in a way that is incompatible with the stated purposes, the Directive goes on to qualify this statement: 'Further processing of data for historical, statistical or scientific purposes shall not be considered as incompatible provided that Member States provide appropriate safeguards.' This raises the possibility that, as long as data are collected for specified purpose 'X' (and all the relevant information is provided about X), then it is permissible for data to be processed for certain additional research purposes 'Y' *without* specific notification of these additional purposes to a data subject. It should be emphasised, however, that the principles set out in Article 6 are *independent* of the principles relating to the provision of information set out in Articles 10 and 11.

This means that, even if the *processing* of data for purposes that have not been notified to a data subject is legitimate (due to the applicability of Article 6(1)(b)), information about the processing must *still be notified* to a data subject under Articles 10 and 11. This might, initially, appear perverse. However, sense can be made of this if it is remembered that Article 11 permits exception from the requirement to notify (when data have not been received directly from a data subject) if, inter alia, notification would be impossible or would involve a disproportionate effort.

The qualification of the principle of compatible processing can thus be explained: it allows data to be appropriately processed for research purposes (with additional safeguards) *when* the purposes of the processing have not been specified or made explicit to data subjects *because* it would be impossible or would involve a disproportionate effort to do so. This explanation confirms the strictly limited nature of any permitted processing *without* notification, particularly if the data was received directly from the data subject.

---

[66] Article 10 and Article 11, Data Protection Directive (95/46/EC).

Just as there might be circumstances in which obtaining consent would jeopardise the viability of research, there may be circumstances in which a requirement to provide information might similarly jeopardise research.[67] One can imagine here circumstances where data was obtained directly from a data subject, but some time ago, and the opportunity now presents to use it for research but there is no longer a practicable opportunity to contact or gain consent from the data subjects. The Directive makes no explicit exception for the non-provision of information in such circumstances. The only exception to the requirement to notify is either if it would be impossible or if it would involve disproportionate effort *and* the data have been obtained from a third party.

One additional alternative, also available under Article 11 only, is that non-notification may be permitted if 'recording or disclosure is expressly laid down by law. In these cases Member States shall provide appropriate safeguards.' If Member States wish it, then they may provide for circumstances in which the requirement to notify (where data has been received directly from a data subject) may be restricted beyond the bare circumstances of impossibility or disproportionate effort. If they were to do so, then they would need to ensure that the circumstances satisfied those set out in Article 13.

The strict limits on processing *without* notification must be contrasted with the fact that it is *only* the data subject that needs to be notified of any intention to process personal data *and* that obligation would appear to extend *only* to an intention to process the data while it is in identifiable form.[68] What is more, the Directive also establishes that, as one of its principles of good data processing, personal data are not kept in personal form for longer than necessary. This motivates the de-identification of data as soon as possible and supports the attitude that it is only *identifiable* information that is capable of jeopardising relevant privacy interests. This is a notion that is contested in later chapters.[69]

Rights to access and to object

Two other important rights that the Directive recognises a data subject to have concerning personal data are the right to access and the right to object. Article 12 requires Member States to provide a data subject with

---

[67] Unless it is considered 'impossible' to provide information in such circumstances, which seems to be rather to stretch the meaning of the word.

[68] For more on this see M. J. Taylor, 'Data protection, health research and the public interest in notification', *Medical Law Review* 19(2) (2011), 267–303.

[69] See especially Chapter 6.

the right to confirm whether data relating to her are being processed, the purposes of the processing as well as the categories of data concerned, the recipients of any data disclosed and, importantly, communication in intelligible form of the data undergoing processing as well as any information as to its source. Member States are entitled to establish exemption and derogation from this right to access under Article 13, and 13(2) anticipates such restriction where data are processed solely for the purposes of research or the creation of statistics, so long as, inter alia, 'there is clearly no risk of breaching the privacy of the data subject'. The appropriate safeguards that Article 13 does expressly anticipate, and which would accompany any exemption or derogation from the right to access provided by Article 12, include that the data is not used for taking measures or decisions regarding *any particular individual*. The implication would seem to be that, if an individual's privacy is protected, for example through concealing the identity in any research publication, and the research itself informs no measure or decision taken regarding any individual, then the right to access provided by Article 12 may be legitimately restricted.[70] The fact that an individual might associate themselves with a group identified in the published work seems to be irrelevant.

The possibility of access to *unexpected* findings in research using genetic data is addressed by a recommendation of the Council of Europe, Committee of Ministers, on the protection of medical data.[71] The Committee recommend that access to unexpected findings following genetic analysis *should* be given if it is not prohibited by domestic law, if the person has asked for it and if the information is not likely to cause serious harm to his or her health or 'to his or her consanguine or uterine kind, to a person who has a direct link with his/her genetic line, unless domestic law provides other appropriate safeguards'.[72]

This recommendation is interesting for two reasons. First, it would appear to undermine the position taken within the Directive. It supports the idea that access to genetic data in cases of scientific research *might* be appropriate even where the data itself informs no measure or decision regarding the individual.[73] Also, although it only

---

[70] This certainly seems to have been the approach taken towards the implementation of a restriction to Article 12 within UK law (see section 33, Data Protection Act 1998).

[71] Council of Europe, Committee of Ministers, Recommendation No. R (97) 5 on the Protection of Medical Data (13 February 1997).

[72] *Ibid.*

[73] It should be noted that it may be queried whether there is any inconsistency because it might be questioned whether the qualification of the right to access *does* in fact extend to

recognises the interests of related family members as a potential qualification upon the right to access, and does not waver from the line taken within the Directive that a right to access is exercised only by a data subject herself, it does nevertheless expressly recognise that family members might have interests that should be taken into account within the decision-making process.

In addition to the right to access, the requirement of notification also provides a data subject with the opportunity to object to data processing. Article 14 of the Directive recognises a data subject to have the right to object to the processing of personal data that relates to them (at least where they have not previously consented to it).[74] Where the objection is justified, the processing instigated by the data controller may no longer involve those data. The Directive does not clearly specify when an objection may be justified and Recital 45 only indicates that there may need to be both 'legitimate and compelling grounds, relating to his [or her] particular situation'. Presumably, an allegation that the processing represented an interference with privacy would be subject to scrutiny according to the idea of privacy, and the principles of proportionate interference, described earlier in relation to the European Convention.

One might observe at this point that the analysis of the Directive has confirmed the central position of the term 'personal data' and the significance of being considered a 'data subject'. Only while genetic data is considered to 'relate' to an identifiable individual do any of the principles of good data processing apply. If data can no longer be associated with a particular identifiable individual, then the implication is that privacy is adequately protected by that lack of identifiable association. As noted earlier, this reflects a relatively thin concept of privacy when assessed according to the relational variable.

---

incidental findings that might be of clinical significance to the data subject. The suggestion may be, as the content of the incidental finding is material to a decision on whether to report it to the data subject, and as the decision on whether to report is itself a decision regarding a particular individual, then the data cannot fall within the Article 13(2) exemption. While this is a superficially appealing argument, I am not persuaded by it. The exemption must suppose that there are valid reasons for excluding research data from the right to access. The decision to withhold research data under the exemption cannot itself be understood to represent 'a decision regarding a particular individual' (denying the operation of the exemption) without emptying the exemption of all meaning. At the very least, it would frustrate the operation of the exemption in circumstances where the valid reasons supposed for it were operative.

[74] Article 14(a), Data Protection Directive (95/46/EC).

Not only does it appear to be only individuals that are recognised to have particular privacy expectations but those individuals must 'relate' to the processing of genetic data in question in an *identifiable* way. This also represents a limited range of relevant 'transactions' within a concept of privacy that has otherwise been seen to be expansive along the transactional variable: only transactions that 'relate' to an *identifiable* individual in terms of 'content', 'purpose' or 'result' are captured within the scope of the operative concept of privacy.

The justification for these choices, regarding either relational or transactional variables, in terms of the relevant foundational norms is not clear. There is some considerable uncertainty about whether the range of interests recognised, first within the Universal Declaration and then again in the European Convention, is sufficiently captured through the concept of 'personal data'. That is not to underestimate the difficulty if the scope of protection were to be expanded. Even within the relatively narrow range of interests recognised in the detail of the Directive, there remain many uncertainties. Indeed, as we have seen illustrated by the question of priority regarding the alternatives to consent set down in the Directive, some of this uncertainty may actually flow from unresolved issues concerning the concept of privacy reflected within the foundational instruments themselves.

Recognising that questions such as 'When is genetic data personal to an individual?' and 'What represents a necessary and proportionate interference with privacy?' can only be answered in a context dependent way does not help a researcher, or a potential research subject, seeking certainty. To get a clearer idea how different interests might be expected to be reconciled, at least in the case of genetic data and research, we can turn to legal standards that are intended to apply specifically in the context of research using genetic data. It needs to be emphasised, however, that the legal protection available throughout Europe is as stated up to this point. What follows is a consideration of the extent to which other, more specific, international instruments might provide a way of further interpreting these standards – in the way that the Helsinki Declaration was offered as supplementary material earlier – so as to further clarify relevant expectations.

Each of the standards considered hence is supposed to be at least consistent with the responsibilities established by the Universal Declaration, the European Convention or the Data Protection Directive 95/46/EC (and sometimes all three). I do not consider national legislation here. There are in fact relatively few pieces of national legislation that are specifically targeted at genetic data. The Estonian Human Genes Research Act (2003) and the Latvian Human Genome Research

Law (2003) are applicable to the respective national genome research programmes.[75] While the Hungarian Biobanks Act,[76] the Portugese law on genetic information[77] and the Lithuanian Law on Biomedical Research are of more general application, they should remain consistent with the standards described here.

SECTION II INTERNATIONAL LEGAL STANDARDS APPLICABLE SPECIFICALLY TO GENETIC DATA

Is it possible to develop our understanding of the normative, transactional or relational aspects of the legal concept of privacy by reference to other international legal standards that apply specifically to genetic data? Do they help us to understand *why* genetic data will engage a right to privacy? If so, then what are the implications for the responsibilities that one would owe when conducting research using genetic data, including when might privacy interests be trumped by other considerations?

The Universal Declaration on the Human Genome and Human Rights (UDHGHR) was adopted by UNESCO in 1997.[78] The preamble of the Declaration recognises not only that research on the human genome may 'open up vast prospects for progress in improving the health of individuals and of humankind as a whole', but that such research should respect freedoms and human rights, as well as prohibiting all forms of discrimination on genetic characteristics. Normatively, this seems consistent with the instruments already considered but, arguably, only because it is equally vague.

In 2003, UNESCO agreed the International Declaration on Human Genetic Data.[79] While this is a more comprehensive statement regarding the expectations regarding the processing of genetic data in a research context, it is no more enlightening when it comes to explaining the underlying normative justification for those expectations. It simply reaffirms the principles established in the Universal Declaration on the Human Genome and Human Rights.[80]

Additional to the Council of Europe treaties of more general significance, the CoE has negotiated a treaty with particular relevance to the processing of genetic data: namely, the Convention on Human Rights

[75] Privileged Project, 'Region A – Stage Two', Regional Working Report, p. 7. www.privileged. group.shef.ac.uk/projstages/regional-reports/.
[76] Hungarian Parliamentary Act on the Protection of Human Genetic Data and the Regulation of Human Genetic Studies, Research and Biobanks, No. XXI of 2008.
[77] Law 12/2005 of 26 January 2005 on Personal Genetic Information and Health Information.
[78] www.unesco.org.   [79] *Ibid.*   [80] See the second to last paragraph of the Preamble.

and Biomedicine (1997, ETS 164). The normative underpinning of this convention is again established simply by reference back to the more general treaties (including the Declaration and the Convention). Perhaps, the only thing of note within this Convention, regarding its normative perspective at least, is the explicit statement that the 'interests and welfare of the human being shall prevail over the sole interest of society or science'.[81] While consistent with the position described by the other legal standards considered, it does make it clear that no qualification on the expectations of individuals regarding access to their genetic data should be justified on purely utilitarian reasoning. Beyond this, we do not find much further enlightenment regarding the relevant normative base for any concept of privacy contained within international law and engaged by research using genetic data.

Transactional variable

Do these other instruments provide any clearer idea what *kinds* of access to genetic data will be expected and by whom? What expectations are expressed regarding when it is (not) necessary either to notify people of research uses of genetic data or to seek their consent? Do they recognise rights to access or to object any more specific than those contained within the Directive?

The UDHGHR contains an extremely clear statement that research, treatment or diagnosis affecting an individual's genome shall only be undertaken with the prior, free and informed consent of the person concerned.[82] Also, the right of each individual to decide whether to be informed of the results of genetic examination is presented in entirely unqualified fashion.[83] Despite the lack of qualification within the UDHGHR one might doubt any intention to insist that they would not, or should not, be qualified in practice. The UDHGHR is intended to *promote* certain principles without any indication that each should be considered an absolute requirement. This does, however, make it difficult to assess just how far the expectations are intended to run and to what extent this may indicate that access should extend beyond the access anticipated by the Directive in a research context.

---

[81] Article 2.
[82] Article 5(b). Note that 'If the latter is not in a position to consent, consent or authorization shall be obtained in the manner prescribed by law, guided by the person's best interest.'
[83] Article 5(c).

UNESCO's subsequent, more comprehensive, statement on the expectations that one might have regarding the processing of genetic data, the International Declaration on Genetic Data (the 'International Declaration'), is in many ways little clearer. For example, it states that the 'prior, free, informed and express consent' should be obtained for the collection of human genetic data and that only compelling reasons may justify any limitation on this principle. No clarification on what might constitute such 'compelling reasons' is given, however, beyond noting that they must be consistent with the international law of human rights.[84] Assertions that human genetic data may only be collected for specified purposes, and not used for discriminatory purposes, similarly end with the vague conclusion that, actually, any processing is permissible so long as it is consistent with the Universal Declaration on the Human Genome and Human Rights and the international law of human rights.[85] What is more, the International Declaration only applies to a relatively narrow definition of genetic data. It only considers genetic data to be information 'about heritable characteristics of individuals obtained by analysis of nucleic acids or by other scientific analysis'.[86] Any statement about the expectations one might have regarding genetic data will inevitably be constrained by this definition. The standards published by UNESCO are then, ultimately, of little use when it comes to developing our understanding of the operative legal concept of privacy, at least according to its normative and transactional elements. It may be more useful when it comes to understanding the relational aspect of the relevant transactions (as we shall see below). What is more, the International Declaration does contain an interesting statement about the importance of *transparent* and ethically acceptable procedures concerning the collection, processing, use and storage of human genetic data – a point that will be seen to have some relevance when reviewing the position of the Directive on the issue of transparency regarding notification of an intention to process genetic data for purposes *post* de-identification.[87]

The CoE Convention on Human Rights and Biomedicine establishes as 'a general rule' that 'an intervention in the health field may only be carried out after the person concerned has given free and informed consent to it' and that the 'person concerned may freely withdraw consent at any time'.[88] Article 12, dealing with predictive genetic tests, states that they should *only* be performed for 'health purposes or for scientific research linked to health purposes, and subject to appropriate

---

[84] Article 8(a).   [85] Article 5(iv); Article 7.   [86] Article 2(a).   [87] Article 6(a).
[88] Article 5.

genetic counselling'. This certainly goes beyond any other limitation on the purposes for which genetic data may be processed. However, the strength of these expectations is undermined by Article 26, which states that restrictions may be placed on the rights that the Articles recognise so long as they meet similar conditions to those established by Article 8 (2) of the European Convention on Human Rights. In this respect, the more specific convention establishes some more explicit expectations, but then suggests that they may be qualified without giving any more guidance as to when this may be appropriate than the more general instruments.

Relational variable

The greatest variation from the position apparently taken within the Directive may be found within the approach taken by some international instruments towards the idea of genetic data itself. Most significantly, some international instruments adopt a concept of genetic data that is explicitly *not* individualistic. For example the Council of Europe, Committee of Ministers, Recommendation No. R (97) 5 on the Protection of Medical Data (13 February 1997) states that 'the expression "genetic data" refers to all data, of whatever type, concerning the hereditary characteristics of an individual or concerning the pattern of inheritance of such characteristics within a related group of individuals'.[89] This has implications for the way that the recommendation unpacks and explicit mention is made at a number of points of the interests of related family members. It should be noted, however, that these interests do continue to be mentioned as qualifications to the interests of the data subject. The differences may then, ultimately, prove rather superficial, with the idea of privacy *protected* not so very different from that immanent within the Directive itself: for example, the already mentioned recommendation that the data subject be given a right to access and rectify genetic data *unless* the information is likely to cause serious harm to consanguine or uterine kin or to a person who has a direct link with this genetic line.[90] This qualification may be much more explicit than that contained within the Directive, which only permits Member States to qualify the right of access[91] if necessary to protect the fundamental rights and freedoms of others,[92] but it still stops short of recognising related family members to have a right of access themselves. Similarly, despite recognising that the

---

[89] Appendix to Council of Europe, Committee of Ministers, Recommendation No. R (97) 5 on the Protection of Medical Data (13 February 1997); Section 1.
[90] Article 8(c).   [91] Article 12.   [92] Article 13(1)(g).

genetic data processed may relate to a group of individuals, it is still only the recommendation that it is the data subject that is informed of the processing.[93] The alternatives to this individualistic attitude towards the exclusivity of the genetic data and the information concerning its processing are considered in the next chapter.

It does seem that the dominant conception of privacy protected by the expectations of international legal instruments is principally individualistic in nature. This seems to be confirmed by a consideration of even those instruments specifically concerned with genetic data that recognise that family, groups, communities and wider organisations have interests in the data. These interests are typically represented by way of qualification upon the fundamental rights and freedoms *of identifiable individuals* rather than as entitlements to claim such things for themselves. One of the closest to doing so would appear to be the UDHGHR. This declaration states that no research concerning the human genome should 'prevail over respect for the human rights, fundamental freedoms and human dignity of individuals or, where applicable, of groups of people'.[94] The inclusion of the phrase 'or, where applicable, of groups of people' would appear to signal that groups of people may themselves possess, rights, freedoms and/or dignity capable of infringement. However, none of the substantive principles contained within the UDHGHR seems to carry this observation through into a recognised expectation of groups of persons per se.

Reflections

The idea of informational privacy immanent within the Universal Declaration and the European Convention has been distilled into a concept of 'personal data' that represents a particularly narrow view of privacy when judged according to the relational and the transactional variables. The justification for this rests upon relatively poorly defined norms.

Acknowledgment of only a narrow spectrum of the relational variable is found within insistence that it is only individuals that might have their privacy infringed. What is more, according to the Directive at least, those individuals must be either identified, or identifiable, before their preferences regarding access to genetic data will be protected as privacy interests.

---

[93] Para. 5.1, Appendix to Council of Europe, Committee of Ministers, Recommendation No. R (97) 5 on the Protection of Medical Data (13 February 1997).
[94] Article 10.

The foundational instruments, the Universal Declaration and the European Convention, have recognised that privacy can be infringed in a wide range of ways. However, as the idea of informational privacy has been drawn down into the Directive, and managed through the concept of personal data, so the range of relevant transactions has also been more clearly specified. Only data that 'relates to' identified, or identifiable, persons is recognised to be data capable of impacting upon an individual's privacy. Even if you define the phrase 'relate to' to mean 'is capable of impacting upon an individual's privacy', then the range of potentially relevant transactions has still been limited by the fact that the data must bear this relation to a particular identifiable person. Data that relates to a group of persons, even if it has an impact upon multiple identifiable individuals, would thus appear to fall outside of the scope of 'personal data' and legal protection.

Only uses of data that relate to a particular identifiable individual are presented as potentially privacy infringing. This represents a thin concept of privacy; and, it may have implications for the ability of the Directive to capture the concept of privacy inherent in the European Convention. While the Court has been reluctant expressly to determine the boundaries of the Article 8 right to private life, it has indicated that the interpretive potential of data should be taken into consideration when evaluating its ability to impact upon an individual's privacy. Certainly, any insistence that data must have as its focus *a* particular identifiable individual – discarding the idea that the same data might, if interpretive contexts are fluid, impact upon the fundamental rights and freedoms of multiple individuals through subsequent association with them – would seem inconsistent with that recognition that interpretive potential should be taken into account. This is an idea that is picked up in the next two chapters.

The Directive also represents a relatively thin notion of privacy, and this time it may be drawing its inspiration directly from the concept of privacy contained within the foundational instruments, because it captures only a relatively narrow range of preferences that might be expressed in relation to determining the conditions of access to genetic data. If privacy is concerned with norms of exclusivity, and the conditions of exclusivity may determine access as well as separation, then a proper protection of privacy might actually require access to genetic data in some circumstances.

At the very least, preferences for access would need to be taken into account before it could be said that the public interest in proper privacy protection had been satisfied. There are a number of ways in which the concept of privacy, presented within the Directive, fails adequately to account for the possibility of such preferences. The first example considered was that of non-consented access to genetic data for research purposes. There is no express provision for preferences for such access to be taken into account. Also, if Member States do provide for such access, then there is no indication *how* the interests in non-consented access might be balanced against the preference for consent, in different circumstances.

This can be contrasted with the situation regarding notification and compatible processing. A preference for research access to genetic data to be permitted, notwithstanding the requirement that data only be processed consistent with specified purposes, *is* expressly recognised (although not as an interest in privacy). But the requirement of notification is inconsistently qualified. Only if data have been obtained through a third party may the obligation to notify be set aside for reasons of impossibility or disproportionate effort. The fact that it might sometimes be impossible to conduct research with notification where data have been directly obtained from a data subject (e.g. where data was gathered historically) is not acknowledged, even though exactly the same privacy interests might be at stake.

If we are to hope for a regulatory system that is capable of accounting for the broadest range of privacy preferences regarding research uses of genetic data, then we must hope for a system that is capable of moving beyond a narrow concept of personal data. If we hope for a regulatory system that can provide *legitimate* protection of privacy, and not arbitrarily restrict research uses of genetic data which are compatible with proper privacy protection, then we must hope for one that rather more clearly articulates how competing interests are to be reconciled in the public interest. Unfortunately, rather than recognising that the foundational legal instruments adopt a narrow relational aspect to their operative concept of privacy, we have moved to a position where the Data Protection Directive also restricts the transactional aspect beyond that required to protect fundamental rights and freedoms. In this sense at least, the law may be moving in the wrong direction.

Part II

The critique

5   Data in common

The last chapter considered how the law provides privacy protection by establishing certain expectations of those processing genetic data. Although a range of legal instruments were initially considered, it was suggested that the legal concept of informational privacy has been gradually distilled (perhaps inappropriately but certainly unfortunately) into a series of expectations that are represented by the Data Protection Directive and triggered by the gateway concept of 'personal data'. In Part II, I seek both to unpack and to defend the claim that this direction of travel (towards exclusively organising privacy protection around the concept of 'personal data') is moving us towards a regulatory framework that is systemically incapable of providing proper privacy protection, or protecting the public interest in such proper protection. I will take the Data Protection Directive in particular, and the concept of personal data that it contains, as the specific target of this critique. In more general terms, however, it is a critique of any attempt to equate proper privacy protection with expectations that relate exclusively to data identifiably associated with a particular individual.

The lawful processing of personal data will, within those legal regimes that are consistent with the requirements set out by the Directive, typically require that data subjects are notified before their personal data are used for specified purposes, including research purposes, and also entitle them to consent, or at least object, to such processing. Alternatively, privacy is supposedly protected by data controllers. 'de-identifying' data, and no reasonable expectations are considered to persist in data that has been effectively de-identified at the individual level. There are a number of difficulties presented by this approach.

I will begin this chapter by examining the adequacy of the premise that data that engages privacy preferences relates only to *a particular* identifiable individual. In the next chapter, I will develop this argument and challenge even the premise that data relating to *identifiable individuals* should be the exclusive concern. While the difficulties described in the next chapter might only be addressed through significant legal reform, those indicated here might be effectively addressed through relatively modest change.

What is more, as well as providing better protection in some areas by more fully accounting for preferences that may be associated with different identifiable individuals, such modest change would also clarify the law and help to facilitate appropriate research access. If regulation were to reflect even just a slightly broader concept of privacy than it currently does, then it might more easily recognise the responsibilities of (potential) research participants to other identifiable individuals. This would help to constitute a regulatory framework cognisant of the interests of *all* those identifiably affected by the use of genetic data for research purposes and would not necessarily expect a particular individual to have exclusive control over access to data of significance to both them and others.

If the current understanding of 'personal data' persists, then the law will continue to fail individuals to whom genetic data might be identifiably associated in significant ways. These identifiable individuals might each have claims on the conditions of access to data capable of affecting them: separately preferring particular norms of exclusivity and preferring legal establishment of different conceptions of privacy. There is no suggestion here that their preferences ought automatically to succeed. The suggestion put forward is simply that if they may have preferences regarding (non) access to certain genetic data, then the law should be prepared at least to *acknowledge* them. Ideally, a regulatory framework would be capable of accounting for their interests and demonstrating, in ways acceptable to them, that when their preferences were not to be protected the infringement was justified (and not merely arbitrary).

Terminology

Within clinical research, the person that serves as the starting point for the genetic study of a family is commonly known as the 'proband'. The 'proband' will have a particular relationship with the healthcare professional, usually a clinical geneticist, to whom she provides information. This relationship may well create specific rights and responsibilities that do not apply to other identifiable individuals discussed during a consultation. There is then a need to distinguish between a 'proband' and 'others' within a clinical context. However, even outside of the clinical context, there may be relevant differences between the responsibilities owed to an individual from whom information is directly taken and others, e.g. different responsibilities may be owed to a participant in research when compared with family members mentioned during a research interview. This chapter seeks to critique the adequacy of the data protection regime to protect the privacy of these 'other' identifiable individuals and seeks to describe the failure to recognise that they may have similar interests to the participant as often arbitrary. As we are concerned here with the law of data protection, I will use the term *primary* data subject to describe the non-clinical equivalent of a 'proband': the individual that is the direct participant in research and the immediate focus of the researcher's interest.

It may or may not be that a researcher's hypothesis raises issues that are obviously of concern to a primary data subject's broader family, group or community. The genetic nature of research will, however, often involve asking questions about family members, their medical histories etc., and when it does so, they may be identifiable within the context of the research data collected. If they are identifiable, and data that relates to them is recorded, then they will be described here as *secondary* data subjects. Admittedly, this use of terminology betrays at an early stage my preference for these individuals to be brought within the data protection regime, but I do not intend to include them simply by definitional fiat. I will explain why I consider such individuals should be regarded as 'data subjects' within the *existing* definition of data protection and what kinds of protection this may provide them. I accept that, at the end of the chapter, the reader may have rejected my claim that secondary data subjects are 'data subjects' within current data protection terminology. It remains important to be able to distinguish between two types of identifiable individual: those that are participants in research and those that are involved only by association. We may discuss the inadequacies of the current data protection regime regarding the latter group irrespective of the label we attach to them or whether we agree that they should *currently* be considered to be data subjects.

Recognising secondary data subjects to be data subjects in their own right is not simply about extending the reach of the data protection regime or increasing the responsibilities of data controllers. Recognising secondary data subjects is also, in large part, about bringing into perspective the preferences of a primary data subject. It is about recognising their preferences to exist within a broader context of familial and social interests and ensuring *only* appropriate protection. In this way, the clarification that I am seeking over the legally protected expectations of secondary data subjects is relevant both to facilitate research and to protect interests *beyond* interests in research itself. Information about family members is routinely taken as part of a genetic consultation. While often used for research purposes, this information is also, quite obviously, important to the provision of care and treatment.[1] At times, the information will be relevant to the care and treatment of more than the primary data subject. Uncertainty about what kinds of identifiable information can be gathered about secondary data subjects without having to treat them as primary data subjects in their own right is undesirable and unfortunate for a number of reasons.[2] Explicitly addressing the issue of *secondary data subjects*, and ensuring (only) proportionate privacy protection of *primary data subjects*, would allow those responsible for processing genetic data to have a clearer view of their responsibilities. It should also avoid any disproportionate interference with research activity.

Family members (and other affected individuals)

Chapter 3 described two categories of genetic data: that providing information about what the code is and that providing information about what the code means. If data in either category were to be gathered from a primary data subject, then this may have implications for individuals genetically related to them. Information about an individual's genetic architecture may have significance for others owing to the hereditary nature of genetics: it can indicate a relative risk of possessing similar architecture. Therefore, it also has implications for family members if that architecture is associated with significance.[3] It will be argued that the protection provided by a properly implemented Directive ought to extend to secondary data subjects if they 'relate' to data in a relevant fashion because of its having implications for them in terms of architecture or significance. Of course, they might not relate to data in the *same way* as a primary data subject, but any relevant variation in the nature of the relationship should be recognised through reconciling and, where necessary, qualifying their respective rights and responsibilities. Appropriate balance is not achieved by denying that secondary data subjects might be affected in material ways at all, simply because a primary data subject might typically relate to genetic data in 'more significant' ways. This can be particularly obvious when, for example, a primary data

---

[1] British Society for Human Genetics and Joint Committee on Medical Genetics, 'A joint response to the Ministry of Justice consultation paper on the use and sharing of personal information in the public and private sectors', Published Response to Data Sharing Review Consultation Exercise, 2. www.bshg.org.uk/documents/official_docs/Response to Data Sharing Review 140208 (AHamd).doc.

[2] Human Genetics Commission, *Inside Information* (London: HGC, May 2002), 69–70.

[3] J. Kaye, 'Abandoning informed consent', in R. Tutton and O. Corrigan (eds.), *Genetic Databases: Socio-ethical Issues in the Collection and Use of DNA* (London and New York: Routledge, 2004), 128.

subject dies or exercises her preferences in ways that would be considered inconsistent with expected patterns or reasonable preferences and her actions have a negative impact upon their relations.

The opportunity to provide appropriate protection, with the necessary balancing of interests, lies immanent within current data protection legislation. Recognising this protection would, however, require a shift in current thinking. With such a shift would come the opportunity explicitly to limit the rights of both primary and secondary data subjects when appropriate to do so. This, in turn, would limit the responsibilities of researchers processing their data. Researchers should be able to identify clearly what responsibilities they have to *both* primary and secondary data subjects, and those responsibilities should be proportionate to any risks that are posed to the privacy of each. This extends to include circumstances where questions might be asked directly about other family members, and clarity needs to be brought to the law so that researchers understand when it is permissible to ask questions about identifiable others and what their responsibilities are to any secondary data subject identified during the course of their research.

Member States have consistently failed to provide expressly for the possibility of multiple data subjects within national data protection law. Rather than recognise the common interests in genetic data by acknowledging the possibility that family members might be data subjects in their own right, there is some evidence (in the UK at least) that the courts are moving instead towards an understanding of 'personal data' that denies the possibility of secondary data subjects.

Structure

The argument presented here proceeds through three sections. Section I considers whether information that is common between persons, in the way that much genetic data is common between family members, could be defined as 'personal' data for each of them. It explains why family members might have preferences regarding the processing of relatives' genetic data, and it shows how the Directive's definition of 'personal data' may already be compatible with genetic data being the 'personal data' of secondary data subjects. Section II seeks to explain why, despite the possibility that family members' data could already be included within the definition of personal data contained within the Directive, it does not appear that this interpretation is being preferred within Member States. Recognising secondary data subjects undoubtedly creates the possibility that data subjects' rights could conflict. Unfortunately, the Directive does not explicitly identify how any such conflict ought to be managed. Indeed, beyond the definition of personal data itself, the construction of the Directive arguably anticipates a single data subject: it establishes a framework of rights and obligations that would cause difficulties if family members were recognised to be data subjects in their own right. To avoid such difficulties, national courts are motivated to interpret the law in a way that denies the possibility of secondary data subject. Certainly, it seems that English courts are adopting an interpretation of personal data that is consistent with the denial of secondary data subjects. Even if other authorities do not take this approach,[4] the inconsistency that would follow from different approaches being taken at a national level is as undesirable as a blanket refusal to acknowledge secondary data subjects.[5] Section III suggests how the Directive might be modified by Member State action and, inter alia, English law re-directed. It is proposed that secondary data subjects must be recognised within the data protection framework if the objectives of data protection are to be achieved. This could be by a more explicit balancing of interests between multiple data subject and between primary data subjects and secondary data subjects (and between secondary data subjects), as well as between multiple data subjects and others (including researchers and data controllers).

If this kind of change is not caused by review of the Directive itself,[6] then it could, and should, be done by Member States acting under the discretion currently granted them by Article 13 of the Directive. Member States have a responsibility, under the European Convention, to exercise this discretion, as it is necessary to ensure adequate protection of fundamental rights and freedoms. However, despite the existing imperative, there is a danger that (notwithstanding the extensive jurisprudence concerning Article 8 of the European Convention on Human Rights) if Member States relied upon the discretion contained within Article 13, then they would work out the relevant balances in quite different ways. While some variation in implementation is inevitable (and even desirable), as well as permitted through the mechanism of a directive, consistency could be improved by explicit mention of secondary data subject within the Directive. Review of this aspect of the Directive is, therefore, preferable in terms of consistency of ambition

---

[4] See Chapter 4, note 51, p. 81 above.

[5] If family members were to be denied protection in a way that left fundamental rights and freedoms unprotected, then they might claim a failure to protect their rights under Article 8 of the Convention. It would be better if the need for such protection were explicitly addressed through the Directive so that a consistent approach might be promoted.

[6] Although the Directive is currently under review there has been no suggestion that the concept of personal data is being considered for amendment. http://ec.europa.eu/justice/policies/privacy/review/index_en.htm.

but also in providing the necessary motivation. Notwithstanding the current responsibilities that countries already have under the European Convention of Human Rights, it does not appear that states are relying upon Article 13 to ensure that the Directive is implemented to take account of the common interests in genetic data at all.

SECTION I   DATA SUBJECTS AND GENETIC DATA IN COMMON

As described in the previous chapter, the Directive makes the related concepts of 'personal data' and 'data subject' central to its operation. It will be remembered that the Directive is *only* concerned with the processing of personal data and so the data protection principles have no application unless there is an identifiable person to whom particular data might be said to 'relate'. This makes it important for a data controller (or anyone assessing compliance with the Directive) to establish whether there is such an identifiable person. This is important not only for determining whether the Directive has application in principle; compliance with the data protection principles will often require a data controller to be able also to identify a data subject in practice.[7]

Given the significance of identifying data subjects it is important that the question of whether data might be common between multiple persons, and the personal data of each concurrently, has a clear answer. For example, can a family tree constitute the personal data of each (living) member of the family represented? Is it possible for data to 'relate' to more than one identifiable person in a particular context? How might one confidently establish who is a/the data subject in that context? If multiple (and potentially conflicting) responsibilities could be incurred through the Directive recognising secondary data subjects, then how should such conflicts be managed? Unfortunately, the Directive does not directly answer any of these questions. It does not address the possibility of personal data being common between persons, nor the related possibility of multiple data subjects. Indeed, given the importance of 'data subjects', the Directive is remarkably vague about how they might be identified at all. [8]

---

[7] For example, in order to process data 'fairly and lawfully', it will sometimes be necessary to gain the 'consent' of a data subject (see Articles 7 and 8 (and Recital 30) of the Directive).

[8] Although Recital 26 to the Directive does offer some help in the interpretation of 'identifiable', it does so in the most inclusive of terms: 'to determine whether a person is identifiable, account should be taken of all the means likely reasonably to be used either by the controller *or by any other person* to identify the said person' (Recital 26) (emphasis added).

Defining data subjects

A data subject is defined by the Directive simply as the identifiable natural person to whom personal data relates.[9] As we have already seen, the Directive leaves the key conceptual category of 'personal data' unclear – at least in part, because the term 'relate' is so remarkably imprecise. Those responsible for enforcing and those responsible for complying with the Directive (not to mention those supposed to benefit from it) are largely left to work out for themselves how data must 'relate' to an identifiable individual in order for it to be personal data. They have not always done so in a consistent fashion.[10]

WP29's attempt to unpick the definition of 'personal data' was described in the last chapter, as was their conclusion that data should be understood to be personal data if it relates to a data subject in *any one of three* different ways: by 'content', 'purpose' or 'result'. As noted at the time, there is every reason to believe that data might satisfy at least one of these requirements in relation to more than one individual concurrently. Even data that is most 'obviously about' one person (and so satisfies the 'content' element in one context) might be used to inform decisions about another, with the result of affecting their fundamental rights and freedoms.[11]

This analysis of the definition of 'personal data' by WP29 would surely suggest that the same data may, depending upon the context of the access, be the personal data of more than one person? How does the *possibility* that the definition relates to multiple persons compare with the interpretation and application of the definition *in practice*? In 2004, Booth *et al.* sought to investigate how supervisory authorities, responsible for monitoring, investigating and where necessary instigating relevant legal proceedings,[12] understood the requirement that data must

---

[9] Article 2(a).

[10] The existence of inconsistencies was recognised in the European Commission's first report on the implementation of the Data Protection Directive: Report from the Commission of 15th May 2003 (COM(2003) 265). Improvements in harmonisation were recognised in a follow-up report, but it was still noted that a number of countries continued to fail properly to implement the Directive: Communication from the Commission to the European Parliament and the Council on the follow-up of the Work Programme for better implementation of the Data Protection Directive (COM(2007) 87). http://europa.eu/legislation_summaries/information_society/l14012_en.htm.

[11] An easy example here might be the questions that insurance companies ask about the health of family members when calculating risk profiles and insurance premiums.

[12] See Article 28 of the Directive for further details of the responsibilities of Supervisory Authorities.

'relate to' an identifiable individual.[13] We found two kinds of requirement regularly invoked by authorities when explaining why particular
kinds of data 'relate' to a particular individual in relevant fashion. These
requirements were labelled 'Identificatory Potential' and 'Relevant
Affect'. 'Identificatory Potential' referred to a requirement that personal
data must be capable of contributing towards the identification of an
individual in some way: there must be something about the data in
question that contributes towards the association between that data
and a particular person (even if additional information is required before
the association is possible). 'Relevant Affect' referred to a requirement
that personal data must be capable of affecting the individual in some
relevant way other than through identifiability: identification alone was
not enough. 'Relevant Affect' could be demonstrated, for example, by
(potentially) infringing fundamental rights and freedoms. In this way, it
shared similarities with WP29's category of 'result'.

Despite obvious overlaps between the practice of the supervisory
authorities and the principles laid down by WP29,[14] there were considerable inconsistencies identified between the authorities. When considering their responses as a whole, however, the twin requirements of
'Identificatory Potential' and 'Relevant Affect' did provide a reliable way
to establish what might constitute a 'core' of 'personal data'. Not all
authorities would necessarily recognise each requirement, or indeed
attach equivalent significance to either as a requirement, but the implication of the positions described by the supervisory authorities supported the claim that any data capable of satisfying both requirements
had a very strong claim to be regarded as 'personal data'. If one returns
to the question of whether the Directive's definition of personal data may
recognise multiple data subjects, then the application of these two
requirements would seem to point towards a way of recognising
(multiple) data subjects that appears consistent with both the practice
of the data protection authorities and the position in principle described
by WP29.

Can data 'relate to' more than one individual?

If it is the Directive's aim to protect individuals' fundamental rights and
freedoms in the processing of personal data, then *any data* sufficiently

---

[13] Booth *et al.*, 'What are personal data?'
[14] Which is perhaps not surprising as WP29 is made up of representatives from national
supervisory authorities.

'personal' to *both* contributes towards an individual's identification *and* to enable infringement of their fundamental rights and freedoms ought surely to fall within the scope of the protective regime. To protect only a particular class of persons when these two conditions were met, if they represent reasonable expectations of privacy protection, would be arbitrary.

It is certainly plausible that data might contribute towards the identification of more than one individual. Within the context of an information system, 'identification is the association of data with a particular individual',[15] but that association takes place within a context that may be fluid. As contexts change, the possibility that data may be associated with *different* individuals is raised. Indeed, the idea of 'indirect' identifiability recognised by the Directive[16] captures the idea that it is through a combination of data that identification becomes possible.[17] Different combinations might associate particular data with specific (particular) but different people. Recital 26 would suggest that, when determining whether a particular combination of data enabling 'indirect identification' is possible, the only significant assessment is whether 'the means likely reasonably to be used either by the controller or by any other person to identify the said person are available'. If 'indirect' identification is distinguishable from 'direct' by the need for data to be linked, then the only relevant question is the relevant likelihood of *different* people being identified through different links. One only needs consider a particular example in practice, such as a photograph of a school class, to recognise that the possibility of multiple identification is likely to depend entirely upon the actuality and fluidity of available context(s) in practice. If I show an old school photo to my work colleagues, they might recognise me, but are unlikely to be able to identify anybody else. If I post the same photo on Facebook, then the identification of multiple others becomes much more likely using 'means reasonably likely to be used'. There is certainly nothing about the concept of identifiability to suggest that the same data is *not* capable of simultaneously contributing towards the identification of multiple persons.

It is also equally plausible that the same data might be capable of 'affecting' more than one person in relevant fashion. If I publish the school photograph alongside the revelation that we were all exposed to a

---

[15] R. Clarke, 'Human identification in information systems: management challenges and public policy issues', *Information Technology and People* 7(4) (1994), 6–37 at 8.

[16] Article 2(a).

[17] For example, if people share an address, then the same postcode (as data held in common) might identify different people when joined with some other information, e.g. given name or height.

particular virus on a school trip to the Lake District, then that data might 'affect' each of those identified in the photograph in relevant fashion. A rather less fanciful example might be found in the fact that details of X's communicable disease or carrier status will regularly be information capable of affecting others. Even a relatively restrictive understanding of the concept of personal data, such as would require *both* Identificatory Potential and Relevant Affect, would then seem to place no obvious barrier to recognising that information might be the personal data of multiple individuals.

Can *genetic* data 'relate to' more than one individual?

In 2004 the Article 29 Data Protection Working Party published a Working Document on Genetic Data.[18] Within it, the Working Party noted that genetic data might be described as possessive of a number of distinctive characteristics. They summarised these characteristics as follows:

while genetic information is unique and distinguishes an individual from other individuals, it may also at the same time reveal information about and have implications for that individual's blood relatives (biological family) including those in succeeding and preceding generations, Furthermore, genetic data can characterise a group of persons (e.g. ethnic communities);

- genetic data can reveal parentage and family links;
- genetic information is often unknown to the bearer him/herself and does not depend on the bearer's individual will since genetic data are non modifiable;
- genetic data can be easily obtained or be extracted from raw material although this data may at times be of dubious quality;
- taking into account the developments in research, genetic data may reveal more information in the future and be used by an ever increasing number of agencies for various purposes.

The first of these characteristics might offer some insight into why genetic data could be considered *incompatible* with the possibility of multiple data subjects. It is widely believed that, except for monozygotic twins, every human being has a unique genetic architecture. Two points can be made in response to this. The first is that it must be remembered that not all genetic data possesses the same characteristics. Some genetic data 'can reveal parentage and family links'. Some can be 'extracted from raw material'. Some can 'characterise a group of persons' and only

---

[18] Article 29 Working Party, 'Working Document on Genetic Data', WP91, 17 March 2004.

some may be 'unique'. The second point is that, even when 'genetic data' can be 'uniquely associated' with one individual *in one context*, it might still be associated with others in other contexts.[19] A tiny minority of genetic information (perhaps even none) may be described as uniquely related to a single individual across all plausible informational contexts.

The WP29 description of genetic data's characteristics seems consistent with the idea that it might, simultaneously, constitute the personal data of more than one person. An example of genetic data demonstrating the qualities of 'Identificatory Potential' and 'Relevant Affect' in relation to multiple persons simultaneously was reported in the *New Scientist* magazine. A 15-year-old boy in America identified a previously anonymous sperm donor as his biological father.[20] The boy had used the services of an Internet-based company, called FamilyTreeDNA.com, which offers a 'genealogy driven DNA testing service'.[21] The company put the boy in contact with two men who had Y chromosomes closely matching his own.[22] The boy used the fact that the men had similar surnames to guess the surname of his biological father. He then used information about the date and place of birth of his biological father, which had been provided to his mother at the time she received the donated sperm, to track him down (using the services of another online company: omnitrace.com). Genetic data shared between the boy, his father and the two strangers was thus used to identify the father indirectly and, one must assume, 'affect' him in significant (and relevant) ways. There would, therefore, appear to be no obvious reason to believe that genetic data might not relate to more than one individual any less readily than any other type of data. Indeed, genetic data would often appear particularly capable of satisfying the requirements of 'Identificatory Potential' and 'Relevant Affect' in relation to more than one person at the same time.

The capacity of genetic data to affect more than one person in profound ways was also held by the Icelandic courts to support the possibility that family members can hold personal interests in common genetic data. In *Ragnhildur Guðmundsdóttir* v. *The State of Iceland*[23] a daughter successfully claimed a legitimate interest in determining

---

[19] Indeed, the familial searching of forensic databases relies upon the possibility of partial matches between 'unique' DNA profiles to establish possible family connections.

[20] A. Motluk, 'Anonymous sperm donor traced on internet', *New Scientist* (3 November 2005), 6.

[21] www.familytreedna.com/ (last accessed September 2006).

[22] Motluk, 'Anonymous sperm donor traced on internet'.

[23] No. 151/2003, Icelandic Supreme Court.

whether her deceased father's medical records were transferred to a Health Sector Database. This was because hereditary information might be gathered from the records and this hereditary information could have been associated with her as well as her father: it may be perceived as common data between them. The Icelandic Supreme Court ruled that:

> the argument of the Appellant is accepted that, for reasons of personal privacy, she may have an interest in preventing information of this sort about her father from being transferred into the database, and therefore her right to make the claims that she is making in the case is admitted.[24]

As genetic data is increasingly held, upon increasingly networked data-bases, the point made by the court in this case grows only more significant. If a particular piece of data is capable of being identifiably associated with a number of specific individuals, and is capable of affecting the enjoyment of the fundamental rights and freedoms of each of them, then it ought to be acknowledged as 'personal data' if the concept of privacy established by the Data Protection Directive is to be protected.

When the Article 29 Data Protection Working Party considered the issue of genetic data, they explicitly recognised, and implicitly sup-ported, the argument that genetic data ought, at least sometimes, to be considered to be the personal data of more than one person:

> One of the fundamental features of genetic data consists both in its marking out an individual from others and the fact that this data – and more precisely: the characteristics to which it refers – is structurally shared by all the members of the same biological group.[25]

They also recognised that 'it can be argued that' family members some-times have a right to this data that is structurally shared:

> In this context, questions arise as to whether or not genetic data belong exclusively to the single, specific individual from whom they are collected … To the extent that genetic data has a family dimension, it can be argued that it is 'shared' information, with family members having a right to information that may have implications for their own health and future life.[26]

They did not go so far as to state expressly that family members ought to be recognised to have this 'right' *as data subjects*. Their claim that family members might sometimes be entitled to common data seemed to be informed at least as much by consideration of ethical principle as it did

---

[24] *Ibid.*, Part II.
[25] Article 29 Working Party, 'Working Document on Genetic Data', 7.   [26] *Ibid.*, 8.

legal obligation. In fact, WP29 originally seemed decidedly unsure about how any 'right' to access 'shared' genetic data ought to be reflected within law. Only one of the alternatives described by WP29 was the recognition of family members as data subjects in their own right:

> At least two scenarios can be imagined. One is that other family members could also be considered as 'data subjects' with all the rights that follow from this. Another option is that other family members would have a right of information of a different character, based on the fact that their personal interests may be directly affected.[27]

They stopped short of recommending either of these alternatives as their preferred option at the time. This appears, at least in part, to be due to a lack of opportunity to consider fully the implications of either approach.[28] It is important that the Working Party recognised that the most appropriate way of protecting the legitimate interests of family members *might* be to recognise them as data subjects in their own right. It confirms the possibility that such an interpretation would be consistent with the Directive. It is also important, however, to understand why they thought that recognising family members to be data subjects might also give rise to 'various conflicts' that they were not in a position to resolve readily (and for which we might therefore already infer the Directive did not explicitly provide).

SECTION II   WHY MIGHT RECOGNISING MULTIPLE (GENETIC) DATA SUBJECTS BE PROBLEMATIC?

Raising the possibility of multiple data subjects raises the possibility of conflict between those data subjects.[29] Although data might 'relate' to more than one person there is no reason to suppose that a common interest will give rise to a common understanding of how data should be processed. As previously indicated, under Directive 95/46/EC, a data subject is entitled to certain rights in relation to the data. These include, inter alia, a right of access and, in certain circumstances, a right to the rectification, erasure or blocking of personal data.[30] The exercise of any one of these rights by one data subject might potentially conflict with the preferences of another in a significant way. The nature of family relationships is sufficiently diverse to make it near impossible to predict how one member of a family would feel about, or be affected by, their

[27] *Ibid.*   [28] *Ibid.*

[29] M. J. Taylor, 'Data protection: too personal to protect?', *SCRIPT-ed* 3(1) (2006) (www.law.ed. ac.uk/ahrc/script-ed/vol3–1/taylor.asp).

[30] Article 12(b).

relatives gaining rights of access, rectification, erasure or blocking to data common between them. In particular, circumstances can be imagined in which parties might wish to prevent family members from having access to data originally gathered from them.[31] Similarly, the right to object to processing might also bring family members into conflict. Should secondary data subjects have the same rights to object to processing as would be enjoyed by a primary data subject? If so, then could they prevent processing to which the primary data subject had explicitly consented?

Alongside the rights of access, etc. that data subjects have to their personal data, and in fact to facilitate the exercise of these rights, data controllers have a duty to provide data subjects with certain information about data processing. WP29 themselves drew attention to the possibility that this requirement alone might cause considerable difficulty in certain circumstances. Health professionals might quite regularly find themselves in a position where they have gathered data about a primary data subject but also appreciate that same data both to possess identificatory potential and to satisfy the requirement of relevant affect in relation to a family member. In such circumstances, they might be reluctant to discharge a responsibility (under Article 11 of the Directive) to provide information about the processing of that data to the family member as a secondary data subject.[32] Such reluctance might be attributable to an alternative professional or legal obligation, such as a duty of confidence to the primary data subject, or it might simply be due to a wish to avoid the administrative inconvenience of having to provide information to multiple persons (particularly if they are not present and may be difficult to reach). One has the added complication that such persons may not be expecting, and may not wish, to receive the information in question. The health professional may also, therefore, in addition to any legal or professional duty or practical inconvenience, consider it unethical to notify a secondary data subject about the processing.

Without a mechanism to ensure competing interests are appropriately adjudicated, data controllers could quickly find themselves under an

---

[31] See for example the scenario described by Wai-Ching Leung and the discussion that immediately follows: W. Leung, 'Results of genetic testing: when confidentiality conflicts with a duty to warn relatives', *British Medical Journal* 321 (2000), 1464–6.

[32] Article 29 Working Party, 'Working Document on Genetic Data', 6. The important exception to this requirement is discussed more fully later, but, in short, where data has not been obtained directly from the data subject the information need not be provided where 'the provision of such information proves impossible or would involve a disproportionate effort' (Article 11(2); Recital 40). Again this underlines the importance of knowing who the data subject is with respect to any particular piece of data.

inappropriate and unjustifiable burden. None of the responsibilities that a data controller has to data subjects is currently qualified to take (explicit) account of the possibility of multiple data subjects.[33] For example, while the possibility of an exemption to the responsibility to provide information (under Article 11) has been seen to exist if discharge of that responsibility would either be impossible or involve a disproportionate effort, it is not clear that this could be calculated on a cumulative basis. That is, while it might not be 'disproportionate' apropos an individual (given the individual's interests in having that information), cumulatively these responsibilities could represent a significant (and disproportionate) administrative burden upon a data controller.[34] The aggregation of individual difficulties is not addressed, either favourably or otherwise, by the Directive. Instead, the Directive recognises rights that, if they were to be recognised in relation to multiple data subjects, would almost inevitably cause conflicts that the Directive does not resolve.

The lack of clarity within the Directive, on the subject of multiple data subjects, provides an obvious temptation to resolve any ambiguity against them. If a data controller is not given clear guidance on how to resolve potential conflicts, then the option of denying that they have any obligations to a secondary data subject will obviously seem attractive. This may be especially true if denying that a secondary data subject has any rights not only appears to be a perfectly lawful (and more convenient) option but also appears to be the only way to protect what are seen to be the legitimate expectations of the person with whom the data controller is primarily concerned.[35] This precisely mirrors the situation that we have with regard to the possibility of multiple data subjects and genetic data: denying family members the status of data subjects allows a data controller to avoid acting in a way that would unjustifiably infringe the legitimate interests of either the primary data subject or themselves. What is more, it may appear to be the only way of avoiding such infringement open to a data controller because the rights of a secondary

---

[33] For discussion of, inter alia, the implications for a data controller of recognising multiple data subjects to enjoy a right of access to personal data see Chapter 7, and also Deryck Beyleveld and Mark Taylor 'Patents for biotechnology and the data protection of biological samples and shared data', in Jean Herveg (ed.), *The Protection of Medical Data: Challenges of the 21st Century* (Louvain-la-Neuve: Anthemis, 2008), 127–48.

[34] This point is also made in A. Lucassen, M. Parker and R. Wheeler, 'Implications of data protection legislation for family history', *British Medical Journal* 332 (2006), 299–301 at 301.

[35] Use of the term 'primary concern' is not meant to imply any judgment of value or desert. It is simply meant to recognise the varying nature of the relationship between data controller and multiple data subjects.

data subject are not obviously qualified in a way that would allow a data controller to deny them in other circumstances.

If it were not possible to ensure that the rights enjoyed by multiple data subjects could be properly qualified (by a commensurate respect for the rights and freedoms of others), then the legitimate interests of primary data subjects could only be protected through the marginalisation of secondary data subjects within the framework of data protection. It is not within the power of data controllers (or relatives themselves) to effect such a marginalisation. There is, however, an early indication that English courts at least may help to avoid some of the difficulties threatened by multiple data subjects by constructing a concept of personal data that favours only one data subject. The interpretive approach described within *Durant* v. *FSA*[36] has almost certainly reduced the likelihood of English law recognising the possibility of multiple data subjects.

English law and secondary data subjects

The Data Protection Act 1998 implements the European Data Protection Directive throughout the United Kingdom, and the definitions of 'personal data' provided by the 1998 Act and the Data Protection Directive are broadly similar.[37] It was in the context of establishing the extent of the responsibilities of a data controller that the English Court of Appeal considered the meaning of 'personal data' under the 1998 Act in the case of *Durant* v. *FSA* [2003]. While the Court was not dealing with genetic data, or shared data, or indeed with the possibility of multiple data subjects, the judgment issued nevertheless informs an understanding of the Court's approach to defining the limits of the 1998 Act. The case has proven controversial, but the Court has not taken subsequent opportunities to revisit its judgment and so we must understand *Durant* to continue to reflect accurately the English law position on 'What are personal data?'[38]

---

[36] [2003] EWCA Civ 1746.

[37] '"[P]ersonal data" means data which relate to a living individual who can be identified (a) from those data, or (b) from those data and other information which is in the possession of, or is likely to come into the possession of, the data controller, and includes any expression of opinion about the individual and any indication of the intentions of the data controller or any other person in respect of the individual', s. 1(1) Data Protection Act 1998.

[38] Although an understanding of the courts' approach to interpreting the definition of personal data has been supplemented in other ways by the decision of *Common Services Agency* v. *Scottish Information Commissioner* [2008] UKHL 47. See p. 143.

Durant v. FSA [2003]

This case followed a complaint by Mr Durant to the Financial Services Authority (FSA) about Barclays Bank. He had sought from the FSA, inter alia, information that had been gathered during the course of their investigation into his complaint about the bank and which was now retained by them both electronically and in manual files. Mr Durant claimed a right of access to the relevant information contained within FSA records under the 1998 Act. His right of access turned, inter alia, on whether the data was properly classified as 'personal data'. When Auld LJ considered what makes data 'personal' within the meaning of the 1998 Act he found that,

> Whether [data constitutes personal data] in any particular instance depends on where it falls in a continuum of relevance or proximity to the data subject as distinct, say, from transactions or matters in which he may have been involved to a greater or lesser degree ... In short, it is information that affects his privacy, whether in his personal or family life, business or professional capacity.[39]

As noted earlier, if 'affect' is considered to be (part of) the test for personal data there appears no reason to suspect that personal data could not be held in common between multiple persons. However Auld LJ unpacks the idea of 'affect' within his judgment in a way that challenges this claim. Whether more than one person can be 'affected' in a relevant way depends upon how the 'continuum' he describes is understood and, at least just as importantly, where the threshold between personal and 'non' personal data is found upon that continuum. While it is not clear from Auld LJ's judgment exactly how one should assess 'relevance or proximity' there are clearly a number of options; and according to some of them they have little to do with 'affect'. For example, if one were to assess 'relevance or proximity' simply in terms of the 'content' or 'purpose' element of the data *at the time of collection*, then this might bear little relation to the 'affect' or 'result' that the information derived from the sample might have upon the individual subsequent to its analysis.[40]

It is of course true that, according to Auld LJ, the continuum of 'proximity' and 'relevance' he describes is simply supposed to indicate

---

[39] Para. 28.
[40] An example of this is provided at n.20 above. The biological father identified was the individual arguably most significantly affected by the boy's actions but the information used was gathered from biological data originally collected from strangers and not in circumstances where the collection of that data was either 'obviously about' the father or with the purpose of informing any decision about him.

whether information affects an individual's privacy. It is perfectly possible to see how consideration of either proximity or relevance might, in many circumstances, inform such an understanding and it does not prevent the possibility of multiple data subjects. Indeed, it would be unfair to criticise the continuum described for not yielding a complete answer to a question it never addressed. The point made here, however, is that even if 'affect' continues to be seen as the overriding consideration, introducing the terms 'proximity' and 'relevance' inevitably shapes English law's concept of 'personal data'. What is more, the terms have been introduced in a way that makes it less likely that the law will recognise the possibility of multiple data subjects.

Passing the threshold

While not specifically concerned with the possibility of multiple data subjects, Auld LJ developed two notions that he expressed the hope 'may be of assistance' in assessing whether the relevant threshold upon the continuum(s) described has been passed. Rather than the specification of the continuum itself, it is these two notions that make it less likely that English law will recognise the possibility of multiple data subjects:

> The first [notion] is whether the information is biographical in a significant sense, that is, going beyond the recording of the putative data subject's involvement in a matter or an event that has no personal connotations, a life event in respect of which his privacy could not be said to be compromised. The second is one of focus. The information should have the putative data subject as its focus rather than some other person with whom he may have been involved or some transaction or event in which he may have figured or have had an interest, for example, as in this case, an investigation into some other person's or body's conduct that he may have instigated.[41]

If the courts take up the suggestion that a data subject needs to be the 'focus' of the data 'rather than some other person with whom he may have been involved or some transaction or event in which he may have figured or have had an interest', then this would most clearly undermine the possibility of multiple data subjects.[42]

Given the ambiguity that exists around the notion of 'personal data', it might be considered that any guidance from the courts on the issue should be welcomed. The approach advocated certainly would have its

---

[41] Para. 28.

[42] Incidentally, it would also appear to introduce something other than simply 'identification' or 'affect' into the equation that calculates whether data is an individual's 'personal data'.

advantages. It would have the effect of restricting the responsibilities of a data controller, minimising the possibility of the interests of a data subject inappropriately restricting their ability legitimately to process personal data, and it would remove the possibility of inappropriately resolved conflicts between data subjects. It would achieve this, however, by simply removing family members from the category of potential data subjects entirely. We should be fully aware of all the consequences of adopting this approach, together with any alternatives, before we welcome it as a resolution to the problems of multiple data subjects.

Problems with *not* recognising multiple data subjects

It is trite to note that the Directive aims to provide data subjects with protection that they would not otherwise have. It is equally obvious that, if family members are found to fall outside the framework of the Directive with respect to common data, then they fail to enjoy this additional protection. Given the object of the Directive,[43] this might cause problems for more than just the unprotected individuals. If individuals identifiably linked to data capable of affecting their fundamental rights and freedoms are not protected by the regime established by the Directive, then the Directive may not achieve the 'free flow' of information that it aims to secure. If individuals ought to be protected if they can be identifiably associated with data capable of affecting their fundamental rights and freedoms, then the most significant problem with not recognising multiple data subjects is that people do not receive adequate protection in these circumstances.

Inadequate protection

Suggesting that the system provides inadequate protection is not the same thing as suggesting that it does not provide any protection at all. Indeed, there are a number of occasions on which the Directive explicitly provides for the interests of individuals other than the (primary) data subject to be taken into account. Consideration of the provision for 'third parties' in the Directive can however help to explain why their interests are not provided for *adequately*.

One example of the Directive allowing for the interests of third parties to be taken into account by data controllers is to be found within the list of criteria for making data processing legitimate in Article 7. Article 7(f)

---

[43] See the early recitals, e.g. Recital 2.

provides that personal data may be processed if 'processing is necessary for the purposes of the legitimate interests pursued by the controller or by the third party or parties to whom the data are disclosed'. This raises the possibility that a family member, even if not considered to be a data subject, might be legitimately informed of genetic information gathered from a relative if this is in pursuit of their 'legitimate interests' (even if the relative did not consent to this).

Justifying disclosure to a third party is not, however, the same thing as justifying a claim by the third party that data is disclosed. Article 7(f) permits disclosure by a data controller in some cases but it does not require it upon request by a family member (not recognised to be a data subject) *in any circumstances*. It is important to recognise that this is not due to a fear that this would unjustifiably trespass upon the rights and freedoms of the (primary) data subject. Article 7(f) concludes with the specific qualification that such disclosure shall only be legitimate where the interests of the data controller or third party are not 'overridden by the interests for the fundamental rights and freedoms of the data sub-ject'. It would always be possible to deny disclosure (under 7(f)) because it would be inconsistent with proper protection of the interests of the primary data subject. It is, however, never possible for a third party to claim that, in the circumstances, they are entitled to access the data because in the circumstances their interests in the processing have priority.

The lack of authority (and protection) that this grants a family member (not recognised to be a data subject) is reflected in the fact that there is no responsibility upon a data controller to inform a family member of the data that they process of significance to them (in terms of identificatory potential and relevant affect) in any circumstances. If a third party is unaware of the processing of information, then she is clearly in no position to request that a data controller permit its disclos-ure or to object to its processing. It was to avoid just such debilitating ignorance of the processing of information relating to them that led to the Directive's insistence upon the provision of information to data subjects in the first place. Denying family members any entitlement to notification, in any circumstances at all, leaves them in ignorance and frustrates any attempt by them to ensure their own interests are appro-priately taken into account by others.

It might be that there are few cases when the interests of a primary data subject in fundamental rights and freedoms, especially interests in privacy and the confidentiality of personal data, could be justifiably overridden by the interests of family members in data that is held in common between them. It must be conceivable, however, that such a case could arise[44] – particularly, for example, if the primary data subject is deceased. At the moment, however, the data protection regime seems to be moving in a direction that would deny a family member the status of data subject even if the individual about whom the data was originally gathered had died. In such circumstances, if multiple family members might have an interest in the continued processing of their data, how would multiple (perhaps conflicting) preferences be managed? This has, of course, been to focus entirely upon the law of data protection. There are other ways in which family members' interests might be protected and a number of countries have pursued alternative routes to protection that apply in particular circumstances. The drawback of such approaches is that they can complicate an already confused picture. International research, seeking to process genetic data and remain compliant with the rules on access to such data applicable in every participating country, would benefit from the rules regarding family members to be harmonised through more positive engagement with the possibilities of multiple data subjects.

Alternative responses

In Israel, s.20(5) of the Patient's Rights Act 1996, provides that confidential patient information may be shared with relatives, overriding a patient's dissent, if an '[e]thics Committee has decided, after giving the patient an opportunity to voice his opinion, that disclosure of the medical information is vital for the protection of the health of others or the public, and that the need for disclosure overrides the interest in the information's non-disclosure'.[45]

In Portugal, the law on genetic information[46] provides that 'citizens have the right to know if a medical record, file or clinical or research folder contains genetic information about themselves and their family,

---

[44] There are certainly indications that medical professionals consider family members' interest in genetic data held between them to be, at times, sufficient warrant to breach deeply held duties of confidence (see, for example, S. Barnoy and N. Tabak, 'Conflicting loyalties in the communicating of genetic information: a test of Israeli nurses', 16th World Congress on Medical Law 2006, Toulouse France). The US case of *Tarasoff* v. *Regents* (1976) 17 Cal. 3d 425, P.2d 334 and the UK case of *W* v. *Edgell* [1990] 1 ALL ER 835 both established that the duty of confidence, ordinarily owed by medical professionals, might be set aside to protect third parties in certain, albeit relatively extreme, circumstances. Philip Leith has convincingly argued that third party interests are consistently undervalued by our legal system: P. Leith, 'The socio legal concept of privacy', *International Journal of Law in Context* 2(2) (2006), 105–36.
[45] http://waml.haifa.ac.il/index/reference/legislation/israel/israel1.htm.
[46] Law 12/2005 of 26 January 2005 on personal genetic information and health information.

and the right to know the purposes and possible uses of that information, the way of storage and periods of conservation'.[47] The exclusive right to access identifiable data held in a biobank provided by the Hungarian Biobanks Act,[48] can extend in exceptional cases to close relatives if necessary to inform their healthcare.[49] There are then circumstances in which individual countries have recognised that family members can, in particular circumstances, have good reason to *access* genetic data held primarily about a relative. Such good reason has been understood to extend in some cases to access when that primary data subject is both alive and objecting to such access. The circumstances in which relatives are understood to be entitled to express preferences independent of, and in opposition to, the preferences of the primary data subject are understandably limited. The point is, however, that they are acknowledged. What is more, the relevant 'social unit' (as assessed according to the relational variable) is not only extended within some jurisdictions beyond the primary data subject to include secondary data subjects. In at least one country, there is legal recognition for the idea that the processing of personal genetic data should be informed by the views of a wider community identifiably associated with research and potentially affected by it.

There is a legal requirement in Taiwan that requires group consent to research involving aboriginal people.[50] In the context of a particular research project using genetic data, namely the Taiwan Biobank, this basic legal requirement is supported and supplemented, through an Ethical Governance Framework that insists upon family or community consent being collected alongside individual consents.[51] The process of obtaining such group consents involves consultation with community leaders and a representative panel of participants as well as ongoing engagement and dialogue with relevant communities through the

---

[47] Article 6, no. 9. Access to biological samples might also be given to close family members 'if necessary to a [*sic*] better knowledge of [their] own genetic condition.' Article 18, no. 7. www.privileged.group.shef.ac.uk/wp-content/uploads/2010/02/region-b-stage-2.pdf, 6. Grateful thanks to Dr Rafael Vale e Reis for the collection and translation of this material.

[48] Parliamentary Act No. XXI of 2008 on the protection of human genetic data and the regulation of human genetic studies, research and biobanks.

[49] See www.privileged.group.shef.ac.uk/wp-content/uploads/2010/02/region-a-stage-2.pdf, p. 4. Grateful thanks to Prof. Judit Sándor, who provided this information.

[50] Article 21 of The Indigenous People Basic Law of 2005. For more, see J. Wright, 'Privileged project, stage two regional report: governing the privacy–research interface in the Nordic region and Taiwan', Privileged Project Website (2010), 17–18. www.privileged.group.shef.ac.uk/wp-content/uploads/2010/03/nordic-region-plus-taiwan-report-stage-2-privileged-jwright.pdf.

[51] Wright, 'Privileged project, stage two regional report', 17–18.

vehicles of education and benefit sharing.[52] It does not appear that group consents are intended to be an alternative to individual consent. Instead, the process of securing seeks to ensure the support of the community for the processing of data that might be said to relate to them as a group.

This approach clearly has the advantage that it allows for particular local needs to be identified and addressed. It reflects, as do the national provisions on access, that there is a recognition that identifiable individuals – other than the immediate participants in research – may have an interest in the conditions governing access to genetic data and would wish to express relevant preferences on the processing of that data. The difficulty with such local responses is, however, both that they present a discordant picture of regulation to those considering international research *and* that it will be difficult, as research collaborations are increasingly international, for particular protections to be tracked through into other jurisdictions. If the interests that these national responses recognise are genuine (and there appears no reason to doubt this) then there should be *recognition* of them within the European framework. Of course, that is not to say that they should be overriding. As emphasised earlier, the ideal is not necessarily to give everybody what they would want but at least to make clear that any decision has taken reasonable account of their privacy preferences. Within the EU at least, a similar balance should be found between different parties (due to us operating within the normative expectations of the ECHR) and, if this is the case, then striking that balance within data protection law may be the simpler, more elegant solution.

SECTION III   ADDRESSING THE BALANCE

Potential conflicts of interest between rights-holders are not a novel problem. In cases of conflict, it is not an appropriate response to deny a category of persons any rights at all. Instead, conflicts should be resolved in accordance with the underlying normative bases of the rights claims involved. Invariably, this will mean appropriately qualifying the rights held by all interested parties to ensure adequate and appropriate protection for all. In the case of privacy claims, the normative bases may be many and varied and, for many people, rather uncertain as their privacy norms follow established patterns of behaviour rather than being shaped by deliberate normative preferences. The interests recognised by

---

[52] *Ibid.*

the Directive are, however, amongst others and as noted above, those provided for within the European Convention of Human Rights and the Council of Europe, Convention on Data Protection (1981).[53] There is an extensive pre-existing jurisprudence concerning the balancing of rights acknowledged by the European Convention.

In so far as the interests concerned are those recognised by Article 8 of the Convention, any question concerning the resolution of conflict should be resolved consistent with the established practice of balancing an individual's 8(1) right to a private and family life with a State's entitlement to restrict the enjoyment of that right under 8(2). As we saw in the last chapter, identifying the point of balance between these two provisions is not necessarily a straightforward process if you rely directly upon the articles contained within the ECHR. What was reasonably clear from the jurisprudence surrounding the ECHR, however, was that although the relational variable of the concept of privacy protected by the Article 8 right to a private life might be relatively narrow, the transactional element was both broad and inclusive. If it could be shown that activity interfered with *an identifiable individual's* enjoyment of private or family life, then Article 8(1) would most likely be engaged (even if such interference might ultimately be considered justifiable). There seems little doubt that secondary data subjects might be identifiably associated with data, and also that the processing of that data might be capable of affecting them in relevant ways, such that their rights to a private and family life might at least *sometimes* be engaged by such processing. The national implementations of protection for family members seem to anticipate just such circumstances. The EU Data Protection Directive represented an opportunity to work out and specify more clearly how the respective interests of primary and secondary data subjects were to be appropriately qualified. Its failure to do so not only risks leaving identifiable individuals unprotected, it also creates a need that is currently being addressed (if at all) in bespoke fashion at a local level. This creates the possibility of just the kind of inconsistency that the Directive was supposed to avoid.

How should data be understood to 'relate to' another individual in order for that data to be personal data?

When determining how data must legally relate to an individual to constitute personal data we must establish which factual relationship(s) will

---

[53] Convention for the Protection of Individuals with regard to Automatic Processing of Personal Data, Strasbourg, 28.I.1981.

count. When a court determines the relevant kind of relationship, it must operate within the context established by both the literal text of the Directive and its legislative purpose. The Directive explicitly requires that a data subject be either 'identified or identifiable'. The Directive further indicates (through Recital 26) that when assessing whether an individual is identifiable account should be taken of those 'means likely reasonably to be used'. It therefore seems reasonable to suggest that an individual can only be considered 'identifiable' if data exists, or can be foreseen to exist, within a context permitting association between it and a particular individual by 'means likely reasonably to be used'. The linking of specific data with a particular person, the hallmark of that individual's identification, can only take place in an informational context permitting of such association. If such a context might also place an individual's fundamental rights and freedoms, in particular their right to privacy, at risk, then the data in question must surely be said to 'relate' to the person concerned. Only if data could be said to 'relate to' an individual in a way that was capable of 'affecting' their enjoyment of their fundamental rights and freedoms ought it to be termed 'personal data' within the context of the Directive. While this may seem vague and imprecise, it might be noted that it mirrors the principles that could be discerned from the preferences of the supervisory authorities currently charged with monitoring the implementation of the Directive in practice: data must both possess 'identificatory potential' and be capable of having a 'relevant affect'.

Put simply then, data ought to be understood to relate to an individual if it is possible that the data might be associated with her via means likely, reasonably, to be used, and this might affect her fundamental rights and freedoms, especially privacy. This should be assessed by reference to the interpretive potential of the data, in the relevant circumstances, and not determined by interpretive pedigree. The fact that information was originally generated through an inquiry that had a particular individual as its focus does not insulate other identifiable individuals from the potential privacy infringing effects of that information when recorded as genetic data. There is no reason to doubt that genetic data might satisfy these requirements of personal data simultaneously with regard to multiple persons. There seems no justification, within the context of a protection of the fundamental rights and freedoms of identifiable persons, for denying this. Accepting it would, however, expand the class of recognised 'data subject' and would undoubtedly give rise to more explicit conflicts. Such conflicts of interests ought, however, to be recognised and appropriately resolved rather than simply denied. Examples of how conflicts might be effectively and appropriately resolved already exist within the Directive.

Expanding the exemptions

Those parts of the Directive concerned with information provision provide a clear illustration of how rights and obligations can be appropriately qualified. It has been noted that limited restrictions upon the right to be provided with information exist only when the data has been obtained by a data controller from a third party.[54] The specified exemptions could quite easily be extended to include cases where provision of the information would represent a disproportionate interference with the fundamental rights and freedoms of others. Appropriate wording could even be straightforwardly copied across from Article 7(f). Such an extension of the exemption would allow a data controller, who had gathered data from a relative, to avoid providing information to family members when it would be *inappropriate* to do so owing to an unjustified interference with the fundamental rights and freedoms of a primary data subject. Other potential conflicts, such as those introduced by recognising a secondary data subject's right to access, rectify or erase data, could be resolved in similar ways.[55] While Article 13 does not permit Member States to restrict the Article 14 right to object, that right only requires a data controller to cease processing where the objection is 'legitimate'. Failure to accommodate the interests of others would undermine the legitimacy of any objection. The expansion of the relevant exemptions, that would be necessary as a corollary to the recognition of multiple data subjects, thus exists within the wherewithal provided by the Directive.

The requirements to gain consent, notify, provide access to data, etc. would each need to be expressly qualified to ensure that they did not inappropriately interfere with the privacy rights of others. This exercise would give Member States the opportunity to address the potential conflicts between the privacy preferences of *all* of those affected by the processing of personal data in relevant ways. This may result in the expectations of primary data subjects, as currently represented, being recast. At times, this would extend the responsibilities of those processing personal genetic data – obviously most notably, in the context of this argument, to secondary data subjects in some circumstances – but, at other times, the responsibilities would be reduced as the interests that *others* held in genetic data took priority. Examples, here, might include

[54] It is Article 11 (and not Article 10) that is most likely to have applicability here anyway, because it is unlikely that a data controller will have obtained the data directly from a secondary (or tertiary) data subject.

[55] Indeed the Directive indicates that restrictions should be placed upon the rights to information and access in a number of circumstances, see Recitals 41, 42 and 43 for more.

clarifying that the responsibility to notify data subjects of research purposes *can be qualified*, even if data has been obtained directly from a data subject, when necessary and proportionate to preserve the integrity of the research. In such cases, being able to give reasonable account for each of the interests engaged, and for the way in which they are adjudicated, would be consistent with the idea of the public interest advanced in Chapter 2. Denying the opportunity to account for the interests of secondary data subjects is not in the public interest.

There is arguably a responsibility upon Member States to exercise their discretion to ensure that the fundamental rights and freedoms of all those within their jurisdiction are properly protected.[56] Unfortunately, they have not consistently done so and, in particular, secondary data subjects appear to have been marginalised as a category. Rather than explicitly recognising that they may have preferences with regard to the processing of genetic data, and explicitly accommodating those within a framework that justifiably prioritises the interests of a primary data subject only where necessary, they, and other individuals who may have an identifiable interest in access to genetic data, have been denied account of their preferred norms of exclusivity.

---

[56] Such a responsibility is incurred, inter alia, by being party to the European Convention (Article 1).

6   Anonymity

It was argued in the previous chapter that legal frameworks centred upon the idea of 'personal data' could be usefully extended to include more explicitly a broader range of *identifiable* persons. Arguing that the existing data protection framework should be interpreted to offer protection to secondary data subjects is to argue a relatively small broadening of the relational aspect of the idea of privacy that the law currently protects. It does not, for example, question whether anonymous data rightly falls outside of the regulatory framework established by data protection law. On the contrary, if de-identification is perceived to be a way of protecting privacy (and reducing the obligations of a data controller), then any efforts directed towards extending the range of identifiable data subjects (and the scope of data protection legislation) might make the anonymisation of data seem more attractive. Certainly, anonymous data has far fewer protections, and therefore fewer regulatory hurdles, associated with it than personal data under the information governance regime anticipated by Data Protection Directive 95/46/EC. However, is it correct to assume that anonymous data is incapable of affecting an individual's privacy? To what extent could, and should, privacy protection be extended to include anonymous data?

Structure

I begin this chapter by considering what the terms 'identifiable' and 'anonymous' mean, both in the abstract and in the context of law and research using genetic data. We see that – both in principle and in practice – the deceptively simple idea of identifiability is fiendishly difficult to apply reliably without taking context into account: identifiability refers to a particular associative potential of data and the realisation of that potential relies upon the availability of a relevant interpretive framework. Again, we find the idea of interpretive potential important to an assessment of the significance of data.

Data can be identifiable in one context, anonymous in another, and it may shift between these states depending upon the availability and accessibility of relevant interpretive frameworks. In fact, the halfway house between theses two states, represented by pseudonymisation, acknowledges this contextual nature of identification; the term implies that the availability of the contexts enabling identification are both limited and controlled.

The variability in the possibilities of identification challenges the somewhat simplistic distinction drawn by data protection law between identifiable and anonymous data. It also poses problems for a regulatory framework organised around the idea that a data controller owes responsibilities to an identifiable data subject. What if a particular context determines that a data subject is identifiable to some but not to others? *Who* must be able to identify the data subject? Must the possibility of identification be a realistic one or is a purely hypothetical possibility sufficient? What does realistic mean?[1]

A consideration of the responsibilities placed upon data controllers demonstrates that, providing the *possibility* of identification (by anyone) is assessed from the perspective of a data controller, then it is possible for a data controller to meet a number of the responsibilities that the data protection framework would place upon her even if the data is, to her, not identifiable. By the same token, if identifiability by others cannot be anticipated by a data controller, then it will be hard to discharge her responsibilities even if data is, as a matter of fact, identifiable to certain persons with access to both it and relevant interpretive frameworks.

If a data controller *can* discharge certain responsibilities to data that she is not capable of identifying herself, but can anticipate that others with access might associate the data with particular persons, then it will be suggested here that she *should* be understood to owe responsibilities in relation to that data under the current data protection framework – even though the data is, to her, effectively anonymous. If third parties have access to data, then anonymity is not assured by the data controller's own inability to associate the data with a particular person. The identifiability of data by third parties is a relevant concern when considering the impact that data might have upon particular individuals' enjoyment of their fundamental rights and freedoms, especially privacy.

---

[1] The previous chapter addressed the possibility that, with changing context, *different* individuals are identifiable to different (or even the same) person: there are multiple data subjects. Here the focus is on the variability in identifiability of a particular person. When one recognises that the variable of identifiability applies to each of the different individuals referred to in the last chapter, then one gets a sense of the difficulty in applying the concept of personal data in practice.

Simply recognising that data controllers may owe responsibilities in relation to data that third parties may relate to identifiable individuals does not exhaust the responsibilities owed to anonymous data. There are other responsibilities, some not so easily accommodated within the existing legal framework, brought to light if one challenges certain key assumptions underlying the current construction and operation of the law. The first assumption is that data *can* be effectively dissociated from particular individuals on an enduring basis; the challenge here is to the idea of a distinction between 'identifiable' and 'non-identifiable' data at person level. The second is that identification is *only* about association with particular individuals *as individuals*; and the challenge here is to the idea that identifying individuals *as members of groups* cannot infringe their privacy. Each of these two challenges suggests a more fundamental shift in privacy protection than may be provided within the context of current data protection law.

None of the above is intended to demonstrate that the Directive's concern with identifiability is mistaken. The de-identification of data, so far as possible in a particular context, does undoubtedly *reduce* the possibility of certain kinds of risk.[2] However, both group and individual harms may still flow from the use of data considered by a data controller to be anonymised, particularly if that data is subject to fluid interpretive frameworks, due to the associative potential of such data. An absolute failure to acknowledge this potential represents a significant weakness in privacy protection. As has previously been noted, any advantages attached to extending a protective framework to include anonymous data would, of course, need to be proportionate to any burdens incurred. Relevant burdens would be those experienced by data controllers in meeting such responsibilities. The chapter concludes with a suggestion that reducing the regulatory distinction drawn between anonymous data and identifiable data might actually have a number of advantages for researchers.

In summary, this argument will present three claims that it is suggested the law must address. (1) Researchers owe certain responsibilities even if data is currently anonymous to them: namely a responsibility to manage the identificatory potential of data to third parties. (2) Individual personal-level data should be treated in a similar way to identifiable data even if currently anonymous (to anyone). (3) Even if individual

---

[2] Although it might also introduce additional risks of certain kinds. For example, the possibility of feedback of clinically relevant (incidental) findings is reduced or eliminated through de-identification of data used for research purposes. Hence, the significance of context.

identity is not a concern, then group harms should be considered. None of these claims undermines the importance of anonymisation as a means of offering important protection to individual, or even group, privacy. Collectively, however, they do support the argument that the clear distinction between 'anonymous'and 'identifiable' data currently drawn by the law is hard to defend.

Undoubtedly, it would be a challenge to address each of these claims in a way that was proportionate, did not unjustifiably burden researchers with additional responsibilities, continued to encourage de-identification where appropriate, but also found alternative methods of protection where de-identification was insufficient to the task. To tempt individuals to take up this challenge, however, one might encourage an appreciation that reducing the significance of anonymity may be a good thing from a research perspective.

SECTION I TERMINOLOGY

On the one hand, anonymity seems a simple idea. It does, after all, describe an absence of information. This would seem to suggest that the term should describe a state less complicated than alternatives. Instead, it seems anonymisation is a rather complicated business. Superficially at least, being anonymous is associated with being nameless.[3] However, when the word is being used to imply the opposite of 'identifiable', then the notion of a 'name' itself appears complex. To give but one example, the graffiti artist Banksy is notoriously protective of his or her identity.[4] Banksy is, nonetheless, 'famous' and the work is associated by many with the name 'Banksy'. As previously noted, at least within the context of an information system, 'identification is the association of data with a particular individual'.[5] This would seem to suggest that the work is *identifiable* even though it is not associated with the artist's 'real' name. Is the work *both* anonymous *and* identifiable? Clearly, the term anonymous is being used here in two different ways. It is possible for artwork to be identifiable (i.e. associated with a particular individual), even though the artist remains anonymous (i.e. one of the names – the

---

[3] The word 'anonymous' is defined by the Oxford English Dictionary as '1. Nameless, having no name; of unknown name ... 2. Bearing no author's name; of unknown or unavowed authorship. 3. Unacknowledged, illegitimate, rare' (Oxford English Dictionary, 2nd edition, 1989).

[4] D. Usborne, 'Staying anonymous is 'crippling', says Banksy', *The Independent Newspaper*, May 2007.

[5] R. Clarke, 'Human identification in information systems: management challenges and public policy issues', *Information Technology and People* 7(4) (1994), 6–37 at 8.

'real' name – is unknown). The work is, and simultaneously is not, anonymous depending upon *which* name you are seeking to associate with it. While the term 'anonymous' remains meaningful, it can be confusing when it is not clear which association is being denied. If we are only concerned with a lack of association with a particular *person*, then Banksy's artwork is certainly *not* anonymous.

To try to avoid either contradiction or unnecessary confusion, the word 'anonymous' will be used here simply to imply the opposite of identifiable. It will be considered irrelevant whether a *particular* name, or data, is known: the only significant consideration is whether the data in question can be associated with a particular individual. If data can be associated with a particular individual, then it will not matter which identifying characteristics – or data fields – are used to do so. This means that data may be identifiable even if (a particular) name remains unknown or some other quality (e.g. geographical location) remains unassociated with the person. This use of the term is preferred here both because the law speaks only of identifiability (and so I use the term anonymous to describe a state of non-identifiability) and because (and perhaps somewhat ironically, unlike Banksy) it is often not their name that people are concerned with being associated with.

This is an important point and so I will expand briefly upon it through an example. If an individual walks into a room, even if you do not know her name, then that individual might be identifiable to you. You might, for example, recognise her to be the president of the company for which you work. If she then goes berserk and wrecks the boardroom, other employees may be associating that action with her before the end of the working day. Whether they know any of her given or family names, whether they know where she lives, or how old she is, they all know who they are gossiping about: they have identified her in a particular context through the use of an identifier that has meaning in that context. The importance of common 'identifiers', such as name, address or national security number, is largely due to their instrumental value in facilitating this process of linkage between person and *other* data *across* a wide range of contexts.[6]

When data is being used in this way to facilitate identification, the novel association is *not* with the identifying data itself – the identifying

---

[6] Although it should be noted that certain identifiers do come to be closely associated with an individual's sense of identity and so possess inherent (rather than merely instrumental) value. This can be seen with the sense of violation experienced in identify theft which goes beyond the inconvenience of having to change a number of assigned identifiers.

data must already be known by both gossiping parties if identification is to take place. To function as an identifier, data used to make an association must already be familiar in *both* contexts. In fact, when you link an action to a person through an identifier, there are two *separate* associations taking place. To return briefly to the example of the destructive company president: if someone tells you that 'Poppy wrecked the board room', then it only tells you something about a particular person if you already know who Poppy is. The information provided only draws a link between the action and a particular person, if the identifier used (in this case name) is otherwise linked to that person. There has to be a separate and discrete association between the identifier and a particular person before that person is identifiable.

This independent association between particular person and identifier might be facilitated through a 'look-up list' designed for the purpose, such as a company members' directory, or broader circumstances (you might already know who Poppy is for many different reasons). There must, however, be this separate association between data functioning as an identifier and person before identification will take place. The range of data that could function as an identifier is limitless and it need not be intended to be an identifier: any one of those pieces of data that is associated with an individual in one context might also be associated with them in another, and might be *the data* that enables the linkage across those two contexts and the association of *additional* data with an individual. It is the fact that *any* data might function as an identifier that makes absolute anonymity almost impossible to guarantee if data is held at the individual level. While no individual data may be uniquely identified with a particular individual with certainty, a combination of relatively commonplace details can easily mark an individual life out as unique. Our lives represent a unique portfolio of what are typically rather common details. Through combining such details, we might construct an increasingly distinct profile matching decreasingly few individuals.

It is, however, important to recall that data will only function as an identifier if there is *already* secondary linkage between that data and a particular person in another context. Any 'new' information that you learn about a person through linkage is not the information that has served to facilitate that linkage. (If there is no 'new' information, and *all* relevant information is functioning as an identifier, then you do not learn anything new about the person.) Again a simple example might help make the point. Imagine that someone robbed in the street described their attacker as over 6 feet tall, covered in tattoos, and wearing top hat and tails. The only people able to identify the attacker will be those that already know an individual who fits this description. The *only* thing they learn new is that this individual (or someone matching her description) has been accused of committing a street robbery. This is important because identifiers themselves, when acting as such, are not disclosive of their own information content. If they disclose any information, it is not the information *functioning as an identifier in the context*.

I have gone to some length to describe the ideas of anonymity and identifiability, and the possibilities of different data acting as identifiers, because the relationship between data functioning as an identifier, and data associated with it, will have some significance later. Certainly, myriad words are used in the literature to describe a specific kind of relationship between identifier and context. The use of these words is notoriously inconsistent and I wish to rely later upon the point that identifiers are not, themselves, disclosive. To try to avoid confusion over any of the terminology used, I seek to be absolutely clear about the four different terms that I will use to describe materially different contexts on the spectrum of identifiability between the extremes of uniquely identifiable and completely anonymous,[7] neither of which is likely to be realised in practice.

Information such as name, address or national identity number can be described as *generally identifiable*.[8] This is because the relevant interpretive framework enabling linkage between these data items and particular persons is widely available and, in combination at least, the identifiers are relatively discriminating. Also, general identifiers are so well known that they typically indicate, through their format and content, the context in which they need to be placed to enable association with a particular individual.

Information can be described as *identifiably coded*. This is a form of pseudonymisation, and in this case the availability of the relevant interpretive framework, or identifying context, is restricted. Information such as a specially constructed study number (i.e. a specific identifier) permits cross-reference with a separate database, and that database contains general identifiers. The information is identifiably coded only if the individual processing the data has access to this separate database with its general identifiers. (The distinction between this and 'generally

---

[7] These terms are consistent with Article 3 of Recommendation Rec(2006)4 of the Committee of Ministers of the Council of Europe to Member States on research on biological materials of human origins. (Adopted by the Committee of Ministers on 15 March 2006 at the 958th meeting of the Ministers' Deputies).

[8] Although not everyone may have access to the specific 'look-up' list, such as the ability to 'decode' a national identity number, the contexts permitting identification through a general identifier are widely available and not as restricted as when data is 'identifiably coded'. There is not, however, a bright-line distinction between 'generally identifiable' and 'identifiably coded'; there will be varying degrees of restriction on possibility of identification.

identifiable' depends upon the accessibility of the separate database and the general identifiers.) In practice, information might be identifiably coded either by restricting access to the 'look-up list' or by reducing the likelihood of it being used by deliberately obscuring any indication as to relevant identifying context.

Information can be described as *linked anonymised*. This is a second form of pseudonymisation. In this case, information is identifiably coded but the individual processing the data does *not* have access to the separate database and its general identifiers. It must be possible for some other person to do so. The category of linked anonymised might be further separated into those circumstances where the individual processing the data is aware of the possibility that another individual can perform the linkage and 'break the code', and those circumstances where they are unaware of the possibility.

Information can also be described as *effectively anonymised*. This is information that cannot be linked to general identifiers. The association with a particular person will be frustrated because there is no way effectively to link the information to a single individual in the available contexts or, more likely, because it matches multiple individuals and so no particular individual. Effectively anonymised information might still be information that is, or could be, associated with a group.

Describing data as *completely* anonymous would be to assert that the relevant context either does not, or could not, exist that associates the information content of the data with a particular individual. Given that interpretive frameworks making links between data and people may always be freshly constructed, by anybody, this is an extremely hard claim to justify. Effective anonymisation would not require the impossibility of re-identification. It would simply demand that those processing the data could not reasonably expect such contexts, enabling association with a particular individual, to be accessed by anybody.

How do these terms map against the legal concept of personal data described in Chapter 4? Where is the *legal* threshold of identifiability in relation to these terms? Can a researcher meet data protection responsibilities in relation to any identifiably coded, linked anonymised or effectively anonymised data, or only a fraction thereof?

SECTION II   DATA PROTECTION AND ANONYMOUS DATA

In the context of the law of data protection, identifiability is treated rather crudely as a binary idea: personal data either satisfies the requirements of identifiability or it does not. The relevant question then becomes

'At which point, along the spectrum of identifiability described above, does the Directive establish the legal threshold of identifiability?' How available must an interpretive framework possessing the relevant associative potential actually be? To whom must it be available? When must it be available to them? Answers to these questions have important implications for the rights and responsibilities established by the Directive and any legal framework that operates with the notion of identifiable data.

As we have previously seen, the definition of personal data provided by the Directive is of little direct assistance. Article 2(b) states that 'an identifiable person is one who can be identified, directly or indirectly, in particular by reference to an identification number or to one or more factors specific to his physical, physiological, mental, economic, cultural or social identity'. As we have seen, *all* forms of identification rely upon an association being made between (at least) two pieces of data held in (initially) distinct contexts: data originally linked with a particular person in one context is associated with *the same data* in another context. The significance is invariably that this same data, in the other context, is linked with 'other data' not previously associated with the person in question. The significance of 'direct' and 'indirect' identification is then unclear.

It may be that 'direct' is supposed to imply that the data constitutes a 'general identifier' and so might be more readily associated 'directly' to a particular individual. 'Indirect' identification may imply that rather more links are required in the chain of association, as would be the case if the data were 'identifiably coded': data that must be linked with additional data, which is then linked in turn with 'general identifiers' before identification becomes possible.

The number of links in the chain of association is not, however, as significant as the availability of the interpretive frameworks themselves. Some indication of the required availability or accessibility of such frameworks within the definition may have been more useful than this particular distinction (although, as we shall see, there is some such indication within the Recitals to the Directive).

It seems that the imprecision within the Directive has led to some quite different approaches being taken in the implementation of the Directive. The survey of data protection authorities by Booth *et al.* discussed in the last chapter found a significant variation in response to the question whether certain kinds of data might 'always', 'sometimes' or 'never' be personal data.[9] Given the significance attached to the legal

---

[9] Booth *et al.*, 'What are personal data?'

threshold of identifiability, it might be considered surprising to find that the threshold has not been drawn consistently across the EU.

Recital 26 to the Data Protection Directive does provide some guidance on when data should be understood to be identifiable: 'to determine whether a person is identifiable, account should be taken of all the means likely reasonably to be used either by the controller or by any other person to identify the said person'. However, the fact that this explanation occurs within a Recital to the Directive, which is not legally binding, leaves it open for different jurisdictions to establish the legal threshold in slightly different places.

The UK Data Protection Act 1998 provides one example of an implementing statute that presents rather a different conception of identifiability from that contained within the Recital to the Directive. The UK Act focuses upon whether data is identifiable *to the data controller* rather than to any other person. This is to establish the relevant threshold of identifiability in a significantly different place from that indicated by the Recital.

As the shape and distribution of both the benefits and the burdens imposed by data protection law shifts considerably with a shifting threshold of identifiability, there may be considered room for different legal systems to consider the appropriate balance to lie at different points. I do not take up here the problems of inconsistent regulation for researchers. The question that I wish to pursue for now is whether there is anything about the responsibilities that the Directive expects of a data controller that would suggest the threshold of identifiability ought to be drawn in one place rather than another.

The burden of compliance and the UK implementation of identifiability

As noted earlier, Article 2(a) of the Directive states:

'personal data' shall mean any information relating to an identified or identifiable natural person ('data subject'); an identifiable person is one who can be identified, directly or indirectly, in particular by reference to an identification number or to one or more factors specific to his physical, physiological, mental, economic, cultural or social identity.

The implication is that an individual is identifiable if she can be identified, directly or indirectly, by *anybody*. This implication is supported, and only slightly adjusted, by Recital 26 of the Directive:

Whereas the principles of protection must apply to any information concerning an identified or identifiable person; whereas, to determine whether a person is identifiable, account should be taken of all the means likely reasonably to be used either by the controller *or by any other person* to identify the said person; whereas the principles of protection shall not apply to data rendered anonymous in such a way that the data subject is no longer identifiable. (emphasis added)

Recitals are not legally binding, but they offer an authoritative guide to the content of a European directive. In this case, Recital 26 would seem to offer unequivocal indication that data should be understood to be identifiable if it may be associated with a particular individual by *any* person using means reasonably likely to be used. From this it would follow that the Directive requires the legal threshold of identifiability to be set at a point that may well include linked anonymised data *if any person* (not limited to the data controller) may break the code using means reasonably likely to be used.

However, the Data Protection Act 1998 establishes the threshold of identifiability at a point that would exclude identification using information inaccessible to a data controller even if accessible to others. The 1998 Act defines 'personal data' as

data which relate to a living individual who can be identified

(a) from those data, or
(b) from those data and other information which is in the possession of, or is likely to come into the possession of, the data controller,

and includes any expression of opinion about the individual and any indication of the intentions of the data controller or any other person in respect of the individual.

No further guidance is offered within the 1998 Act on how the term 'identifiable' is to be understood or when information should be understood to be 'likely' to come into a data controller's possession. The emphasis is, however, clearly placed upon assessing whether a living individual is identifiable *to the data controller*.[10]

If it were only the possibility of identification by the data controller that were relevant, then English law could recognise data to be anonymised – and would attach no responsibilities to it under the law of data protection – even though it might be perfectly anticipatable that others, e.g. through a data access agreement or the publication of the data, could relate the data to particular individuals using means reasonably likely to be used. This would seem a blatant failure to provide

---

[10] It should be noted that identifiability alone is not itself enough to make data 'personal data' under English law. Data must relate to an identifiable person but it must also do more than that: it must be capable of affecting an individual's privacy. See *Durant* v. *FSA* [2003] EWCA Civ 1746 [28].

protection that the Directive clearly anticipates should be provided.[11] Why might the UK parliament have stated that the legal threshold of identifiability should be drawn here? It can only be because they were concerned with the implications of doing otherwise. The most obvious concern would be with the burdens that would be imposed upon a data controller if they cannot identify the data subject.

Can a data controller meet responsibilities to an anonymous data subject?

There are a number of responsibilities that a data controller has when processing personal data. A number of these have already been mentioned in the context of other discussions. For now, the focus will be upon the responsibilities that a data controller has directly to a data subject: the responsibilities that one might expect would be most difficult to discharge if a data controller is unable to identify a data subject themselves, namely, the responsibility to notify data subjects about the processing of their personal data (Articles 10 and 11), to respect their right to access their personal data (Article 12), and, to respect their right to object to the processing of their data in certain circumstances (Article 14).

Notification

We have seen that Article 11 applies when data have been collected through a third party. In such circumstances, it might be difficult for a data controller to discharge her obligation to provide information to a data subject *unless* such information could be provided through the third party. In this context, it is important to remember that the responsibility to provide information under Article 11 is qualified. An inability to provide the information, owing to the provision of the information being impossible or involving disproportionate effort, excuses a data controller of the responsibility. In this context, it seems that the responsibility to notify can be appropriately qualified so as not to impose any unreasonable burden in cases where the data are not identifiable to the data subject.

Meeting a responsibility under Article 10 might, however, be more problematic if a data controller cannot identify the individual to whom data relates. We have seen both that Article 10 applies when data has

---

[11] See p. 145.

been gathered directly from a data subject and that it is not expressly qualified in a similar way to Article 11. If data is gathered directly from an individual, then there will typically be an obvious opportunity to provide her with relevant information: at the time it is gathered. However, if the data controller does not recognise the data to be identifiable at the time of collection, then she may fail to appreciate the need to provide this information. Somebody conducting surveys in the street may deliberately avoid collecting generally identifiable data precisely because she wishes to avoid the responsibilities associated with collecting 'personal data'.

What is more, if the responsibility to provide information about the purposes of processing is an ongoing obligation, and contact details have not been collected at the same time as other data, then it might be impossible, or at least involve disproportionate effort, for a researcher to re-contact for the purposes of personal notification. In circumstances such as these, where notification might actually be impracticable for a data controller, then Article 10 would seem to impose an unreasonable burden upon her *unless* one either adopts the narrow idea of identifiability contained within the UK Act or introduces appropriate qualification.

Access and objection

We have seen that Article 12 provides a data subject with the right to access her personal data. Before a data controller could responsibly provide access to personal data, she would have to be assured of the individual's identity. If a data controller was not in possession of the information that would enable her to identify a data subject, and she was unlikely to process such information using means reasonably likely to be used, then it is difficult to see how it could be considered reasonable for her to discharge a responsibility to provide access. If this were the expectation, then one would expect the Directive to have provided qualification in cases of impossibility or disproportionate effort. No such qualification is contained within Article 13. I would suggest that the only way that such a responsibility could be discharged, if the data is anonymous to the data controller, is if the data subject herself provides the information that would enable the data controller to associate the subject with data the controller holds. This might be difficult if the data subject has not been informed of the collection of the data in the first place.

We have also seen that a data subject has the right to object, under Article 14, 'on compelling legitimate grounds relating to his [or her] particular situation' to the processing of her personal data. Again, the possibility of a data controller meeting this responsibility with data that is to her effectively anonymous must surely depend upon the ability of a data subject to provide the data controller with the information required to associate her with the data. In this case, however, if data is effectively anonymous because it *could* relate to more than one person, then it may be inappropriate to give a single individual the opportunity to veto the processing relating to each of them. This may be a difficult question, but it is one that must be answered if it is the possibility of identification by a third party and not just the data controller that is relevant.

It can be seen that, in the case of notification, access and objection, the responsibilities upon a data controller are not easily met in relation to anonymous data without some further development of the position described in the Directive. Admittedly, there are other responsibilities placed upon a data controller that might be more easily met regardless of the identifiability of the data subject, e.g. the responsibility to ensure that data is kept securely. Even in these cases, it is only reasonable to apply them if a data controller is aware (or at least could or should be aware) that she is processing data that is identifiable *to others* using means reasonably likely to be used. The Directive establishes a regime within which failure to register is a criminal offence. It cannot reasonably be understood to apply to individuals who have no way of recognising themselves to be processing personal data, although this caveat is far from clear if one simply considers the text of the Directive.

It may be reasonable for a data controller to meet data protection responsibilities *if* it is reasonable for her to anticipate identification by others using means reasonably likely to be used *and* the discharge of the responsibility is neither impossible nor would involve a disproportionate effort. In such circumstances, *and with this caveat*, then I would suggest that these responsibilities *should* be discharged even if data is anonymous to the data controller. The alternative would seriously compromise the privacy protection anticipated by the Directive. This is particularly obvious in cases where data is to be widely distributed, e.g. through publication.[12]

---

[12] The possibility of identification by others following publication of data considered anonymous by the body responsible for determining the purposes of processing was clearly demonstrated when AOL released 'anonymised' details of searches that had been made through its Internet search service. M. Barbaro and T. Zeller, Jr., 'A face is exposed for AOL searcher no. 4417749', *New York Times*, 9 August 2006.

In fact, and despite the express wording of the 1998 Act, it seems the UK courts are interpreting it in this way. In the case of *Common Services Agency* v. *Scottish Information Commissioner* [2008],[13] Lord Hope said:

> The question is whether the data controller, or anybody else who was in possession of the barnardised data, would be able to identify the living individual or individuals to whom the data in that form related.[14]

In practice, then, it appears that even English law will recognise data to be personal data when somebody other than the data controller is capable of identifying the data subject. This suggests, however, that the need for clearer qualification of the responsibilities of a data controller when she reasonably perceives data to be effectively anonymised is pressing; even in a country that has implemented the Directive in a way that would seem to deny the possibility.

The argument to this point may have raised a question in the mind of the reader. If a data controller *can* discharge, suitably qualified, responsibilities when data is effectively anonymous *to her*, then should she not discharge those responsibilities? Is it to introduce an irrelevance, and an unnecessary uncertainty, to consider whether *others* might be able to associate the data with a particular person? In the next section, I consider whether there might be reasons for protecting anonymised data even if association with a particular person is not anticipated using means reasonably likely to be used by the data controller *or others*.

Reasons to protect anonymous data

There is little doubt that many of the expectations relating to privacy are related to concerns over the association between data and particular persons: identification. The responsibility imposed by the data protection framework to reduce the identifiability of data[15] is not, however, typically about frustrating identification by a data controller. As described earlier, data can only function as an identifier if it is previously known. Identifiers, when functioning as such *simpliciter*, are not disclosive of any new information. Informational relationships are only changed through the association of particular persons with 'new' data. Such association can occur in two ways with data that is considered 'effectively anonymous'. The first is through unexpected re-identification,

---

[13] UKHL 47.   [14] Para. 26.

[15] This follows from the responsibility only to keep data in identifiable form for as long as necessary in order to perform the purposes of processing for which it was collected. See principle five, Schedule 1, Part 1, Data Protection Act 1998.

or fresh association, at the individual level. The second is through the association of particular persons with data, not as individuals per se, but as members of particular groups: group association.

Zorro's mask and re-identification

If re-identification and fresh association are good reasons to place obligations upon a data controller, then they remain good reasons even if a data controller is unable to identify a data subject or expects others to be able to do so. The risks posed to an individual's privacy do not reduce if data is less identifiable to a data controller, if they remain (or become) identifiable to others. There are certain things that a data controller can do to data to reduce the likelihood of an individual being identified by others. She might, for example, strip data of items that function as common identifiers, they could remove or obscure particularly unusual data items in an individual record, or they may aggregate data. However, if data is kept at the individual level, then it will be extremely difficult to remove the possibility of (re)-identification by a third party or the data in question being freshly associated with a particular person in another context. The difficulty is that, if a data controller loses control over the context, then it may be virtually impossible for her to anticipate each of the different interpretive frameworks that might *ever* be applied to the data. Even if it is entirely reasonable for her to consider data to be effectively anonymous today, that position may well change tomorrow.

Indeed, at times, steps deliberately to reduce the chances of identification today might actually facilitate it in the future. Zorro's mask may have been adopted to prevent the association of activities with the name and character Don Diego de la Vega, but the mask itself becomes a liability if ever removed. Unique identifiers, adopted as pseudonyms to protect identity now, might eventually serve as a means of linking activities that might not otherwise have been associated with each other. In this way, steps taken to obscure an identity can sometimes *facilitate* identification if the informational context changes in a way that was not anticipated or intended.

The possibility of linking pieces of information and, through that linkage, enabling re-identification of an individual is a growing possibility with improvements in information technology. As 'context' is so important when determining the relative uniqueness of a portfolio of information, the publication of information can be particularly problematic as control is lost over that context. There has been concern expressed recently about whether certain genetic data, published as anonymous, might be associated with particular individuals.[16]

The concern led to certain resources being taken out of the public domain despite criticism from researchers. One of the reasons for the criticism of the decision to remove the resources was that the possibility of identification relied upon the genetic data itself acting as an identifier: the linkage could only be made by someone who already possessed the genetic data in question and could already link it with a particular individual.[17] The criticism thus relies upon the premise previously described: data that functions as an identifier is not disclosive of its own information content. What *could* be uniquely inferred from the publication of the data was (only) an individual's participation in a particular research study. If confidentiality had been assured with regard to participation, then that alone may be considered reason to restrict access to identifiable data.

While the possibilities of identifying people within published datasets that contain no general identifiers are currently relatively limited, this situation may change in time. Increasingly, different parts of the portfolio of information that relate to particular individuals are becoming electronically catalogued and cross-referenced. As individuals increasingly make sections of their own genome available through publicly accessible websites, they are gradually compromising their ability to prevent the re-identification of their own, and others', genetic data, in other contexts.[18] This is not intended to be alarmist. The point is simply to underline that as data flows through increasingly rich interpretive contexts, one might need to exercise some degree of precaution when assessing the possibilities of future association.

It is important to underline that the Directive insists that it is means *reasonably likely to be used* that are important. It should not be sufficient for a simple theoretical possibility of re-identification to trigger the relevant protections. Paul Ohm, in his article 'Broken promises of privacy',[19]

---

[16] N. Homer, S. Szelinger, M. Redman, D. Duggan, W. Tembe, J. Muehling, J. V. Pearson, D. A. Stephan, S. F. Nelson and D. W. Craig, 'Resolving individuals contributing trace amounts of DNA to highly complex mixtures using high-density SNP genotyping microarrays', *PLoS Genetics* 4(8) (2008), e1000167.

[17] N. Gilbert, 'Researchers criticize genetic data restrictions', *Nature* (2008) (4 September). Published online. www.nature.com/news/2008/080904/full/news. 2008.1083.html#B1.

[18] D. Greenbaum, J. Du and M. Gerstein, 'Genomic anonymity: have we already lost it?', *American Journal of Bioethics* 8(10) (2008), 71–4. http://dx.doi.org/10.1080/15265160802478560.

[19] P. Ohm, 'Broken promises of privacy: responding to the surprising failure of anonymization', University of Colorado Law Legal Studies Research Paper, No. 09–12, University of Colorado (2009). http://ssrn.com/abstract=1450006.

seeks to demonstrate the inability of anonymisation as a technique reliably to protect privacy. He ably demonstrates that a number of techniques are currently available to re-identify supposedly anonymous data. While it is important to recognise that anonymisation is imperfect as a privacy protecting technique, it is also important that one does not undermine the significance of reducing the possibilities of identification or deride the possibility that data might be rendered effectively anonymous *within particular contexts*.

Ohm claims that data 'can either be useful or perfectly anonymous but never both'.[20] This claim seems to ignore the significance of context to identificatory potential. Data can be perfectly anonymous *in a given context* with specific, and limited, interpretive frameworks applicable to that data. It is the shift in context that is important to undermining the data's anonymity. Admittedly, the significance of genetic data is that it is known that a context might exist within which that data is uniquely related to a particular individual. The important point to remember here, however, is that identification requires not only the possibility of a relevant interpretive framework. It also relies upon its accessibility.

Certain obligations to reduce the future identifiability of data should be understood to continue to apply even if data is currently reasonably understood by a data controller to be effectively anonymous both to them and to others. The obligation should be to seek to maintain proportionate control over the future contexts within which the data may be placed. That said, if appropriate security and integrity of data can be maintained, then there may be reasons to think that reducing identifiability in certain contexts may be undesirable (see discussion of re-contact and continued control below).

In short, the data protection regime may need to be much more sensitive to context than it is currently. Identifiability per se is not likely to be key to addressing individual concerns regarding association with genetic data. Identification itself is unlikely to tell you anything that you do not already know about an individual. It is the *association of other information* with a particular person that is the relevant consideration. It is for this reason that identifiability by third parties brings with it particular risks of the unknown and the feared; and it explains why *fresh association* may be just as important a threat to privacy as re-identification.

---

[20] *Ibid.*, 4.

Fresh association

Even if re-identification of an individual were to be an absolute impossibility, there remain good reasons to doubt de-identification as a method of protecting individuals' privacy. It may not even protect them from harms that can be caused by individual-level association with data. The argument here draws upon the distinction made in Chapter 3 between data and information. Even though data may not be associated with a particular individual, that does not mean that the *information* generated from the data will not be. Interpretive frameworks may be applied to data that result in information being applied at the individual level.

The information need not be that which typically operates as an identifier; *any* information that allows an association to be made between research data and a particular individual may engage preferences on the part of that individual regarding access to that data. Recognising a shared characteristic between a wholly anonymous research subject and a (different) identifiable person can be significant for that identifiable individual if the research attributes that shared characteristic with significance, e.g. anonymous aggregated data suggests that people who drive silver cars are less likely to be injured in accidents than people who drive cars of other colours.[21] If this statistic positively affects the insurance premium of the people who drive silver cars, then each individual identified as a member of this group may be affected in material ways by research using 'anonymised' data. Unfortunately, not all associations with data may be so positive.

Historically, genetic differences have been used as the basis of informing perceptions of many minority populations.[22] It is not difficult to imagine some of the different ways that particular individuals might still be both associated with, and impacted by, research conducted upon those with whom they share particular characteristics. They include the possibilities of stereotyping, stigmatisation and discrimination. Such impacts might be materially felt in a number of areas of life, including, most obviously, insurance and employment. There are, however, other kinds of 'external' harm to which members of specific groups might be subject in specific circumstances as well as a series of 'internal' harms

---

[21] S. Furness, J. Connor, E. Robinson, R. Norton, S. Ameratunga and R. Jackson, 'Car colour and risk of crash injury: population based case control study', *BMJ* 327 (2003), 1455.

[22] J. L. McGregor 'Population genomics and research ethics with socially identifiable groups', *Journal of Law, Medicine and Ethics* 35(3) (2007), 356–70

that might be disruptive to an individual's sense of identity within a particular group.[23] Unfortunately, we cannot assume that unwanted examples of genetic research are confined to history. Some relatively recent examples of contentious research being conducted with members of different groups are discussed below.

The risks of fresh association are not only borne by members of already defined groups. As genetic information is associated with profiles that apply to increasing proportions of the population, so more of us may find that genetic research conducted with others' data informs perceptions that impact upon us. We may find ourselves treated in particular ways owing to membership of groups that we ourselves do not recognise. Privacy protection that focuses exclusively upon data that relates to particular identifiable individuals may be extremely limited in the kind of protection that it can provide to the interests that we perceive as members of such groups.

Anonymity and failure to protect group interests

Anonymisation will often be attempted by ensuring that the data held could apply to more than one individual. This will be done either through aggregation of data or through ensuring that description of a particular case is generalised. The difficulty with this, as a means of protecting an individual's privacy, is that the data may still be associable with individuals. It is just that it may also be associable with a great many more individuals than would otherwise be the case.

If assumptions are made about membership of a group, then the fact that they have been formed in the context of aggregated data is little consolation to individuals if they are disadvantaged by any subsequent inference. Unfortunately, there are already examples of research using genetic data negatively affecting individuals as members of a group (as well, presumably, as identifiable individuals).

The attempts in the early 1990s by researchers to find a genetic cause of the Havasupai's diabetes resulted in profound conflicts between researchers and members of the tribe over whether the full extent of the research conducted was consented to by members of the tribe.[24] Similar concerns had been expressed by the Nuu-chahnulth of Vancouver Island, Canada, when genetic samples provided for one purpose (to discover the cause of rheumatoid arthritis) were used for other purposes.[25] Proposals

---

[23] See pp. 151–3.
[24] R. Dalton, 'When two tribes go to war', *Nature* 430 (2004), 500–2.
[25] McGregor, 'Population genomics', 362.

to establish a genetic database on Tongans floundered when the ethics policy focused on the notion of individual informed consent and failed to take account of the traditional role played by the extended family in decision-making.[26] There have, in the past, been associations drawn between sickle cell anaemia and African Americans and the BRCA1 gene mutation (associated with breast cancer) and Ashkenazi Jews.[27] As research continues to draw associations between particular genetic combinations (haplotypes) and other significant variables, (genetic) profiles will be constructed and inferences facilitated even if not originally intended. The possibility of new group (genetic) profiles being generated, and specific individuals being subsequently affected by this, is something that data protection law fails to address.

As noted above, the concerns are not limited to specific, minority, ethnic groups. Survey evidence shows that people are concerned that genetic information will be used in ways that might disadvantage them (or others) by, inter alia, government, the police or commercial companies. Superficially, it might be thought that their concerns would indeed be effectively met by the anonymisation of data. However, anonymisation does not protect an individual from differential treatment as a member of a group, because of the possibilities of fresh association at the group level.

For as long as perceptions about membership of groups – and impressions about 'group profiles' – are formed using data shared by more than one person, then the processing of the data, its purposes, etc. falls outside of the scope of current regulatory control.

Private data cf. identifiable data

Some of the harms identified with the use of 'group data' are undoubtedly associated with identifiability. They are the kinds of harm that follow an individual's identification with a group if that group is subject to stigmatisation or discrimination. Not all harms are, however, of that nature. McGregor proposes two different types of harm that might follow genetic research using socially identifiable groups: 'tangible harms' and 'dignitary harms'.[28] The first of these are harms which, following stigmatisation or discrimination, may result in a loss of economic benefits. One can imagine this kind of harm being experienced by an individual following identification with a particular group by others.

---

[26] B. Burton, 'Proposed genetic database on Tongans opposed', *BMJ* 324 (2002), 443.
[27] McGregor, 'Population Genomics', 359.   [28] *Ibid.*, 363.

'Dignitary harms' are, however, the kinds that might be experienced by an individual, as a member of a group, whether or not she is associated with that group by others. Dignitary harms to a group 'undermine the value and worth of the group in the eyes of others and the group itself'.[29] If, for example, migration studies undermine a group's sense of cultural history, then that harm does not depend upon the identification of a particular individual as a member of a group. That harm follows the violation of a norm of exclusivity – it intrudes into a particularly significant cultural narrative – without naming any individuals. Some data can be 'private' even if it is not 'personal'.

The privacy concerns associated with data will be determined by the underlying norms and the transactional and relational control that they imply. Those sharing data do not, necessarily, expect the responsibilities of those processing their data to be discharged simply by managing the relationship between data and context in a way that protects their identity. There are alternative expectations that can be plausibly constructed and which might be tested empirically before being dismissed.

In some cases these expectations might ground objections to de-identification and to the proposition that de-identified data (at the individual level) can be used for any purpose at all. There are, in fact, reasons to suspect that there will be cases where individuals do *not* want data to be de-identified. For example, individuals might expect, or at least prefer, that a data controller be able to re-contact them if research happens to yield results that could be of use to the individual. There are undoubtedly several important issues associated with re-contact, particularly in the case of clinically relevant incidental findings, but it is at least arguable that, in some cases, the research participant (and sometimes also the researcher) would *prefer* the possibility of re-contact in some circumstances. A pressure automatically to de-identify might frustrate that process.

Re-contact, even if only theoretical, can also be important from a researcher's perspective if seeking to validate the results and/or to provide an audit trail to support the integrity of the research. Moreover, given the value of linkage, a dataset may be more useful in the future if identifiers are not destroyed. This may be significant to both researchers and research participants keen to see the utility of any research contribution maximised. Any systematic anonymisation of data denies the individual (or the group) an opportunity to express that preference.

---

[29] *Ibid.*, 363.

It is also important to return to the point that some data may be 'private' even if it is not 'personal', to emphasise that this is an observation with applicability to more than members of a group. Preferences regarding access to research data may exist in relation to data that *has* been effectively de-identified at the individual as well as the group level. For example, Beyleveld and Histed discuss the case of the Roman Catholic woman whose information is used to develop a contraceptive. They explicitly rely upon this distinction between data that is defined as personal by the law and that which might be considered private by the individual.[30] A fixation upon identifiability can fail to miss this important point. It is possible for data to fail the 'personal data' test but, nevertheless, represent an acute vulnerability vis-à-vis privacy protection if access to the data provokes clear preferences.

Are we overprotecting identifiability?

Thus far, the narrative has aimed to persuade the reader that preferences regarding access to genetic data might reasonably be expected to persist in data that is anonymous. It has also been suggested that data controllers could meet at least some of the responsibilities that the data protection framework would place upon them in relation to anonymous data, at least, if certain caveats were applied regarding impossibility and disproportionate effort. It might also be desirable to introduce some additional responsibilities, regarding control over the dissemination of effectively anonymous data and accounting for group interests in genetic data. It might be imagined that, involving as it does additional burdens, all of this would seem a rather unattractive proposition from the perspective of a researcher. However, this assumption deserves closer examination.

The proposal is that *if* additional responsibilities were to be recognised in the processing of anonymous data, then it would be appropriate to erode the 'bright-line' distinction that the law currently draws between identifiable and anonymous data. This might be seen to have a number of benefits from a researcher's perspective as well as a research participant's.

It can be practically difficult for a researcher to gather de-identified information for a number of reasons. The first is that information is not usually gathered in an anonymous form. Any retrospective use of a dataset will, therefore, often involve the use of data that is currently held

[30] D. Beyleveld and E. Histed, 'Betrayal of confidence in the Court of Appeal', *Medical Law International* 4(3&4) (2000), 277–311.

in identifiable form. If a researcher is to avoid accessing identifiable data, then this will involve access to either a partial or a modified dataset. The researcher obviously cannot undertake the work required to provide such a dataset herself. Organising access will involve the current holder of the identifiable data applying processes of redaction, compiling anonymous case notes, or establishing a system of structured access to records, etc. Each of these things requires sometimes considerable time and effort. The resource to provide this level of research assistance is not always available and an insistence upon it presents an additional research hurdle.

Any insistence that a researcher *only* use data that has been de-identified would, therefore, create significant practical and methodological problems for certain kinds of research. Such difficulties would be particularly acute if the research required access to large, complex, retrospective collections of identifiable data. Then, there may be little possibility of any other individual (with lawful access to the identifiable data) de-identifying the data for them or, therefore, for the research proceeding.

Also, the attractiveness of keeping data identifiable from a research perspective has already been mentioned and deserves emphasis owing to its importance for ongoing research, and for research linkage, as well as for the validation of previous research.[31]

An insistence upon de-identification can then cause a series of significant problems for researchers. What is more, I hope to have demonstrated that, while reducing identifiability in certain contexts will be important to research participants, the idea that *only* identifiable data presents a risk to privacy does them a disservice. There is no 'bright-line' distinction between identifiable and de-identified data and, even if there were, to insist that individuals only have interests in identifiable data may leave certain important preferences regarding access to genetic data unaccounted for. Recognising that privacy may extend to anonymous data, and that preferences regarding anonymous data ought, in some cases at least, to be taken into account by researchers, would be to increase their responsibilities. So long as these responsibilities were proportionate to the risks, and did not require any impossible or disproportionate activity on their part, this might, however, be welcomed by researchers if it increased the accessibility of identifiable data.

There will be cases where researchers will prefer to operate with data that is not effectively anonymous. Imposing proportionate responsibility

---

[31] Medical Research Council, 'Human tissue and biological samples for use in research: operational and ethical guidelines', Medical Research Council Ethics Series, 2001, p. 2.

in such cases might ease access to identifiable data. If people can be reassured that the data to which researchers gain access cannot be used in ways that are inconsistent with their preferences – at least not without those preferences being reasonably accounted for – then the justification for withholding access will, in some cases at least, dissipate.[32]

Reflection

A proper understanding of anonymity makes the issue of context central to its analysis. Underlining the significance of context does, however, inevitably complicate the picture. When 'context' itself is associated with the idea of 'interpretive frameworks' (described in Chapter 2), this serves effectively to undermine any 'bright-line' or binary distinction between the states of 'identifiable' and 'non-identifiable' data. The law, on the other hand, seems to rely upon being able straightforwardly to characterise data as either identifiable or not. The variability in contexts and the relative availability of different kinds of interpretive framework determine just how fluid the states of 'anonymity' and 'identifiability' are in practice: it is perfectly feasible for data to be 'anonymous' to one person and 'identifiable' to another, anonymous today and identifiable tomorrow. While the transience of any given piece of data through the alternate states of relative identifiability and anonymity depends upon the availability of relevant contexts, the key point is that it is the context that determines whether data is identifiable or anonymous and contexts can, and do, change, and this is a reality that it is hard for the law currently to accommodate.[33] The focus here is identifying problems with the concept of anonymity that the law seems to rely upon and the deficiencies of that concept when it comes to protecting individual's privacy adequately.

Recognising the fluidity of interpretive frameworks undermines any claim that anonymity in a particular, occurrent, context sufficiently demonstrates protection of an individual's interest in not being identified. This applies to an interest in the revelation of individual identity but

---

[32] Admittedly this is a rather large 'if'. It would be too much of a deviation to consider here how this might be achieved, but I would agree with the suggestion made by Jane Kaye in relation to population genetics that it might involve going beyond broad consent and introducing additional safeguards: J. Kaye, 'Abandoning informed consent', in R. Tutton and O. Corrigan (eds.), *Genetic Databases: Socio-ethical Issues in the Collection and Use of DNA* (London and New York: Routledge, 2004), 117–38 at 132.

[33] Particularly when the individual that is identifiable in different contexts might also change. (This was, however, discussed in the last chapter.)

it also applies to an interest in the identification of a group to which one might be associated in the future. Indeed, the notion of anonymity, enshrined within law, may be particularly deficient at protecting notions of group privacy. What is more, and just as importantly, it is possible that privacy interests may not be engaged simply by identifiability. That is, there are reasons to suggest that privacy interests may be engaged by data even if an individual may not be identified. There may be relevant privacy expectations with regard to (anonymous) data that even effective control of identifiability might not safeguard.

Appreciating the limited benefits of anonymisation supports the claim that the privacy protection that de-identification provides may sometimes come at too great a cost. Any system that encourages the de-identification of data as a matter of course may undermine important interests (other than privacy) in circumstances where the privacy protection provided by anonymisation in that context cannot justify the sacrifice. These include circumstances where the data subject's own (non-privacy) interests are at stake, but also the interests that others might have (researchers included) in access to identifiable data (and the public interest in them having such access). Relevant protections may be provided in other ways, e.g. by ensuring that the possibility of identifiability in future contexts by others is taken into account, and, where future association is unavoidable, by providing protection from unfair use of that data (e.g. anti discrimination protection – see Chapter 8).

7 Human tissue

A number of distinctions have so far been identified that have been described as arbitrary from a perspective concerned with regulating the interpretive *potential* of genetic data. The idea that genetic data can, in any given context, only be said to 'relate' to a single individual has been criticised as unjustified. Similarly, the failure to extend protection to individuals as identifiable members of groups has revealed the law to protect only a narrow relational conception of privacy. The vulnerabilities exposed by recognising the relationship between genetic data and multiple individuals may be normatively indistinguishable from those exposed by similar relationships between genetic data and particular identifiable individuals: normatively indistinguishable, that is, even when assessed from the (relatively conservative relational) perspective of the values immanent within the European Convention of Human Rights. If one were to cast one's net for relevant normative patterns and preferences more widely, then one could readily find examples of preferences expressed by members of families or broader social groups that are not accommodated within the jurisprudence of the European Courts, the Data Protection Directive 95/46/EC, or the other international frameworks for information governance concerned with 'personal data', but that are nevertheless consistent with expressed preferences vis-à-vis association with genetic data in particular circumstances. This is because the law has, hitherto, adopted a relatively narrow concept of privacy protection according to both the relational and the transactional variables.

Any insistence that ensuring the applicability of data to *more than one* person – through either anonymisation or aggregation – effectively protects all norms of exclusivity can be challenged. Not only might particular norms attach to data related to groups of persons but, moreover, the law does not account for the interpretive potential of data within fluid interpretive frameworks and the possibilities of downstream association between such data and particular persons *or* groups (or between such data and other data with which persons or groups would prefer not to be associated). Collectively, these problems contribute to a position of inadequate privacy protection: inadequate, it must be remembered, not because particular preferences are not accommodated by the law but because the law does not even account for the norms of exclusivity that they represent.

When considering the justification for particular regulatory distinctions, there is another distinction that needs to be assessed. If reviewing the adequacy of privacy protection applicable to research using genetic data, then the distinction between recorded genetic information and biological material is an important one to consider. It is important because, although the law currently draws a distinction, there is no material difference between the interpretive *potential* of the two data types to yield information through analysis and interpretation. Any insistence upon treating them differently needs, therefore, to be justified with reference to something *other than* interpretive potential. Certainly, there are particular kinds of 'transaction' associated with human biological material that are inapplicable to the acquisition and use of genetic data as such. The possibility for transactions of distinct types (e.g. bodily contact) allows for the associated possibility that certain norms of exclusivity may be associated with biological material that would be inapplicable to information: there are recognised distinctions to be drawn between 'informational' and 'physical' privacy that regulation might track. However, do the qualities of the transactions in which biological material might be involved *post separation* warrant treating such material differently from other kinds of genetic data? Are there relevant distinctions between biological samples and recorded genetic information concerning the potential privacy affect that each might have and the norms with which they might be associated?

It will be argued here that, if one restricts one's consideration to only *prepared* data – which would include human tissue, post separation, readied for analysis as a *sample* – then the transactional distinction between biological sample and other kinds of genetic data is only a matter of interpretive pedigree. *Whichever normative framework is preferred*, to draw a regulatory distinction on the grounds of interpretive pedigree alone would be arbitrary (from that normative perspective so far as it informs norms of exclusivity) because it is the *interpretive potential* of the data that affects the possibilities of exclusivity being affected: an interpretation of a sample is as capable of infringing norms of exclusivity, and affecting individuals through relevant association(s), as an interpretation of previously recorded data. For that reason, there is no clear distinction between biological sample and recorded information from a privacy perspective; and a refusal to include biological samples within the data protection framework would be arbitrary. What is more, there is no material distinction from the perspective of the norms established by the Data Protection Directive itself and, for this reason alone, any exclusion of biological samples from the scope of the Directive should be subject to internal review. However, if one *were* to collapse the distinction and bring biological samples into the fold of data protection, then this would prompt consideration of the adequacy of the data protection framework to protect norms as they apply to biological samples as established by other instruments. It is argued here that there would not be any inconsistency between the protections offered by the Directive and those expected by the norms of relevant international instruments *except* perhaps in one particular regard. There is one respect in which the data protection framework might be considered deficient. One might consider that the *finite* nature of biological material requires distinction from the infinite nature of information and that this finitude also requires that it be treated, and regulated, differently from information as such.

I recognise that this may appear to have painted a rather contradictory picture. I have suggested that it is arbitrary to distinguish between biological sample and information but also conceded that it is possible that the finite nature of biological material may require that it be treated, and regulated, differently from information as such. However, closer inspection reveals no contradiction. The data protection framework is not concerned with information *as such*. The data protection framework is concerned with *recorded* information: data. It is true that one of the things that characterises information is its seemingly infinite capacity for replication, transmission and onward dissemination with no attrition to the original information. It is also true that biological material is, on the other hand, materially affected through the act of analysis and can be consumed over time. However, *recorded* data can be finite with similar effects to a biological sample: each is vulnerable to destruction. Although the method (and perhaps inevitability) of loss may differ, the result from the perspective of one concerned to conserve the resource if there is loss may be just the same. If there is a responsibility to conserve finite data (in certain circumstances), then collapsing the regulatory distinction between data and sample (post separation) would require reform of the Data Protection Directive. If there is no such responsibility, then the Directive is already fit for purpose (subject to the qualifications already given in previous chapters) and should be extended to include biological samples. If reform *is* required, however, then the duty to conserve data would apply not only to biological samples and any such reform should improve the protection of *any* personal genetic data:

biological sample or recorded information with the potential for genetic interpretation. This would not address any of the limitations discussed previously and associated with the law's focus upon *personal* data. It would, however, avoid a different kind of arbitrary distinction undermining privacy protection by limiting the possibility to capture particular kinds of association within regulatory scope.

Structure

Again the focus within this chapter will be the data protection framework as established by the Data Protection Directive 95/46/EC. Although the data protection framework is most certainly not the only regulatory framework capable of protecting norms of exclusivity regarding biological material, it *is* the framework that is most relevant to the regulation of the processing of genetic *data*. One of the key claims to be made builds upon the earlier argument that biological *material*, in some circumstances at least, should be regarded as genetic data. If this argument succeeds, then the Data Protection Directive represents an important opportunity to protect certain privacy norms surrounding that material. I begin, in Section I, by briefly recapping earlier argument and considering whether, and when, a distinction between biological material and genetic information could be defended either from the perspective of the concept of genetic data or indeed from the perspective of the Directive's own definition of data. It is suggested that, even according to the narrow relational concept of privacy embedded within the Directive, the interpretive potential of recorded genetic information and biological *samples post separation* is indistinguishable. If one is concerned with controlling the acquisition and use of genetic information, then things such as the relative availability and accessibility of particular kinds of interpretive framework are more important than the interpreted data's pedigree. Section II considers whether the inclusion of biological samples within the data protection framework would protect norms of exclusivity regarding biological samples, with relevant norms being taken not only from the Directive but also from other relevant international instruments. Signatories to the Data Protection Directive are committed not only to protecting the privacy norms embedded within the Directive, but also to the norms established by other international instruments. If including biological samples within the scope of data protection would leave certain expectations unfulfilled vis-à-vis protection, then there may be a reason for them to wish to retain a discrete regulatory regime for biological samples. Here I propose that the distinction between biological material pre and post separation is a key distinction observed and one that can be used to justify bringing biological samples post separation within the context of the data protection framework without undermining the norms typically expressed in relation to biological samples. However, finally, in Section III, I recognise the limitation of the current data protection framework with regard to the conservation of biological samples. It is suggested, however, that far from representing a reason to maintain distinct regimes, this particular limitation might reveal a failure in the data protection framework regarding the preservation of genetic data more generally. Incorporating a duty to conserve in such circumstances might go beyond the protection of biological samples and improve the protection afforded to other kinds of genetic data, including recorded genetic information.

SECTION I HUMAN BIOLOGICAL MATERIAL, SAMPLES, DATA AND INFORMATION

An obvious objection to treating biological material as information is that it is to confuse a source of information with information per se in an inappropriate way.[1] To unpick this objection we need to rely upon the earlier analysis of the distinction between data and information. There is, it was argued, no *material* difference between interpret*ed* and interpret*able* data: once information has been recorded, there is no distinction between it and other data similarly recognised to be susceptible to interpretation; interpretive frameworks have to be applied afresh to either before information can be gathered. In terms of the absolute possibility to gather information, there is then no distinction between a biological sample prepared for analysis and genetic data recorded in some other medium. There may be relevant distinctions between human biological samples and recorded genetic information with regard to the relative possibilities of particular kinds of interpretation in particular circumstances, but such distinctions can be made *within* the categories of interpreted and interpretable data and not just *between* them. In some circumstances the information potentially gatherable from a sample might be more available, more extensive, and indeed more sensitive, than the information gatherable from the product of specific previous analysis and

---

[1] An opinion expressed by, inter alia, the Australian Office of the Federal Privacy Commissioner to the Australian Law Reform Commission (ALRC). See ALRC, 'ALRC 96 essentially yours: the protection of human genetic information in Australia' (ALRC, 2003), para. 8.29.

recorded as genetic information.[2] The idea that they are merely a 'source' of information does not then justify excluding *samples* from a data protection framework.[3] It rather encourages it.

Not only does it make sense, conceptually, to distinguish between data and information only for as long as information is understood to transcend the physical state, but it is not possible to maintain such a limited concept of information within the context of the data protection framework established by the Directive. In order to be meaningful, the Directive *must* be understood to apply to *sources* of information *rather than* information as such (if information as such is to be understood to be distinct from the object of analysis yielding information) and this is effectively conceded by the fact that the Directive draws no distinction between data and information.[4] While the definition of personal data contained within Article 2 does not state that 'sources' of personal information ought to be protected within the data protection framework described by the Directive, and nor do any of the Recitals to the Directive specifically indicate that 'information' ought to be understood to include 'sources of information', it remains the case that data (as *recorded* information) must always be interpreted before its meaning can be understood: records must be read. If the privacy protection established by the Directive extends to include the physical record of information, then the viability of any division between (biological) sample and information built upon the former's need for subsequent interpretation crumbles.

It might be claimed that although it is *possible* that both samples and recorded information present particular risks to privacy (as each may be interpreted), nevertheless the data represented by recorded information

---

[2] The Human Genome Project transformed data from one medium to another. Neither biological sample nor the string of As, Ts, Cs and Gs sequenced from it could inform of very much at all without further analysis. However, converting the data into a string of letters made it more accessible, to more persons, for different kinds of analysis. It is the availability, and nature, of the interpretive frameworks that may be associated with data of different kinds that is important.

[3] For discussion of an objection to collapsing the distinction between 'sample' and 'information' founded upon an understanding of 'information' as the comprehension of a representation of the real world rather than the real world itself, see also L. A. Bygrave, 'The body as data? Reflections on the relationship of data privacy law with the human body', Conference on 'The body as data', Federation Centre, Melbourne, Australia, 8 September 2003. Accessible from the Privacy Victoria website: www.privacy.vic.gov.au.

[4] The Directive recognises that 'information' is not to be restricted to the metaphysical; it is not permissible to deny a source of information the status of 'personal data' simply on the grounds that it must be interpreted before information can be gathered from it. See ALRC, 'Essentially yours', para. 8.29.

poses risks that are not posed by the data that is represented by samples. It might be said, for example, that, in the context of genetic data, recorded genetic information is intended, or perhaps predisposed, to provide genetic information in a way that a biological sample is not. Certainly, interpreted data has an interpretive pedigree that interpretable data will always lack, and this pedigree may manifest in ways that increase the likelihood of particular information being gathered. After all, not only is the route to interpretation proven but, in the case of recorded information, it might also be clearly sign-posted through the way in which the information is itself represented: Bob is 6' 2" is recorded information represented in a particular way with the intention to inform. 'Bob is 62' is understood rather differently. In this way the potential to inform can be intentionally indicated by the form of representation (e.g. by the familiar format of a telephone number) or by specific informational context (e.g. indicating field names within a database by title). This contextualised presentation of previously interpreted data may make the information that it contains more accessible than it would otherwise have been. This is not, however, always the case.

Certainly one might distinguish recorded information from biological sample on the ground that the former represents the record of a *prior* interpretation. It is also true to say that, in some cases, the presentation of a record may deliberately seek to make the information content of the record accessible by pointing to relevant, and relatively accessible, interpretive frameworks. However, while this is perhaps true as a generalisation, it should not be assumed that access to previously interpreted information necessarily leaves individuals' fundamental rights and freedoms any more or less vulnerable than access to the original source material. The *accessibility* of information depends entirely upon the availability (and employment) of relevant interpretive frameworks and, while the manipulation of data may seek to make certain information more accessible, it might also seek to obscure it (e.g. through coding), and the source data may remain interpretable in any event.[5]

---

[5] A weather forecast represents a prior interpretation of data and thus provides information with a particular interpretive pedigree. There is nothing to say, however, that the forecast itself need necessarily yield information any more readily than the interpretable data upon which it was based. Indeed, if broadcast in a foreign language, or deliberately coded (as perhaps in times of war), then the information it contains may be considerably less accessible (generally) than the same information would be to one able to interpret the data upon which it was based. In other words, the application of a prior interpretation does not necessarily indicate either the possibility, the availability or the probability of a particular subsequent interpretation. It certainly should not be assumed that the availability of information to one particular individual can be determined by its availability to another.

It is tempting to suggest that access to the source data might actually be *riskier* than access to the product of a prior interpretation, as there is greater uncertainty associated with the analysis that might be applied and the information that might be gathered. For example, when tissue samples were used from the national neonatal database as part of the police investigation into the murder of Sweden's Foreign Minister, Anna Lindh, the samples were subject to analysis and application that had not been anticipated at the time when they were gathered. This analysis would not have been possible if, rather than keeping the samples, the neonatal database consisted simply of the results of the tests that had been conducted on the samples at the time. However, this is in fact simply an example of a case where a sample was used to generate new information through application of a new interpretive framework. New interpretive frameworks can be applied to recorded information (through secondary analysis) in similar ways, and no claims should be made about the dangers associated with either interpreted or interpretable data as, ultimately, both are subject to novel interpretation and association.

The simple fact is that, if we are seeking to establish *interpretive potential*, then we should be concerned with whatever means are likely reasonably to be used in the circumstances to interpret data and not fixate upon whether, in its contingent state, material displays a particular pedigree. The fact of prior interpretation does not directly affect the interpretive potential of genetic data or the possibility of access to genetic information. It might affect the *likelihood* of access of certain kinds in certain circumstances, but that is a separate, albeit important, assessment and is not necessarily tied to the issue of interpretive pedigree. Although interpretive pedigree may be indicative, it is certainly not determinative of the privacy risks at stake. If pedigree is not a sensible proxy to rely upon within the context of privacy protection, then to deny a biological sample the title genetic data simply because it lacks a particular interpretive pedigree is disingenuous and potentially dangerous; particularly if its interpretive potential can be demonstrated in other ways.

SECTION II   PERSONAL DATA, BIOLOGICAL SAMPLES AND NORMATIVE EXPECTATIONS

Despite the fact that data protection regimes typically draw no distinction between data and information, the inclusion of samples within the scope of data protection regimes has been consistently doubted and resisted. Certainly, the Article 29 Working Party has gone from express ambivalence to a clear statement that biological material should *not* be regarded as data within the context of the Data Protection Directive. As well as being contrary to the position taken in many EU countries and the position now expressly taken by the Article 29 Working Party, it is also considered an unlikely interpretation of existing legislation in at least both America and Australia. What is more, it is a position that has been subject to respected academic doubt.[6]

In the face of such opposition, one might be forgiven for wondering whether it remains a question worth asking. Opinion has undoubtedly gravitated towards the idea that the existing Data Protection Directive does *not* extend to include biological material within its definition of data. The idea is kept alive here, however, not simply for the sake of an argument. It is suggested that including biological samples within the scope of the data protection framework is to be preferred not only conceptually, and not only for the sake of the coherence of the Directive, but also *normatively*, given the opportunities it would present to protect certain expectations regarding exclusivity. The Directive's definition of data ought to be understood to include samples (interpretable data) within its scope as well as recorded information (interpreted data). If it can be shown that to do so would better protect some of the norms contained within the international instruments to which states signatory to the Directive are also committed, then this must surely be motivation for reform of the Directive to include biological samples within its scope.

Normative expectations

There is no suggestion that biological samples are perceived to present a *lower* risk of privacy infringement than other kinds of genetic data. There are certainly concerns that have been expressed by people with regard to the provision of both genetic information *and* biological samples.

Although people may be more concerned with disclosing one type or another, information about genetic profiles is something that concerns both groups of people. A report to the European Commission's Directorate General for Research in 2010 concluded that

those who say they would be concerned about giving blood samples to a biobank are more likely to say they are also concerned about giving tissue samples than they are to be concerned about any other type of information; those who are concerned about giving lifestyle information are more likely to also be worried

---

[6] W. W. Lowrance, *Learning from Experience: Privacy and the Secondary Use of Data in Health Research* (London: The Nuffield Trust, 2002). www.nuffieldtrust.org.uk/ecomm/files/161202learning.pdf.

about giving medical records than anything else. So we have concerns based around physiological samples on the one hand, and around personal descriptive information on the other. Genetic profiles appear to span both types of information, and there does not seem to be a strong connection between concern about particular types of information and levels of enthusiasm about participating in biobanks.[7]

Although concerns may be associated with both samples and information, it is also true to say that the norms established by international instruments do indicate that there may be *different* expectations associated with research involving human biological material from those associated with research that only uses genetic information.

Ethical principles related to research involving people and their biological material has been subject to a series of international agreements since the end of the Second World War. The first of these agreements, the Code of Nuremberg,[8] followed the horrors of the research conducted during the war, and was born of a fear that such research might ever be repeated. Given their history, such instruments understandably place a high value upon the informed consent of participants and the Code states that 'the voluntary consent of the human subject is absolutely essential'[9] to any intervention. As we have seen, the Directive does not make consent an absolute requirement of research using personal data. Does this demonstrate the lack of suitability of a data protection framework concerned exclusively with the processing of *data* to research involving human biological material?

Undoubtedly certain risks are associated with research involving interventions upon persons owing to the issues concerning bodily integrity and the risks to health and well-being that interventional research can present. The risks associated with research using genetic information and the risks associated with research using human biological material information, after the material has been removed from a person, can however both be distinguished from such interventional research. The international instruments considered below do in fact acknowledge that different norms are applicable to different kinds of research and, importantly, they support the idea that a distinction is drawn between interventional research and research that relies solely upon data. That distinction does not divide *recorded* information from biological samples

---

[7] G. Gaskell, S. Stares, A. Allansdottir, N. Allum, P. Castro, Y. Esmer, C. Fischler, J. Jackson, N. Kronberger, J. Hampel, N. Mejlgaard, A. Quintanilha, A. Rammer, G. Revuelta, P. Stoneman, H. Torgersen and W. Wagner, *Europeans and Biotechnology in 2010: Winds of Change?*, Special Barometer 341 (European Union, October 2010), 62.
[8] http://ohsr.od.nih.gov/guidelines/nuremberg.html.
[9] *Ibid.*, First Paragraph, first line.

post separation. If one looks at the different approaches taken within the instruments towards a particular issue such as consent, then, if there is a line to be drawn between research involving persons and research involving personal data, research involving a person's biological material *after* the separation of the biological material from the person falls more consistently in line with the norms attached to research using recorded information.

Convention on Human Rights and Biomedicine

The European Convention on Human Rights and Biomedicine places the individual at the centre of its concern. It establishes the general rule that 'An intervention in the health field may only be carried out after the person concerned has given free and informed consent to it.'[10] This general rule, which applies to research as it does to other interventions,[11] tolerates certain exceptions. Within the Convention itself, however, these exceptions are very tightly drawn and appear only to apply when an individual lacks the capacity to consent (Article 17). Whenever an individual has capacity there is an insistence upon informed consent. This establishes a high threshold for compliance and there are a number of circumstances in which an insistence upon consent would undoubtedly frustrate particular kinds of research taking place.[12] The Convention does not accept as valid an argument that requiring consent would render research impossible or impracticable or the validity of the research threatened, or that this would be a reason for not obtaining informed consent: there would appear to be no exception to the need for informed consent contemplated simply on the grounds of the importance of the research. Indeed, Article 2 ('primacy of the human being') of the Convention states that the 'interests and welfare of the human being shall prevail over the sole interest of society or science'. Furthermore, Article 26, which allows for restrictions on the exercise of the rights

---

[10] Article 5.

[11] Research is defined as an intervention by Article 4: 'Any intervention in the health field, including research, must be carried out in accordance with relevant professional obligations and standards.'

[12] This would include research using retrospective studies where it was not possible to contact data subjects, but it might also involve prospective studies where the scale and nature of the data collection (e.g. through linkage of national datasets) would make individual consent an administrative impracticability. Research using genetic databases may be impracticable on the basis of specific informed consent, as the details of individual research projects are unknown at the time consent is taken, but broad consent might still be possible in such cases. See Kaye, 'Abandoning informed consent', 120–32.

recognised by the Convention in cases prescribed by law and necessary in a democratic society in the interest of, inter alia, the protection of public health or for the protection of the rights and freedoms of others, does not permit restriction to be placed upon the requirements for consent 'on a person' (Article 16 and 17). In this way, individual informed consent is represented as a *sine qua non* of valid ethical research and the expectations of consent extend beyond those that the law (discussed in Chapter 4) would recognise. This does not, however, determine whether the arrangements concerning access to a biological sample *post separation* would be understood to be equivalent to the expectations surrounding an 'intervention' in the health field. There are parts of the Convention that would seem to cast doubt upon it.

For example, the prohibition on interventions without consent that extends to predictive tests (Article 12) *can* be restricted under Article 26. It seems that the possibility of justifying a waiver of the consent requirement is understood differently when we are discussing predictive testing from when we are considering interventional research involving a person. This suspicion is confirmed when we move to consider the protocols to the Convention that are directed at interventions involving biological material *removed* from a person. We see a softening of the line that informed consent is an absolute requirement. For example, the Additional Protocol to the Convention on Human Rights and Biomedicine, concerning Genetic Testing for Health Purposes (Strasbourg, 27 November 2008) makes clear (in Article 16) that everyone has the right to respect for his or her private life, in particular to protection of his or her personal data derived from a genetic test, and that this respect is to be manifest through, inter alia, an expectation (according to Article 9), that

1 A genetic test may only be carried out after the person concerned has given free and informed consent to it . . .
2 The person concerned may freely withdraw consent at any time.

At the same time, it also specifically imagines circumstances in which the testing of samples *already taken* might be permitted without consent (Article 14)

When it is not possible, with reasonable efforts, to contact a person for a genetic test for the benefit of his or her family member(s) on his or her biological material previously removed for another purpose, the law may allow the test to be carried out in accordance with the principle of proportionality, where the expected benefit cannot be otherwise obtained and where the test cannot be deferred.

The Additional Protocol thus recognises the responsibilities that individuals may owe others, and acknowledges that, at times, those responsibilities may assume a priority over obtaining the free and informed consent of a data subject. This is not a broad enough acknow-ledgment to suggest that research for the sake of unconnected others might be similarly justified. The preamble, and the effect of the provi-sions contained within the Protocol, stresses 'the particular bond that exists between members of the same family' and the waiver of consent is limited to those cases where it may benefit family members and to testing for health purposes rather than for research. It does, however, support the line that interventions involving tissue *after* separation are to be treated differently from interventions involving tissue before separation.

The Protocol to the Convention that explicitly applies to research is the Additional Protocol to the Biomedicine Convention of 25 January 2005 on research with human beings. Again, however, the scope of activity imagined by this particular protocol is relatively narrow. This Additional Protocol only applies to research involving either physical interventions or 'any other intervention in so far as it involves a risk to the psychological health of the person concerned' (Article 2). Unsurprisingly, as with the Convention on Human Rights and Biomedicine itself, this Additional Protocol attaches great significance to informed consent.

The Convention, with its Additional Protocols, confirms the expect-ation for informed consent if an *intervention* represents a risk to the physical integrity, or involves a risk to the psychological health, of the person concerned. They also confirm that there may be circumstances, where biological material has been previously removed from a person, when consent is not an absolute requirement. They do not, however, specifically address research involving either biological material post separation or genetic information, and it is not, therefore, possible to assess properly the adequacy of the Directive to ensure the protection the Convention would expect if samples were to be treated as data within its scope. In order to get a better perspective on research uses of inter-pret*able* data that *do not* threaten physical integrity, or pose particular risks of psychological harm to the individual, we can turn back to one of the most long-standing statements of internationally agreed principle in the area: the Declaration of Helsinki.

The Declaration of Helsinki

As previously discussed, the Declaration of Helsinki is an authoritative document that seeks to establish a number of important ethical principles for medical research involving human subjects.[13] It is perhaps

---

[13] See Chapter 4.

worth explicitly recognising from the outset that the Declaration is concerned with research involving human participants and research involving only *identifiable* human material *and* data. When considering research using human material and data then, rather than persons themselves, its focus upon identifiability represents limitations similar to those discussed earlier. However, within this limitation noted, the Declaration does make clear that respecting the privacy of research subjects, and the confidentiality of their personal information, is a requirement applicable to research using *both* identifiable human material and data.

The Declaration of Helsinki supports the view that different levels of protection are appropriate to different kinds of research. Although it (inappropriately) draws a distinction between identifiable human material and data, it (appropriately) does not make *that* the relevant distinction. Research using either identifiable human material or data is contrasted with research using human persons per se. The Declaration makes clear that informed consent *must* be obtained for any research involving human persons (paragraph 24). The only exception to this is the circumstance where the individuals are not capable of providing, or not legally competent to provide, consent, and in such circumstances other safeguards are required (paragraphs 27 to 29). In this respect it is consistent with the position described by previously considered instruments. What is notable about the Declaration of Helsinki, however, is that it also deals explicitly with the expectations (of physicians) associated with research use of identifiable interpret*ed* data (i.e. recorded information) and identifiable interpret*able* data (i.e. biological material) and it distinguishes such research from research involving human persons per se.

As previously noted, the Declaration recognises that there may be situations where consent would be impossible or impractical to obtain for such research or would pose a threat to the validity of the research. In such situations the Declaration recognises that research may be conducted with the approval of a research ethics committee.[14] Thus, the Declaration allows for the requirement to obtain consent to be waived, if research involves identifiable human biological material or data, in circumstances that it would not recognise as appropriate if the research involved human persons. It is important to appreciate that, although recognising that there may be variation from the norm of consent in the case of both data and information, the Declaration *does* recognise the

[14] Para. 25.

norm itself in both cases: consent must normally be obtained in the case of research using *either* identifiable human material or data.[15] This is an important point to emphasise because, by recognising the norm in the case of biological material, the Declaration establishes an expectation that the Directive cannot protect if it excludes identifiable human material from its scope.

If the Directive were to apply to identifiable biological material, then it would provide at least some of the protection that the Declaration requires: not least of all because (explicit)[16] consent would normally be required. According to the argument more fully rehearsed earlier,[17] necessity would be a justification for not seeking consent according to the Directive, but only if the hurdle of proportionality could be cleared. In the case of the Directive, this assessment of proportionality would not need to be made by a research ethics committee (unless specified by a Member State as a suitable safeguard). In this way, the Directive may not currently require quite the level of protection that the Declaration demands for either biological materials *or* human data.

Consideration might be given to whether the Directive could usefully make explicit that, in cases involving research using personal data, such relevant safeguards should include approval by research ethics committee. That said, even without this additional safeguard, extending the reach of the Directive to include identifiable human material as well as data would better enable it to provide legal protection to the norm established by the Declaration when compared to the current situation.

---

[15] In one way, the qualification upon the requirement to obtain consent might not go as far as the Directive 95/46/EC would require. As discussed earlier (see pp. 83–5), a strong argument can be made that a researcher may *only* rely upon an alternative to consent to demonstrate the legitimacy of data processing (under the conditions of Article 7 and Article 8 of the Directive) when lawful, necessary and proportionate to do so. While the Declaration may only waive the requirement of consent under conditions of necessity, it may do so without overcoming the hurdle of proportionality. There is no explicit requirement that the validity of the research is a subsidiary question to the value of the research in the circumstances, Although this may be expected to be the concern of a research ethics committee. In this case, an apparent deficiency may not be manifest in practice.

[16] A human biological sample would constitute data falling within the scope of Article 8 of the Directive. As part of the discussion of the reform of the Data Protection Directive 95/46/EC it has been proposed that genetic data might also be expressly included within the list of sensitive data items in Article 8: European Commission, 'A comprehensive approach on personal data protection in the European Union', Communication from the Commission to the European Parliament, The Council, The Economic and Social Committee and the Committee of the Regions, COM(2010) 609 final, (Brussels, 4 November), para. 2.1.6.

[17] See Chapter 4.

Admittedly, although extending the reach of the Directive to include identifiable biological material would better protect the norms contained within the Helsinki Declaration, this Declaration is not the only source of relevant norms and it does not even constitute a set of norms to which signatories of the Data Protection Directive are themselves explicitly committed. On the other hand, the United Nations International Declaration on Human Genetic Data *does* represent such a commitment.

International Declaration on Human Genetic Data

The International Declaration on Human Genetic Data (IDHGD) was adopted by the General Conference of the United Nations on 16 October 2003. As a Declaration it is not legally binding, but nevertheless represents a commitment by members of the United Nations. It aims, inter alia, to 'ensure the respect of human dignity and protection of human rights and fundamental freedoms in the collection, processing, use and storage of human genetic data, human proteomic data and of the biological samples from which they are derived' while giving due consideration to 'freedom of research' (Article 1(a)).

The IDHGD thus continues the trend of drawing a distinction between 'genetic data' and biological samples. In fact, it even offers a particularly narrow definition of each.[18] Again, this is not a particular distinction that I need to address. The key point here is that it *does* recognise that there is a need to protect biological samples used for research purposes, *and* the need that it recognises could be met in part by bringing biological samples within the scope of the Directive.

According to Article 8(a):

Prior, free, informed and express consent, without inducement by financial or other personal gain, should be obtained for the collection for human genetic data, human proteomic data or biological samples, whether through invasive or non-invasive procedures, and for their subsequent processing, use and storage, whether carried out by public or private institutions. Limitations on this principle of consent should only be prescribed for compelling reasons by domestic law consistent with the international law of human rights.

---

[18] 'Human genetic data' is defined as information 'about heritable characteristics of individuals obtained by analysis of nucleic acids or by other scientific analysis' (Article 2(i)). 'Biological sample' is defined as any 'sample of biological material (for example blood, skin and bone cells or blood plasma) in which nucleic acids are present and which contains the characteristic genetic make-up of an individual)' (Article 2(iv)).

This is precisely the kind of requirement that the Data Protection Directive places upon the processing of personal data and, were it to be extended to include the processing of biological samples, then limitations on the principle of consent would have to be provided by domestic law in a context that ensured 'relevant safeguards' as described above. Also, according to Article 14(c):

Human genetic data, human proteomic data and biological samples collected for the purposes of scientific research should not normally be linked to an identifiable person. Even when such data or biological samples are unlinked to an identifiable person, the necessary precautions should be taken to ensure the security of the data or biological samples.

If identifiable biological samples were to be brought within the scope of the data protection framework, then researchers operating within the EU (and those researchers wishing to demonstrate compliance with the norms established by the framework) would be motivated to ensure either that biological samples were not identifiable (and so were outside the scope of the Directive) or that the identifiability of samples was reduced to the minimum necessary (and so fulfil the requirement only that data be 'adequate, relevant and not excessive in relation to the purposes for which they are collected and/or further processed').[19] What is more, this might also point the way to the first steps that could be taken to protect *unidentified* data.

There is no suggestion here that the protection offered by the Data Protection Directive would align precisely with that anticipated by the IDHGD. It is in fact consistent with previous analysis to argue that incorporating biological samples into the protective regime would not, by itself, be enough (and this is partly because of the Directive's fixation upon identifiability). What is suggested here is that there is no reason *not* to include biological samples *and* that inclusion would provide some distinct advantages. While still imperfect, the scope of possible protections would be extended. There is, however, one particular norm that most certainly could *not* be met by bringing biological samples into the scope of the Directive. What is more, it is presented as applicable *only* to biological samples. If there are norms applicable exclusively to biological samples, then this undermines the claim that they may be effectively protected under a regime designed to address recorded information and it may provide a reason to reconsider the merits of seeking to protect privacy interests in genetic data through a single regulatory framework.

---

[19] Article 6(c), Data Protection Directive 95/46/EC.

International guidance on the use of genetic data within biobanks

The Organisation for Economic Co-Operation and Development (OECD) is a forum within which the governments of thirty democracies, including members of the EU, the USA, Canada, Mexico, Australia, New Zealand and Japan, come together to address economic, social and environmental challenges arising through the effects of globalisation. While a Recommendation of the OECD is a non-legally binding instrument, it represents an important political commitment on the part of member countries. In 2009 the OECD issued guidance on the use of genetic data within biobanks.[20]

The guidelines deal in depth with many aspects of establishing, maintaining and providing ongoing access to biobanks and explicitly recognises the importance of research access. The OECD guidelines recognise that:

Research involving human genetic or genomic information analysed in conjunction with other personal or health data has become increasingly important for the understanding of complex (multi-factorial) diseases.[21]

The guidelines set out eight general principles before discussing some of the detail relating to good practice. The third principle requires operators and users of a Human Biobank or Genetic Research Database (HBGRD) to respect human rights and fundamental freedoms and to secure the protection of participants' privacy and the confidentiality of their data and information. The fourth principle is that

The operators of the HBGRD should consider and minimise risks to participants, their families and potentially identifiable populations or groups whose specimens and data are included in the HBGRD.

This represents an important statement of the need to consider risks to families and identifiable populations and groups as primary concerns (rather than simply as potential justifications for limitations upon the rights of identifiable individuals). The guidelines represent an alternative understanding of the relevant relational variable to that evident within the Declaration and the Directive and, in this way, can be understood to be supportive of the arguments made in previous chapters. Unfortunately, it also points to some of the limitations of the Directive as it is currently understood.

---

[20] OECD, 'Guidelines for Human Biobanks and Genetic Research Databases (HBGRDs)' (October 2009). www.oecd.org/sti/biotechnology/hbgrd.
[21] *Ibid.*, 2.

When it comes to assessing the distinction between sample and information specifically, it is noteworthy that, with one exception, the guidelines make no distinction between the standards to be applied to biological material and those applicable to information. Throughout the guidelines, as with the Declarations just considered, the norms established by the guidelines are equally applicable to both biological material and data. However, there is an exception, and it is an important one because it is a requirement that is applicable to biological material only. The guidelines note that:

Given the potentially finite nature of some human biological materials, the operators of the HBGRD should formulate criteria for prioritising applications for access to the human biological materials.[22]

Do the guidelines then identify a particular characteristic of human biological material that, when recognised, undermines the suitability of the inclusion of physical material within a directive aimed at regulating recorded information?

SECTION III   THE FINITE NATURE OF DATA – A RELEVANT DISTINCTION?

The finite nature of some human biological materials, when compared to the endlessly replicable nature of information as such, demands a particular kind of protection that the Directive does not appear to anticipate. This limitation of the Directive has been recognised by others. Wright *et al.* recognise the finite nature of certain biological material and suggest that this is one of the reasons the Directive cannot provide an adequate framework to regulate the use of tissue in genetic research.[23]

By way of contrast, they note how the finite nature of tissue has been acknowledged within national legislation, providing, as an example, the Portuguese Act on Personal Genetic Data.[24] This Act requires the anonymisation of samples retained for research purposes wherever possible, but also places a responsibility upon researchers to ensure that the rights and interests of research participants, including their privacy interests, are safeguarded. In particular, Article 19, number 14, of Law 12/2005 places researchers under a responsibility to *conserve* samples

---

[22] 7.E.
[23] J. Wright, C. Ploem, M. Śliwka and S. Gevers, 'Regulating tissue research: do we need additional rules to protect research participants?', *European Journal of Health Law* 17(5) (2010), 455–69 at 458, 462.
[24] Law 12/2005.

'which may be necessary for the diagnosis of a family disease, in the context of genetic testing on these individuals and their families'.[25]

The Directive's encouragement of anonymisation would effectively undermine the possibility of conservation for further family (or personal) use in the way that the Portuguese Act anticipates and it contains no analogous responsibility to conserve data. The closest it comes is the obligation that it does recognise regarding security and access. Article 17 (1) states:

Member States shall provide that the controller must implement appropriate technical and organizational measures to protect personal data against accidental or unlawful destruction or accidental loss, alteration, unauthorized disclosure or access, in particular where the processing involves the transmission of data over a network, and against all other unlawful forms of processing.

It would be a relatively small step in terms of the amount of rewording to Article 17(1) to extend the obligation to keep data secure to prevent its destruction when necessary to preserve the rights of access. In itself this may protect the (primary) data subjects' own access to data and impose a limited responsibility to conserve data upon data controllers. Of course, an unqualified obligation to conserve in order to preserve an enduring right to access might be disproportionate. This could, however, be remedied by qualifying the right of access itself (and Member States' entitlement to do so is already recognised within Article 13). Also, if the right of access were extended in line with previous arguments, then the duty to conserve could be understood to extend to the benefit of *secondary* data subjects and may be equivalent to the responsibility to conserve data contained within the Portuguese law. *Both* tissue *and* recorded information represent data that is susceptible to destruction. Recognising a responsibility of conservation, in limited circumstances at least, might represent a step forward in privacy protection if it preserved the opportunity to access genetic data that would otherwise be lost.

Advantages to treating biological samples as 'personal data'

I have argued that the Directive ought to be understood to include biological samples within its scope. It has, however, already been recognised that this argument appears (unfortunately) to be rather

---

[25] H. Moniz and R. Vale e Reis, 'Privacy and research involving genetic databases and biobanks: Stage Two Regional Report – Group B: The description of the regulation within and between the regional members states', Privileged Project Report, 16. www.privileged.group.shef.ac.uk/projstages/regional-reports/.

unfashionable. It bears rehearsing, however, because it not only represents the most conceptually sound interpretation of the scope of the existing Directive. There are also a number of distinct advantages associated with the approach.

Treating a biological sample in the same way as other kinds of personal information is not a novel idea. The Australian Law Reform Commission (ALRC) considered the relationship between 'biological samples' and 'personal information' when they reviewed the operation of the Australian Privacy Act.[26] They recognised that 'the plain and ordinary meaning of the word "information" is unlikely to extend to a genetic sample, as opposed to the information that is derived by sequencing the DNA that the sample contains',[27] but also that the 'plain and ordinary' meaning of 'information' is not always adopted in the context of privacy legislation. They found that, for example, at least one Privacy Commissioner in Australia preferred to interpret 'information' in a more inclusive manner to ensure adequate regulatory protection:

> In the present – and particularly in the likely future – a bodily sample is personal information and should be so defined. While a bodily sample and the genetic data derived from it will almost always be health information, it will also be personal information with relevance to matters other than health. Proper privacy protection in relation to genetic information should not fail for any individual through the narrowness of a definition.[28]

When the ALRC suggested reform of the Australian Law on Privacy they recognised that there might be objections to including biological samples as personal data.[29] Having considered the issue at length, the ALRC recognised that while a distinction could be drawn between 'samples' and 'information' they did not think that it was a distinction that should represent a limit to the reach of privacy legislation. Indeed, they agreed with the Privacy Commissioner quoted above that a failure to extend privacy protection to DNA samples would leave too many gaps in privacy protection and favoured a more consistent approach.[30]

The ALRC's comments were made in the light of a call for reform of Australian legislation; they were not at all confident that existing privacy legislation would, in fact, be interpreted in a way that included samples within the definition of information. They made the recommendation, despite the objections and their doubts, because they saw many benefits

---

[26] ALRC, 'Essentially yours', especially paras. 8.55 to 8.62.   [27] *Ibid.*, para. 8.8.

[28] *Ibid.*, para. 8.68.

[29] *Ibid.*, Paras. 8.70 to 8.86, where the ALRC detail objections associated with efficacy, duplication and complexity.

[30] *Ibid.*, para. 8.32.

attached to such reform. These benefits included ensuring that the obligations associated with the processing of genetic information, including the obligations 'to collect this information only with consent (except in specified circumstances) and to inform individuals, at the time of collection, about how their information is to be handled'[31] extended to the collection of genetic samples.[32] It bears considerable emphasis that similar benefits would obtain under EU law if the Directive were understood to include biological samples.

In addition, the ALRC thought it desirable that the 'rights of access' given under the Australian Privacy Act (and under the EU Directive) be extended to 'biological samples', given the possibility of a legitimate need to obtain such access.[33] The reasons for such a request might include an intention to transfer the samples to a new medical practitioner for re-testing or to arrange new testing of the samples for health-care purposes. This is entirely consistent with the idea, again already expressed, that there may be circumstances in which data subjects (as/ and family members) might expect to be able to access data if that were to their benefit and represented no disproportionate interference with the interests of others.[34] This right of access might only be meaningfully exercised if data controllers are also placed under a responsibility to conserve samples where there may be an expectation of benefit to others. If the right of access were coupled with an expectation that access would be prioritised owing to the finite nature of some samples, then access to genetic data, by those with a reasonable expectation of such access, would be improved.

In the face of any charge of impracticability, it should be remembered not only that this is already a responsibility recognised in particular countries but also that, to be consistent with the interests of the data controllers themselves, the responsibility would be proportionate in the light of any burden imposed.

Reflection

There are some terrible examples of medical research taking place without participants' consent.[35] These examples are terrible not simply because of the absence of consent, but one might imagine that an

---

[31] *Ibid.*, paras. 8.35 to 8.41   [32] *Ibid.*   [33] *Ibid.*, paras. 8.42 to 8.47.
[34] *Ibid.*, paras. 8.48 to 8.52.
[35] M. Angel, 'The Nazi hypothermia experiments and unethical research today', *New England Journal of Medicine* 322 (1990), 1462–4. At times, of course, what constitutes a 'terrible' abuse of power is a rather more finely grained judgment: R. Smith, 'Informed consent: the intricacies', *BMJ* 314 (1997), 1059–60.

adequate system of informed consent would have prevented many of them. Given the abuses, it is both reassuring and unsurprising that ethical codes since the Code of Nuremberg have underlined the importance to be attributed to voluntary participation in any form of human experimentation.[36] However, there has been no argument to this point that consent should be understood to be a *sine qua non* of all research using personal or private information. Consent has been recognised to be an important part of any regulatory system that respects particular norms of exclusivity but it has also been recognised that relevant norms do not always require it. Does this set research using genetic information apart from research using human tissue? Is there something about human biological samples that requires a distinct regulatory regime?

It may be possible to draw material lines between different kinds of risk and different kinds of mechanisms for evaluating respective risk and reward. In particular, the kinds of risk associated with interventional research are different from those involved in research that relies entirely upon data already separated from the human body. There are attempts to recognise distinctions between different kinds of risk, and reward, within international instruments intended to guide medical research, and non-consented genetic research is not condemned in all circumstances. However, it is significant to observe that samples *removed* from the body are consistently treated in a similar way to other kinds of data. When determining how we should respond to the increasing accumulation of personal information about us, and genetic data in particular, we should consider how any response might affect our relationship with the physical material from which information is derived. The significance of the distinction between the physical and the virtual can be seen to be receding. As we prepare to move towards a 'converged world', we should be reluctant to persist in maintaining unnecessary, and inappropriate, legal distinctions that might frustrate effective privacy protection both now and in the future.

[36] http://ohsr.od.nih.gov/guidelines/nuremberg.html.

8   Genetic discrimination

Thus far, the argument has sought to demonstrate the inability of the law of data protection, at least as currently implemented, to regulate research access to genetic data in a way that acknowledges the full range of privacy interests potentially engaged by research using genetic data. In addition, it has been suggested that there is an unwelcome degree of uncertainty in the application of the existing legal framework and this, especially when coupled with the drive to de-identify data, might work against the public interest in both proper privacy protection and appropriate research. Success up to this point might be understood to constitute grounds for reform of the law of data protection. Equally, however, it might be understood to point to the need for alternative ways to secure adequate privacy protection. Rather than seeking to reform the law of data protection, do we need other, perhaps more specific, ways to protect privacy interests in genetic data?

A number of countries have introduced legislation to protect privacy in genetic data, at times specifically in the context of research use of genetic data. Some of these national measures have already been mentioned briefly in previous discussion. For example, the Estonian Human Genes Research Act[1] has objectives which specifically include, inter alia, 'to ensure the voluntary nature of gene donation and the confidentiality of the identity of gene donors, and to protect persons from misuse of genetic data and from discrimination based on interpretation of the structure of their DNA and the genetic risks arising therefrom'.[2] This represents much more specific regulation than any reform of a general data protection framework might hope to achieve.

There might be many advantages to local measures. Regulatory measures at national, and even sub-national, level might be better placed to promote the legitimacy of regulatory instruments by ensuring that they demonstrate an understanding of local concerns (including particular

[1] RTI 2000, 104, 685, available in English.
[2] Section 1(1), Chapter 1, Human Genes Research Act, RTI 2000, 104, 685.

180

privacy norms) and are, therefore, better placed to demonstrate accountability than international regulation. Local governance may be preferred over central direction generally, owing to the fact that it can better support 'self-determination and accountability, political liberty, flexibility, preservation of identities, diversity, and respect for internal divisions of component states'.[3]

There is also some perceived advantage in tackling the issues raised by the acquisition and use of genetic data specifically. The proposals for reform in America mentioned earlier[4] have not been motivated simply by a belief that certain things can be done more effectively at a state level. Human genetic science has a dark history, particularly during parts of the twentieth century. This history includes abuses of fundamental human rights and freedoms across many countries. One of the initiatives in America explicitly recognises within the text of the proposed legislation that this history, when coupled with the significant progress that is being made in the area of genetic science, provides a reason to tackle directly some of the issues raised by that progress. The bill, introduced into the Californian Senate, states that 'the current explosion in the science of genetics, and the history of sterilization laws by states based on early genetic science, compels legislative action in this area'.[5] The attraction of local regulation is thus not simply that it is closer to the individuals that it affects. It also reflects a view that there is something about genetic science, and the human transactions that it might involve and enable, that compels action.

Without undermining any claim that there is an obligation upon governments to respond to the risks associated with advances in genetic science, when it comes to tackling those issues raised by the acquisition and use of genetic data, is a genetic exceptionalist approach justified? This chapter challenges the suggestion that reform should relate only to *genetic* data. However, rather than directly engaging with the question of whether there is anything *special* about genetic data,[6] the challenge I present begins with a straightforward application of the concept of genetic data already developed.

---

[3] G. A. Bermann, 'Taking subsidiarity seriously: Federalism in the European Community and the United States', *Columbia Law Review* 94 (1994), 331–456 at 343.

[4] See Chapter 1, note 13.

[5] Section 1(d), Senate Bill 559. Introduced by Senator Padilla, California Genetic Privacy Legislation (17 February 2011).

[6] For such a discussion I refer the reader to S. Holm, 'There is nothing special about genetic information', in A. Thompson and R. Chadwick (eds.), *Genetic Information: Acquisition, Access and Control* (New York: Kluwer Academic/Plenum Publishers, 1999), 97–105 and R. H. Wilkinson, 'Genetic information: important but not "exceptional"', *Identity in the Information Society* 3(3) (2010), 457–72.

One of the concerns with access to genetic data is that it might be used to inform discriminatory preferences. It is not the only concern but a temporary focus upon it will serve to illustrate the point that I wish to make. The distinction between interpret*ed* and interpret*able* (genetic) data can be seen to imply at least three different kinds of genetic *discrimination*. Identifying the conceptual boundaries between genetic discrimination in a primary, secondary and tertiary sense illustrates some of the potential regulatory difficulties if seeking to focus exclusively upon genetic data.

Analysis of the concept of genetic data reveals certain practical problems that would be unavoidable if regulation sought to establish a boundary coterminous with primary, secondary or tertiary genetic discrimination. To avoid these practical problems, regulatory lines would have to be drawn *across* these boundaries. However, drawing a line across a boundary would inevitably involve just the kind of arbitrary expression of preference that such regulation should be seeking to proscribe. In other words, avoiding practical problems should raise principled objection. Once the problems, of both principle and practice, have been articulated, it is possible to assess whether these burdens are worth shouldering: do the advantages of being able to tackle explicitly some of the issues raised by advancing genetic science justify creating either type of regulatory difficulty? Put another way, is it possible to avoid the difficulties associated with targeting genetic data exclusively and yet still achieve the legislative objectives? To inform this particular consideration, which continues into the final chapter, the possibility of achieving at least some of the regulatory aims through the framework of data protection will be considered.

Structure

Section I relies upon the concept of genetic data previously described (first in Chapter 3 and then summarised again in Chapter 7). It is important to recap briefly some key points because this analysis is directly relied upon to develop a trifold categorisation of genetic discrimination. In Section II, this analytical framework is used to support the claim that an unblinking focus upon the concept of genetic data per se demonstrates the limits of this concept, or the concept of genetic discrimination per se, as the object of legislative reform. If alternative criteria are introduced to justify regulatory intervention, then this undermines any claim that regulation should apply exclusively to genetic data. Here, some thoughts are offered on the implications of this analysis for the effective, and non-arbitrary, regulation of genetic discrimination.

I conclude, in Section III, with the proposal that, while advances in genetic science may provide the motivation, the most appropriate target of reform is not genetic data at all.

SECTION I TERMINOLOGY

Previous discussion has sought to underline the significance of interpretation to the perception of information: data must be understood before it may inform and such understanding depends upon variable interpretive frameworks. Many interpretive frameworks are shared, often deliberately, and we learn, and are taught, to associate particular data with particular kinds of significance. While particular interpretations of data may be commonly recognised, they are not universally known, nor are they unanimously accepted by those aware of them. It is this inconsistency in the availability, and application, of particular interpretive frameworks that leads to a situation where you can hand somebody a sample of biological material and yet they may gather no genetic information from it. They may not even recognise its potential to offer genetic information. On the other hand, an individual may recognise quite specific features of another's genetic architecture simply by watching her enter a room.

This discussion of data and information has sought to establish that, even if genetic information is understood *simply* as information about genetic architecture (rather than genetic significance), then it may be gathered from a wide range of data types and sources. It has *not* sought to establish that all data is equally susceptible to a genetic interpretation. It is almost certainly the case that certain data types are more readily associated with the ability to yield genetic information (of certain kinds and character) than others. As has already been conceded, one way in which the possibility of genetic interpretation may be most straightforwardly demonstrated is through the presentation of the data as itself the 'product' or 'record' of prior genetic interpretation. If data is presented as already possessing a particular interpretive pedigree, then the possibility of such interpretation can be clearly demonstrated by that pedigree. An example would be the result of any test that has been recorded and presented as the result of a 'genetic test'. If an individual acquires the results of a 'genetic test',[7]

---

[7] I adopt here the definition of genetic testing provided by the UNESCO International Declaration on Human Genetic Data (16 October 2003): 'Genetic testing: a procedure to detect the presence or absence of, or change in, a particular gene or chromosome, including an indirect test for a gene product or other specific metabolite that is primarily indicative of a specific genetic change' (Article 2(xii)).

then it will be difficult for that individual to deny the acquisition of
genetic information. The results of a genetic test, representing as they
do the product of prior 'genetic interpretation', is interpret*ed* genetic
data.[8] However, genetic information can also be gathered from data
that can be placed within an interpretive framework capable of generating genetic information: the data is interpret*able*. Examples of such
data have also already been given, and include, for example, the results
of a test for colour blindness or, alternatively, details of the iron
accumulation in an individual's blood. The latter may be interpreted
to reveal haemochromatosis, which *might*, in turn, be recognised to be a
genetic condition.[9]

The distinction between interpret*ed* and interpret*able* data is a
relevant one when seeking to establish a conceptual boundary around
the idea of 'genetic discrimination'. As with the term 'genetic data',
the phrase genetic discrimination has been defined in a number of
different ways. Initially at least, I offer a particularly inclusive
approach towards defining the term. The aim here is not to better
any existing alternative definition by virtue of breadth alone, but
rather to offer a perspective that allows one to accommodate, and
distinguish, different kinds of discriminatory action. Other definitions
of genetic discrimination might then be organised from this perspective and particular boundaries between them more readily identified
and assessed. Recognising that significant problems of practice and
principle may be associated with law reform either respecting or
crossing such boundaries helps to illustrate the difficulties associated
with regulation settling upon any particular definition of genetic
discrimination.

---

[8] Data might also be described as 'genetic data' owing to its indexical relation to genetic
material itself. If the significance of the physical, or causal, link between the data
perceived and the 'genetic' phenomenon was given emphasis, then the data would
remain 'genetic' regardless of whether a particular person had perceived the link (in
the way that animal tracks continue to relate to an animal even if they have not been
interpreted to do so). The contrast that I am attempting to draw is between those
circumstances in which it would be implausible for an individual to deny appreciation
of the possibility of a genetic interpretation (owing to its having already been
demonstrated) and those in which it would be at least arguable that (given that
revelation of genetic information required the subsequent application of an interpretive
framework) the individual was genuinely ignorant of the possibility of genetic
information being gathered from the data in question.

[9] This can indicate whether an individual suffers from the genetic condition
haemochromatosis. For details see the Haemochromatosis Society homepage (www.
ghsoc.org/home.html last accessed 27 May 2004).

Three kinds of genetic discrimination

An inclusive description of genetic discrimination would include any expression of a preference informed by genetic data (about architecture or significance).[10] This would capture any occasion when genetic data was taken into account when making a decision about how to behave towards somebody else. Genetic information, informing such preference expression, may be gathered from data that was, at the time of perception, either interpret*ed or* interpret*able* genetic data. As long as genetic data is informing one's expression of a preference, then one might be said to be acting in a genetically discriminatory way.

If genetic discrimination has been informed by an interpretation of data that was, at the time it was taken into account, interpret*ed* data, then the interpretive pedigree of the data will make it difficult for an individual to deny *genetic* discrimination. Discrimination that is informed by interpret*ed* genetic data might be described as *primary* genetic discrimination, and one of the particular concerns associated with primary genetic discrimination is that it might discourage individuals from seeking genetic tests in circumstances where it might be considered desirable.[11] For example, people may be discouraged from seeking tests in the context of either healthcare or medical research, if they fear the results could be used to discriminate against them.[12] While discriminatory preferences for particular genetic variations might be expressed in a variety of different contexts,[13] people have, for example, consistently expressed concerns over genetic information affecting their employability and insurability.[14]

---

[10] Explanation of these alternative concepts draws upon M. J. Taylor, 'Problems of practice and principle if centring law reform on the concept of genetic discrimination', *European Journal of Health Law* 11(4) (2004), 365–80 and M. J. Taylor, 'Problems with targeting law reform at genetic discrimination', in G. Árnason, S. Nordal and V. Árnason (eds.) *Blood and Data: Ethical, Legal and Social Aspects of Human Genetic Databases* (Reykjavik: University of Iceland Press and Centre for Ethics, 2004).

[11] P. Nemeth and T. W. Bonnette, 'Genetic discrimination in Employment', *Michigan Bar Journal* 88(1) (2009), 42–5.

[12] E. V. Lapham, C. Kozma, and J. O. Weiss, 'Genetic discrimination: perspectives of consumer', *Science* 274(5287) (1996), 621–4. Also, a Breakthrough Breast Cancer survey conducted in September 2004 found that about 28 per cent of women with a family history of breast cancer reported that they would be deterred from taking a genetic test if it had an effect on insurability. See C. Parsons Perez, 'The patient perspective on buying insurance', Presentation to Genetics and Insurance Committee public meeting, 12 July 2005. www.dh.gov.uk/ab/Archive/GAIC/DH_087663#_5.

[13] Anonymous, 'Air Force Academy sued over sickle cell policy', *New York Times* (4 January 1981).

[14] Human Genetic Commission, 'Public attitudes to human genetic information – People's Panel Quantitative Study conducted for the Human Genetics Commission' (London: HGC, March 2001). See also associated preparatory work: G. Voss, 'Report to the Human

The reality is that advances in genetic science will increasingly offer genetic tests that might be perceived as providing useful information within contractual contexts: typified by the contractual relations between employers and employees and insurers and the insured.[15] For as long as individuals express contractual preferences, they will seek novel comparators to inform their assessment of prospective contractual terms and partners. Any new opportunity to inform one's preferences will offer tempting advantage within an environment preoccupied with self-interested dealing. As genetic variations are associated with significance by potential contractors, then knowledge of these variations is likely to assume instrumental value.[16] Even if genetic information alone is not considered sufficient to inform a decision, it may be regarded as a factor worth including within a decision-making strategy. The risks of primary genetic discrimination are then very real.

While *primary* genetic discrimination might be described as the paradigm case, it does not cover all potential cases of genetic discrimination. Indeed, serious problems of ineffectiveness may be prompted by limiting regulation to only primary genetic discrimination; preferences may also be informed by individuals gathering genetic information from interpret-*able* data. While there might be nothing about the nature of the data or

Genetics Commission on public attitudes to the uses of human genetic information', 10 September 2000. www.hgc.gov.uk/uploaddocs/docpub/document/public_attitudes. pdf. It is also in these contexts that some of the earliest examples of primary genetic discrimination have been reported. e.g. D. Vorhaus, 'GINA in action: woman alleges genetic test led to firing', *Genomics Law Report* (Robinson Bradshaw & Hinson, 28 April 2010); J. K. Williams, C. Erwin, A. R. Juhl, M. Mengeling, Y. Bombard, M. R. Hayden, K. Quaid, I. Shoulson, S. Taylor, J. S. Paulen, E. V. Lapham, C. Kozma and J. O. Weiss, 'Genetic discrimination: perspectives of consumers', *Science* 274 (1996), 621–4; L. N. Geller, J. S. Alper, P. R. Billings, C. I. Barash, J. Beckwith and M. R. Natowicz, 'Individual, family, and societal dimensions of genetic discrimination: a case study analysis', *Science and Engineering Ethics* 2 (1996), 71–88. Interestingly, a study of people at risk for Huntington's disease in 2009 found that family history, and not genetic testing, was the major reason for genetic discrimination: Y. Bombard, G. Veenstra, J. M. Friedman, S. Creighton, L. Currie, J. S. Paulsen, J. L. Bottorff, M. R. Hayden, Canadian Respond-HD Collaborative Research Group, 'Perceptions of genetic discrimination among people at risk for Huntington's disease: a cross sectional survey', *BMJ* 338 (2009), b2175 (9 June).

[15] W. Allen and H. Ostrer, 'Anticipating unfair uses of genetic information', *American Journal of Human Genetics* 53(1) (1993), 16–21. Although note that, according to the terms of the UK moratorium on the use of genetic test information for insurance purposes and the Association of British Insurers (ABI) Code of Practice UK, insurers are entitled to petition for particular gene tests to be used (for high-value policies) when they are considered to be of actuarial significance. To date, the only test that has been approved for such (restricted use) is for Huntington's disease.

[16] L. Gostin, 'Genetic discrimination: the use of genetically based diagnostic and prognostic tests by employers and insurers', *American Journal of Law and Medicine* 17 (1–2) (1991), 109–44.

its contextual presentation to make a genetic interpretation obvious, it is possible for the data to be understood to provide genetic information given the application of a suitably (ill-)informed interpretive framework. The example of haemochromatosis has already been given and there is some evidence of discrimination on the basis of a diagnosis of the condition that does not rely upon a genetic test.[17] It remains a clear example of a type of discrimination that may be distinguished conceptually from primary genetic discrimination if diagnosed other than via genetic test. *Secondary* genetic discrimination can then occur when an individual *perceives* data to yield genetic information. Such a perception may be more or less well informed.

Secondary genetic discrimination undoubtedly predates genetic science. Discrimination on the grounds of sex, or indeed any other genetic condition indicated through 'non-genetic' test, including the observation of a distinctive body type (e.g. as associated with particular chromosomal disorders) would constitute examples of secondary genetic discrimination. In such cases the motivation for the discrimination may have little to do with the 'genetic' nature of the condition preferred (avoided). Indeed, it is quite possible that the individuals discriminating did not realise the potential to gather genetic information: they may not have actually possessed a relevant framework. They must clearly have understood the data to inform of something (e.g. they understood an elevated iron count to indicate haemochromatosis) but they may not have recognised its genetic significance (i.e. they did not realise haemochromatosis to be a genetic condition). Secondary genetic discrimination might then be described as either 'witting' or 'unwitting'.

Finally, genetic discrimination may also (or alternatively) be described as the act of expressing a preference for a characteristic that is disproportionately associated with a particular genetic variation. *Tertiary* genetic discrimination may then be described as occurring when a decision-making process is informed by the presence or absence of a property that is not uniformly shared across all genetic variations. The nature of the relationship between the property selected for and any genetic variation

---

[17] J. S. Alper, L. N. Geller, C. I. Barash, P. R. Billings, V. Laden and M. R. Natowicz, 'Genetic discrimination and screening for hemochromatosis', *Journal of Public Health Policy* 15(3) (1994), 345–58. It should be noted that subsequent studies have questioned the continued extent of such discrimination, e.g. M. A. Hall, J. C. Barton, P. C. Adams, C. E. McLaren, J. A. Reiss, O. Castro, A. Ruggiero, R. T. Acton, T. E. Power and T. C. Bent, 'Genetic screening for iron overload: no evidence of discrimination at 1 year', *Family Practice* 56(10) (2007), 829–33. This does not, however, affect the point that diagnoses of 'genetic conditions' can be made other than via 'genetic tests'. See also Bombard *et al.*, 'Perceptions of genetic discrimination among people at risk for Huntington's disease'.

may be statistically weak, but discrimination on the basis of this property may nevertheless have a disproportionate impact upon groups possessing particular genetic variations. Discriminating on the grounds of height, strength or athletic ability might provide examples of tertiary genetic discrimination. Various genetic profiles may be more or less closely associated with particular physical characteristics or abilities and disproportionately affected by selection for (or against) them. The individual expressing a preference for the property selected may, or may not, appreciate that such a preference may place those with specific genetic variations at particular (dis)advantage. This perception may, or may not, be what motivates the discrimination. As with secondary genetic discrimination, the individual discriminating might perceive the relationship between the genetic characteristic and the valued trait to be stronger than others would accept (i.e. they may operate with a contested interpretive framework).

SECTION II   PROBLEMS OF DISTINCTION AND DEFINITION

If regulation were to target genetic discrimination, then the definition of genetic discrimination used would capture acts typified by at least one of these three kinds of discrimination. Regulating the acquisition and use of genetic data associable with anything other than all three kinds would represent an incomplete regulation of genetic discrimination broadly conceived. It may be, however, that the regulatory objectives could be achieved by regulating less than every conceivable instance of genetic discrimination. If the scope of regulatory reform is to be limited, then it is important to be clear about exactly what it does seek to target and what motivations underlie its selection of target.

If the target of legislation were to be genetic data per se, then I would suggest that, in order for it to be workable, the legislation would be forced to regulate only recorded genetic information: interpreted genetic data: primary genetic discrimination. However, this would obviously fail to account for the possibility of genetic information being gathered from 'non-genetic data'.[18] It would have to be accepted that regulation which stopped at the boundary between primary and secondary genetic discrimination could not regulate the inappropriate acquisition or use of all genetic data.

---

[18] See for more detail ALRC, 'Essentially yours', paras. 10.1–10.6.

It might protect certain things, e.g. individuals' access to some genetic testing services, and if it did, then this should not be underestimated as an achievement. It could not address other problems. For example, regulation that only addressed primary genetic discrimination might encourage would-be discriminators to seek less reliable proxies for genetic architecture. If people are discouraged from relying upon genetic tests, then an interest in genetic information may lead them to look for it in other ways, e.g. by asking questions about family history. The point is that regulation that applied only to primary genetic discrimination would *not* prevent people from taking genetic data into account when making decisions, it would simply compel them to use a particular type of genetic data: interpretable genetic data.

However, if regulation were to be extended to include secondary genetic discrimination, then some considerable practical problems of workability would be encountered. There would be controversy over the accuracy of some claims that data *could* be interpreted to yield genetic information. The list of 'genetic conditions' is not certain and the inclusion of particular conditions, such as short-sightedness, homosexuality or height, on that list would be controversial.[19] It is not possible confidently to determine which data people will perceive as interpretable to yield genetic information. At the extreme end of the scale, the Australian Law Reform Commission point out, 'In one sense, almost all information about a person's health and physical well-being can be called "genetic information".'[20]

A definition of genetic discrimination that included primary and secondary genetic discrimination would, therefore, be potentially as extensive as it was indeterminate. Uncertainty would also surround the understanding and intent of the discriminator. It would, for example, be extremely difficult to distinguish between witting and unwitting secondary genetic discrimination or to determine the reliability of any interpretive framework applied to data that others considered non-genetic. Interpretive frameworks are not necessarily made public. However, if the distinction between witting and unwitting discrimination were not made, then people could be captured by regulation when they had no knowledge that the trait they were taking into account had a genetic implication and had no intention to discriminate on genetic grounds.

---

[19] All examples of 'genetic condition' reportedly provided by a 1999 RADAR survey. A. Fletcher, *Genes Are Us: Genetics and Disability: a RADAR Survey* (London: Royal Association for Disability and Rehabilitation, 1999) cited by G. Voss, 'Report to the Human Genetics Commission on Public Attitudes to the Uses of Human Genetic Information', 10 September 2000.

[20] ALRC, 'Essentially yours', para. 3.2.

Practical problems associated with uncertainty regarding what constitutes a genetic condition, and what constitutes evidence of a genetic condition, would continue into the identification of tertiary genetic discrimination. The boundary between secondary and tertiary discrimination would itself be unclear and, for this reason, any attempt to draw a regulatory line *before* tertiary discrimination would be problematic – and not only because it relies upon the assessment of the reliability of particular interpretive frameworks that we have already recognised, and that are hard to capture and interrogate. It would also be problematic because the scope of the regulation would be determined by an orthodox position on the relation between genotype and phenotype. Those individuals adopting an unorthodox position, perhaps generating that genetic information which would be the most difficult to justify, would probably fall outside the scope of regulation: the more unreasonable the association between the characteristic perceived and the genetic trait valued, the less likely it would be to constitute genetic discrimination.

Extending regulation to include tertiary genetic discrimination would, however, not be an unproblematic response. If practical problems are associated with regulating secondary genetic discrimination, then these are multiplied by any attempt (also) to regulate tertiary genetic discrimination. Any attempt to regulate tertiary genetic discrimination could be described as tantamount to an attempt to regulate discrimination on the grounds of any human trait at all.

There are then significant practical problems encountered if one seeks to establish a clear regulatory boundary either between primary and secondary or between secondary and tertiary genetic discrimination.

An alternative approach?

It would be wrong to infer from the way in which I have attempted to distil the concept of genetic discrimination into three different kinds that I seek to imply that regulators would either have to choose between them in mutually exclusive fashion or indeed, have to accept any combination as indivisible categories. The three kinds of genetic discrimination described simply trace a boundary around a paradigm case of genetic discrimination in an increasingly expansive fashion; there is nothing to prevent regulators drawing their own lines in different places. The point is that, unless *all* conceivable instances of genetic discrimination are to be regulated, lines such as these must be drawn: any regulation tackling genetic discrimination must describe and privilege a particular kind of genetic discrimination. The same is true of any regulator seeking to tackle a particular use or access of genetic data.

If a regulator chooses *not* to draw the line between primary, secondary and tertiary genetic discrimination, then she may limit the scope of legislation in other ways. While drawing lines *through* these different conceptions of discrimination may avoid certain *practical* difficulties, it would threaten to introduce certain problems of *principle*. Dividing a coherent concept of genetic data, and only regulating a sub-set thereof, is to concede that neither the pedigree nor the potential of genetic interpretation is alone considered sufficient warrant for regulation.

While there may be nothing wrong with requiring *more* than that genetic data is involved in a particular activity, the shift in emphasis from a concern *simply* with the genetic interpretation (or interpretability) of the data must be acknowledged. Otherwise, it may provide cover for arbitrariness in the operation of the law. If the potential of the data to inform of genetic information is not the defining characteristic of the data regulated, then an unrelenting focus upon genetic data becomes questionable. We can justifiably demand that the 'other' defining characteristic is brought out for examination, and we may find, when it has, that it is more significant – e.g. for the protection of privacy – than the genetic pedigree or potential of data.

Drawing a distinction *within* different kinds of discrimination

While some international treaties condemn the concept of genetic discrimination *tout court*,[21] domestic legislation tends to take a more restrictive approach towards its (definition and) regulation. For example, the US Genetic Information Non-Discrimination Act 2008 (GINA 2008) draws a regulatory boundary around acts of genetic discrimination that encompass instances of both primary (an individual's genetic tests) and secondary (and even possibly tertiary) genetic discrimination ('the manifestation of a disease or disorder in family members of such individual').[22]

---

[21] See, for example, Article 11 of the Council of Europe, Convention on Human Rights and Biomedicine (Oviedo, 4.IV.1997): 'Any form of discrimination against a person on grounds of his or her genetic heritage is prohibited.'

[22] GINA 2008 defines 'genetic information' thus: '(A) IN GENERAL. – The term "genetic information" means, with respect to any individual, information about – (i) such individual's genetic tests, (ii) the genetic tests of family members of such individual, and (iii) the manifestation of a disease or disorder in family members of such individual ... (C) EXCLUSIONS. – The term "genetic information" shall not include information about the sex or age of any individual' (Section 201(4)).

However, not *all* cases of such genetic discrimination are regulated. The Act applies only to discrimination within the context of health insurance and employment. It does not cover life insurance, disability insurance or long-term care insurance or any discrimination at all out-side of the employment or insurance field. Also, it specifically excludes sex from the category of data that might constitute genetic information[23] (despite the fact that, as was recognised above, data recorded regarding sex could clearly facilitate secondary (or tertiary) genetic discrimin-ation). GINA 2008 does not then capture all genetic discrimination broadly conceived, even in the fields to which it applies.

If there is to be a distinction drawn *within* a particular kind of genetic discrimination, and that distinction is not to be an arbitrary one, then there must be some reason for regulation *beyond* the use of genetic data. In the case of GINA 2008, there is a clear priority attached to regulating the discriminatory uses of data in the context of employment and health insurance. If this is the intention, then is it possible to defend limiting the scope of that intervention to particular types of genetic data?

Drawing a line within primary genetic discrimination

One distinction that may be drawn between genetic discrimination and discrimination of other kinds is the *predictive* nature of certain genetic data. Genetic data can be interpreted to inform a perception of the risk that an individual faces of manifesting a genetic condition in the future.

This is one explanation for the categories of data captured by GINA 2008. It is also reflected in the genetic privacy legislation proposed in the State of Vermont; the proposed bill seeks to extend the protections provided by the Federal GINA but also mirrors some of its provisions. The purpose of the bill is to protect explicitly the privacy of genetic information.[24] It aims to ensure, inter alia, that genetic information cannot be disclosed without the informed written consent of the person to whom the information pertains.[25] The bill defines genetic information to include the results of genetic tests as well as information about the manifestation of a disease or disorder in family members.[26] For the purposes of certain sections, however, 'genetic test' does *not* include a test, examination or analysis, if

---

[23] *Ibid.*
[24] 'An Act Relating to Privacy of Genetic Information', Bill H.368, Vermont Legislature, Page 1, Line 7 (Statement of purpose).
[25] Bill H.368, SS.9330(a) (Lines 19–20).   [26] Bill H.368, SS.9331(9) (Lines 10–18).

in accordance with generally accepted standards in the medical community, the potential presence or absence of a mutation, alteration, or deletion of a gene or chromosome has already manifested itself by causing a disease, disorder or medical condition or by symptoms highly predictive of the disease, disorder or medical condition.[27]

One reason for targeting the use of predictive information is a desire to protect people's choice to undergo screening and other forms of pre-symptomatic testing. There is a concern that any fear that predictive information may need to be disclosed to employers or insurers in the future would discourage people from taking testing now. While this is a legitimate concern, Jon Beckwith and Joseph Alper point out that this rationale implicitly recognises the importance of prohibiting discrimination based on any form of predictive medical information, not just those based on some form of genetic data.[28]

It is also pertinent to recall that the preferences informed by genetic data are the preferences of a discriminator interested in details of genetic architecture *only* because of the association with a valued characteristic. The interpretive pedigree of the information informing the perception may indicate the quality of the association but it is no way determinative. At the very least, a concern with unjustified associations would suggest that regulation should include *secondary* genetic discrimination (whether witting or unwitting) or else risk capturing some of the most common associations.[29] Indeed, this would seem to be recognised by the inclusion of information about manifest conditions in other family members within GINA 2008 and the proposed bill in Vermont. Drawing a line through primary genetic discrimination and continuing it *into* secondary genetic discrimination does, however, raise the practical problems discussed above, as well as further problems of principle (discussed below).

Drawing a line within secondary or tertiary genetic discrimination

It might seem that if the objective is to regulate genetic discrimination then an obvious place to draw a regulatory line may be between witting discrimination, on the grounds of perceived genetic architecture, and

---

[27] Bill H.368, SS.9331(10)(C)(ii) (Lines 18–2).

[28] J. Beckwith and J. S. Alper, 'Reconsidering genetic antidiscrimination legislation', *Journal of Law, Medicine and Ethics* 26 (1998), 205–10 at 209.

[29] A study into the experiences of genetic discrimination by those at increased risk of Huntington's disease found family history, rather than the result of genetic testing, the main reason given for genetic discrimination: Bombard *et al.*, 'Perceptions of genetic discrimination among people at risk for Huntington's disease'.

unwitting genetic discrimination, on the grounds of a characteristic which could have been, but was not in fact, used to derive genetic information. The distinction between interpreting data to inform of genetic architecture and interpreting it to inform of something else may also be related to the distinction drawn above between 'predictive' and 'diagnostic' testing. For example, if a test for colour blindness is being used to diagnose colour blindness, then the argument is that the discrimination is on the grounds of colour blindness and not genetic characteristic. If, however, colour blindness is associated with some other disorder by reason of genetic data, and a test for colour blindness is being used as a proxy test for this disorder, then it would be genetic discrimination and should be treated as such.

One of the challenges associated with distinguishing between witting and unwitting secondary (or tertiary) genetic discrimination is that the distinction depends entirely upon the interpretive frameworks applied by discriminators when informing their preferences. Regulating witting, but not unwitting, secondary genetic discrimination would discourage not the use of genetic data but only the witting use of that data. This is a significant problem.

From the perspective of the individual discriminated against, there is little significance to whether a discriminator perceived a genetic connection between the data that informed the discrimination and the trait that she valued. If Bob is denied a job interview at a local firm because of his father's criminal record, then it matters little to him whether the interviewer perceived criminality to be a heritable characteristic due to genetics or due to a shared environment. Similarly, if denied the position because he is assessed to be at elevated risk of carpal tunnel syndrome, then why would he deserve protection only *if* the risk is informed by data associated with genetic characteristics?[30] What if the data were not associated with a genetic characteristic today, but it was tomorrow? What if the reverse was the case and current associations were subsequently abandoned?

While it might be currently the vogue for things to be marketed with associations to DNA technology emphasised, regulation of witting genetic discrimination might reverse this trend. Tests could be labelled

---

[30] Burlington Northern Santa Fe (BNSF) Railroad admitted testing employees, without their knowledge or consent, for genetic markers associated with carpal tunnel syndrome. See US Equal Employment Opportunity Commission Press Release, 'EEOC settles ADA suit against BNSF for genetic bias', 18 April 2001. www.eeoc.gov/eeoc/newsroom/release/4–18–01.cfm. Elevated risk is also associated with being female (women are three times more likely to get carpal tunnel syndrome than men) and with extended periods of assembly line work. BNSF might then have also gathered data about risk by collecting data about current (and past) work practices and gender.

according to the actual property tested for, or the characteristic valued, rather than with any mention of genetics: in the way that 'pregnancy testing kits' need not make reference to the hormones they are assessing, so 'employability' tests might indicate only an individual's susceptibility to particular medical conditions or behavioural traits. The incidence of *witting* genetic discrimination may decline and become increasingly hard to prove. This would be of little comfort to those who continued to be subject to discrimination.

However, if extending protection to *all* secondary genetic discrimination would encounter significant practical problems, and drawing a line between witting and unwitting discrimination would not address the unwanted discrimination, then how might the category of secondary discrimination be subdivided? One response might be to recur to the predictive nature of certain genetic data. This would capture the hypothetical 'employability tests' mentioned above and would also continue to offer protection to those concerned about accessing healthcare services for the purposes of pre-symptomatic testing.

A concern to protect access to healthcare might seek, for example, to include access to genetic counselling services that rely upon family histories, but also to information about cholesterol level, blood pressure, etc.: information that might be linked to some kind of predisposition or susceptibility. As a matter of principle, however, could this justification be restricted to pre-symptomatic data? There is already some empirical evidence to support the claim that concerns with confidentiality may affect disclosure of information to a healthcare professional.[31] People may be concerned with the confidentiality of information *post* manifestation of a disorder and there is little to suggest that *privacy* concerns diminish once a condition is diagnosed as manifest. Discussion of the importance of confidentiality within the healthcare setting is not subdivided according to whether the confidential information held is predictive or diagnostic, or whether it represents interpreted or interpretable genetic data.

There is no need here to dispute the claims that harms might arise as a result of discriminatory uses of predictive genetic information or interpreted genetic data. The point is that the harms that people may be protected from through the regulation of a sub-category of genetic data are not harms limited to such data.[32] If one is justifying selective

---

[31] C. Jones, 'The utilitarian argument for medical confidentiality: a pilot study of patients' views', *Journal of Medical Ethics* 29 (2003), 348–52.

[32] For a fuller discussion of whether harms are particularly associated with 'predictive' 'genetic' testing' see Beckwith and Alper, 'Reconsidering genetic antidiscrimination legislation' and Wilkinson, 'Genetic information: important but not "exceptional"', 460–1.

intervention on the basis of a particular principle, then one needs to be able to demonstrate that the principle has *particular* application to this kind of data and it does not raise any unique issues.

Admittedly, particularity could, in principle, be demonstrated if, while not unique, this kind of data raised issues that were pressing in some other way. For example, if it was *only* this kind of data that was currently unregulated, then one could justify targeting it to bring it into line with other regulated discrimination. In fact, one might suggest that predictive genetic data could be singled out because discrimination against individuals with conditions that are clinically manifest would be already caught by sex or disability discrimination legislation. However, any suggestion that all predictive genetic data could be effectively tackled through legislation designed to regulate sex or disability discrimination is unpersuasive.[33]

I have not sought to engage with the argument of genetic exceptionalism directly, but have inevitably done so tangentially as it has intersected arguments about the reasons for drawing lines within different types of genetic discrimination. In this context it is important to recognise another harm that has been specifically linked to genetic discrimination. Ruth Wilkinson persuasively argues that, as genetic determinism is flawed, that which endorses it is similarly flawed, and this, in itself, may justify the regulation of at least certain kinds of genetic discrimination.[34]

One might expect a critic of genetic exceptionalism, such as Wilkinson, also to be critical of genetic exceptionalist legislation. In fact, Wilkinson herself agrees that 'all legislative or quasi-legislative approaches which prohibit discrimination on the grounds of genetic make-up could be subject to the genetic exceptionalist criticism'. However, despite this, she is concerned that the alternative might only be an attempt to address all 'unfair discrimination' and that this would be unworkable in practice.[35] For this reason, she is in favour of tackling the difficult policy questions raised by genetic information, before, presumably, attempting to extend any conclusions to other kinds of data.[36]

---

[33] Apart from anything else, discriminators may be interested in identifying indicators for human behaviour that falls within the 'normal' range. See further, Nuffield Council on Bioethics, *Genetics and Human Behaviour* (London: Nuffield Council on Bioethics, 2002).

[34] R. H. Wilkinson, 'Unjustified discrimination: is the moratorium on the use of genetic test results by insurers a contradiction in terms?', *Health Care Analysis* 18 (2010), 279–93 at 290.

[35] Wilkinson, 'Genetic information: important but not "exceptional"', 467.

[36] *Ibid.*, 471.

As I have sought to underline the practical difficulties of regulating genetic discrimination, it is important that the impracticability of doing otherwise is given serious consideration.

SECTION III IMPLICATIONS FOR REGULATORY REFORM

If there is a *principle* justifying intervention, such as the prevention of unfair or unjustified discrimination, or the protection of access to health-care services, then that principle can be relied upon to justify regulatory intervention regardless of the interpretive pedigree of the data relied upon to inform the discrimination. Any attempt specifically, and exclusively, to regulate the phenomenon of *genetic* discrimination is challenged to justify the drawing of regulatory lines around, or through, a concept that has neither clear boundaries nor specific significance when it comes to the protection of fundamental rights and freedoms, including privacy. The result is that legislation is pushed to define the nature of the data, and of the information gathered from it, in ways that inevitably fail even to capture completely all genetic (information or) discrimination.

If the only alternative to regulating against unfair genetic discrimination was to regulate all unfair discrimination, then one might encounter even more practical difficulties in achieving effective regulatory reform. However, it might be possible to identify particular contexts (such as the processing of data in health, insurance, employment or research contexts) or limited rights (such as a right to challenge the accuracy and appropriateness of data processed if it relates to a person in a particular way) that would *capture* the uses of genetic data that individuals were concerned about, but not subject to the criticism that Wilkinson rightly levels against any attempt to target all unfair discrimination.[37] I will pick up this thought again later.

Here, I wish only to reiterate that prolonged consideration of the nature of genetic information, and its relevance to a discriminator, helps to illustrate why any attempt to regulate either its acquisition or its use will invariably be either ineffective or arbitrary in its regulation of (some) genetic discrimination. Indeed, the term genetic discrimination may be sensibly defined in ways that would see its regulation failing effectively to control the acquisition and use of (some) genetic information. In short, any law reform centred on the concept of either 'genetic information' or 'genetic discrimination' is doomed to an incomplete regulation of one or the other.

[37] Wilkinson, 'Genetic information: important but not "exceptional"', 468–71.

This, in itself, would not be problematic if the cases of discrimination that were regulated could be shown to have a different impact upon relevant interests, in particular privacy interests, than those that were not. The difficulty is in establishing how instances of discrimination that fall one side of a regulatory line are materially different from instances that fall the other side, and yet are distinguishable by a property that does not extend beyond the concept of genetic discrimination. Drawing lines *within* the concept of genetic discrimination (as will be necessary for the effective administration of justice) inevitably protects individuals from discrimination when certain other individuals, susceptible to similar harms, are not protected from (genetic) discrimination. The law, in so differentiating according to morally irrelevant criteria, is in danger of committing the kind of unjustified expression of preference that it seeks to control.

None of the aforesaid should, however, be taken to question the need for legal reform – nor even to question the need for urgent reform specifically motivated by the current possibility and the future prospect of genetic discrimination. While there may be good reasons for the lawmakers within society to respond to the spectre of genetic discrimination, the question is to what extent the justification for reform supports legislation specifically, and exclusively, targeting genetic data. I suggest that vulnerable individuals might be protected rather more (uniformly and) effectively by legislation that, while encompassing discriminatory practices informed by genetic data, is not defined by them.

Part III

The consequence

9   Potential, promise and possibility

Throughout the previous chapters, the idea that I have sought to advance might be crystallised thus: the law cannot fully protect the public interest in privacy through the idea of personal information alone. This central idea has been advanced by demonstrating the inability of the current regulatory framework, organised as it is around the idea of personal information, to provide adequate privacy protection for the research use of genetic data.

The norms of exclusivity associated with a private life go beyond the current legal concept of personal data, to include data that relates to multiple identifiable individuals simultaneously, and data that (while perhaps not currently associated with any identifiable individual at all) *could* be associated with any number of individuals in different – reasonably anticipatable – contexts. It is the possibilities and implications of *association* that are significant when it comes to understanding the privacy risks posed by research uses of genetic data. These possibilities can only be assessed if one considers the interpretive potential of data. They are missed if one fixates upon its interpretive pedigree, or misunderstands the meaning and significance of identification. Private data is not the same as personal information.[1] Protecting privacy is not just about suppressing or deleting those identifiers which are – in any case – typically non-disclosive of their own information content. Preferences regarding exclusivity are *for* private data to be used in particular ways – for maintaining preferred patterns of association – and while this may, at times, be about preventing particular associations, it may also be about preserving those identifiers that enable the access to data that is preferred, so that the promise of particular data flows may be realised.

---

[1] The point that private information is not the same as personal information is also made in D. Beyleveld and E. Histed, 'Betrayal of confidence in the Court of Appeal' *Medical Law International* 4(3&4) (2000), 277–311. I not only would agree with their claim but would extend the distinction they make to distinguish also between data and information.

In this final chapter, I hope to do three things. First, review some of the limitations that the concept of personal data places upon the current regulatory framework. Second, consider how these limitations undermine privacy protection by encouraging an excessive reliance upon the mechanisms of 'consent' or 'anonymisation'. It will be important to remember at this point that the problems associated with the current regulatory framework are not limited to the under-protection of privacy. The inappropriate frustration of access to genetic data, inconsistent with the operative norms of exclusivity – which occurs when privacy is over-protected – is also inconsistent with *proper* privacy protection. Third, reflect upon how this analysis might inform short-, medium- and long-term reform. This will take into account the previous analysis of the distinction between samples and information and also the problems of targeting any agenda for legislative reform at genetic data exclusively.

If the current protection of privacy is heavily reliant upon a concept that is not fit for purpose, then this has implications not only from the perspective of one concerned with proper privacy protection. It is also significant from the perspective of one concerned to promote and pro-tect the public interest in a regulatory system operating on the basis of reasons that might be defended as reasonable. If the current regulatory framework fails to account for the broad spectrum of privacy preferences engaged by research using genetic data, then confidence in the system to take reasonable account of things that are of value to people is jeopard-ised and its legitimacy is undermined.

Personal information and privacy protection: a dysfunctional relationship

Privacy is concerned with norms of exclusivity that are highly context dependent: particular patterns and preferences vis-à-vis transactions between persons that typically involve preferred access to different per-sons, for different purposes, by different persons, in different situations, with different justifications. Privacy protection is about maintaining these highly variable norms: both protecting the states of separation they represent *and* enabling the access that they expect. When there are different norms in play, then regulation must seek to account reasonably for them all in a process that determines which has priority in any case of conflict. This process should, ideally at least, rely upon justificatory strategies that are acceptable as reasonable by all impacted by the deci-sions reached. There is a public interest in legitimate regulation and this is dependent upon the mechanisms of privacy protection being able to give a reasonable account of different preferences: even if not acceding to them, in particular circumstances, for good public reason.

There is absolutely no reason to assume that preferences for exclusivity – either for access or for separation – apply uniquely to data that is recorded about a particular identifiable individual. It is *association* with data that engages an individual's privacy claim (as it is the possibility of association that characterises a relationship with data as one in which a preference regarding access and separation might most meaningfully be expressed as a preference regarding one's own privacy rather than the privacy of another), and one can be concerned about association with data that one is not currently associated with, concerned about association with data that is (or could be) also associated with (many) others, and concerned about the association of data with a group of which one is, or might be, a member. Here the words of Rabbi Moshe Tendler, when objecting to the early focus on Ashkenazi Jews in genetic research, have particular resonance:

Why are you focusing only on the Ashkenazi Jews, giving the world the impression that we have all the bad genes? ... I walk around, they may not know my name, but I've been identified as a member of the Ashkenazi Jewish community who carries bad genes. They had no right to do that to me.[2]

The idea of 'personal information', at least as captured within existing legal frameworks intended to protect privacy, is incapable of recognising the full range of ways in which people may be associated with data. The idea of 'personal information' is, therefore, incapable of capturing the spectrum of transactions, or relational units, over which persons may have preferences or particular expectations owing to previous patterns of behaviour: it cannot account for all privacy interests.

The limits of personal information

The concept of personal information is limited in some fundamental ways. One of the most significant limitations follows the fact that it consistently references the idea of *information* rather than *data*. Information is a composite concept. It is a composite of data and interpretation. Thus, it only makes sense to think of specific data as representing a particular type of information if one assumes a particular interpretive context. When contexts are relatively static, then one can reliably label

---

[2] Interview on National Public Radio, 'Morning Edition', 6 May 1999, cited in D. S. Davis, 'Groups, communities, and contested identities in genetic research', Hastings Center Report (November 2000).

data with some confidence. However, in the face of fluid interpretive contexts, the idea that particular data can be labelled 'personal information', owing to its association with particular identifiable individuals, is outmoded. Information is only information *because* it has already been interpreted. *Data*, on the other hand, with its infinite potential for varying interpretation, resists definitive classification as a singular type of information. This might explain the decision to focus upon information rather than data, but it also reveals the compromise that has been made for the sake of the appearance of selectivity and manageability. A regulatory system unable to lift its eyes from a definition of 'personal data' as *a particular type of information* is doomed to be always looking back at the interpretive pedigree of recorded information rather than forward at the interpretive potential of the data in question.

The interpretive pedigree of recorded information

We can see a preoccupation with interpretive pedigree evident even in those legal frameworks that use the idea of personal *data*. While the text of these instruments might imply that they are intended to apply to any data that *could be associated with* a particular individual, their interpretation and operation limit their application to data that *does relate* to a particular individual. For example, the explanatory memorandum to the OECD guidelines governing the protection of privacy and transborder flows of personal data states: 'In principle, personal data convey information which by direct (e.g. a civil registration number) or indirect linkages (e.g. an address) may be connected to a particular physical person.'[3] *This clearly indicates that any data, if it may be connected to a particular physical person, should be protected* and it is consistent with the argument that I have been attempting to advance. But the definition of personal data that is actually contained within the guidelines provides that '"personal data" means any information relating to an identified or identifiable individual (data subject)'.[4] The phrase 'may be connected to' has now become 'relating to'. This change represents a considerable shift in emphasis.

---

[3] Para. 41, Explanatory Memorandum to the Recommendation of the Council concerning Guidelines Governing the Protection of Privacy and Transborder Flows of Personal Data (23 September 1980). www.oecd.org/document/18/0,3343, en_2649_34255_1815186_1_1_1_1,00.html#memorandum.

[4] Section 1, Part One (General Definitions), Annex to the Recommendation of the Council of 23 September 1980: OECD Guidelines Governing the Protection of Privacy and Transborder Flows for Personal Data.

In some ways it typifies this move from 'data' per se to a particular type of data: recorded information with a particular interpretive pedigree.

In previous chapters, I have concentrated my analysis upon the Data Protection Directive 95/46/EC. It is the most significant regulatory framework within Europe apropos the regulation of personal data. It is also the framework with which the United States Department of Commerce Safe Harbour Privacy Principles are designed to be consistent, and it is tied closely to other international legal standards, including the OECD privacy principles mentioned above. We can also see, within the language of the Directive, this shift from 'data' to a particular type of recorded 'information' as the primary focus of regulatory concern. Although the Directive uses the phrase 'personal data' rather than 'personal information', it defines 'personal data' as 'any *information* relating to an identified or identifiable natural person ("data subject")'.

This definition of 'personal data' is subject to the problems that will bedevil any concept of data that is defined in terms of recorded information. It is conceptually anchored to a particular, historic, interpretive framework. As contexts shift, the same data might be said to relate to *more than one* identifiable individual. What is more, the fact that data is not currently associated with any identifiable individual says little about the possibility that it might be if interpretive contexts were to change. Recognising the significance of interpretive context to the association of data with any particular individual has an interesting implication: it suggests that there is, in fact, no such thing as anonymous data. There are only, more or less, anonymous contexts. As informational landscapes shift, the same data can be more or less readily identified with different persons. This undermines any claim that regulation *can* effectively distinguish between identifiable and non-identifiable data in a prospective fashion, particularly when control cannot be maintained over the interpretive contexts (e.g. through publication). This does not mean that we should give up on the idea of anonymisation. It does mean that we should concentrate as much on the relevant contexts as we should on the nature of the relevant data they contain.

The problems of distinguishing between identifiable and non-identifiable data are particularly obvious when one considers *genetic* data. Genetic data can relate to multiple individuals and the same data can be more or less identifiable in relation to each of them: as contexts shift and interpretive frameworks change. Genetic data is held in common between relatives, and the possibilities of a significant association between specific data and particular individuals will alter according to the intentions and the resources of those with access to that data. These same things – intentions and resources – will dynamically shape the risks of association: it is interpretive potential, and not pedigree, that should be one's primary concern, and this is a matter of purpose and judgment and has no fixed ontology. A focus upon the interpretive pedigree of recorded information leaves out of sight the range of preferences that different interpretive frameworks might engage.

The limited range of preferences that the concept of personal information is able to account for has a number of implications. For example, if one starts from the premise that preferences should be respected *unless* there is a reason not to respect them, *and* that such a reason should be both transparent and reasonably defensible, then there will be inevitable deficiencies in a regulatory framework if organised around the concept of personal information. Some of these deficiencies are evident when one considers the approach of such a system to the issue of consent.

Consent

If one aims to provide reasonable account for preferences expressed in relation to transactions involving genetic data, then one must aim to create an environment in which such preferences can be meaningfully expressed. However, proper privacy protection is undermined by adoption of the concept of 'personal information' as the gateway to this environment. If one assumes that, in order to be protected, data must relate to an identifiable individual, then one assumes that the only data about which relevant preferences may be expressed is data that is 'about someone'. Not only is this a faulty starting point, but it can lead to the adoption of protective mechanisms that are themselves incomplete. Foremost amongst these is the reliance upon either 'ask or anonymise' in relation to personal data as mechanisms to protect privacy.

If data is interpreted to be *an individual's* information, then that individual becomes the natural reference point when assessing any interference with privacy. There are, however, a number of challenges posed by this analysis – particularly, in the context of fluid interpretive frameworks – and any reliance upon consent to protect privacy should be sensitive to these limitations.

First of all, the individual that the information may be said to be 'about' – described in earlier analysis as a 'primary data subject' – might be in no place to assess reliably the risks to privacy that a particular piece of information poses. This is in no way to dismiss her opinion; it is rather to recognise that her view is unavoidably limited. When information is recorded as part of a larger dataset, then there may be no way for anyone to anticipate reliably exactly what interpretations will be placed upon that data in the future or what kinds of association it will facilitate. This is a particularly pertinent possibility in the context of genetic data recorded for future, as yet undefined, research uses.[5] Reliance upon this means of protection can, therefore, leave certain preferences unconsidered, unexpressed and incapable of consideration.

Use of a *broad* consent might go some way to address such concerns but it cannot guarantee adequate representation of the full range of relevant preferences.[6] This is partly because a broad consent is an unavoidably blunt instrument: even if all preferences regarding future possible associations could be known, then – assuming they provoke different preferences in a particular individual – they would have to be collected together and balanced before one could decide on the relative merits of a broad consent. However, the chances of being able to communicate effectively all of the possibilities regarding future uses of data – and the associations that might provoke – are, in any case, extremely slight.

If the responsibility to provide information about intended uses of data can be discharged by a one-time communication, e.g. when data is collected from a primary data subject, then the information available to inform any broad consent – and, therefore, to inform any analysis of relevant risks and potential benefits – will be especially limited.[7] As we have seen, the responsibility to provide information to a data subject on the purposes of processing, at least as required by the Directive, is not expressly an ongoing responsibility. In such circumstances, a broad consent relies more upon ongoing trust than upon voluntariness.[8] The importance of designing regulatory mechanisms deserving of this trust is barely diminished if the responsibility to provide emerging information about research uses of particular data were to be recognised to be ongoing. This is because of the compromise that a broad consent might represent on behalf of an individual (withdrawal of data from a research database is a crude, and not necessarily an entirely effective, way of fine-tuning one's consent to particular research uses of genetic data), but also

---

[5] Kaye, 'Abandoning informed consent', 120–32.   [6] *Ibid.*, 130–5.

[7] If the data is obtained directly from a data subject, then the information must be provided at the time that the data is collected (Article 10). Alternative time frames are specified if the data is collected via a third party (Article 11). In neither circumstance, however, does it appear that there is a continuing responsibility to provide additional information when it becomes available. For more see M. J. Taylor, 'Health research, data protection, and the public interest in notification', *Medical Law Review* 19(2) (2011), 267–303.

[8] S. Kristinsson and V. Arnason, 'Informed consent and human genetic database research', in M. Hayry, R. Chadwick, V. Arnason and G. Arnason, *The Ethics and Governance of Human Genetic Databases* (Cambridge University Press, 2007), 214.

because of the fact that other people's preferences might also be engaged by research use of genetic data. Reliance upon an *individual's* consent, whether specific or broad, may fail to take into account the preferences of these other people.

Reliance upon consent depends upon there being an individual, proxy or alternative body, competent and capable, to provide consent. If *multiple* individuals are potentially associable with particular data, then consent as a way to account for relevant preferences is problematised. It is difficult to identify reliable methods of obtaining 'group consent' and the difficulties in representing 'the group' in a consistent, constant and replicable fashion are legion.[9] Of course, recognising that multiple individuals may be associated with any given data does not necessarily dilute any claim that each has to express a preference in relation to that data. It simply draws out the possibility that individual preferences may conflict, and that any system intended to account for the broadest range of preferences must be capable of adjudicating conflicting preferences. The use of consent as a mechanism to protect privacy does not deny the need for substantive conflicts raised by uses of data to be resolved, but it can obscure it.[10] This is not to undermine the significance of consent. It is, however, to try and place its significance in context.

Consent cannot alone determine the appropriate route through conflicting preferences and alternate priorities. It cannot step outside of itself as a mechanism for protecting privacy to offer any indication when it need not be sought or when dissent ought to be ignored. Roger Brownsword describes consent as a 'procedural' rather than a 'substantive' form of justification and notes that it cannot comprehensively justify an action as such:

In a community of rights, consent functions as procedural justification, giving the recipient of the consent (B) a complete answer to the consenting agent (A); no wrong is done to the consenting (authorising) agent (A) by the recipient (B); but it does not follow that the recipient agent (B) does no wrong to third-party agents (such as C). In the absence of consent, a wrong will be done to agents whose rights are violated even if, all things considered, the wrongdoing can be substantively justified as the lesser of two evils.[11]

Brownsword makes two important points. The first is that acting in the absence of consent, when background rights are engaged in such a way

---

[9] Davis, 'Groups, communities, and contested identities in genetic research'.
[10] R. Brownsword, 'Consent in data protection law: privacy, fair procesing, and confidentiality', in S. Gutwirth, Y. Poullet, P. de Hert, C. de Terwangne and S. Nouwt (eds.), *Reinventing Data Protection?* (Dordrecht: Springer, 2009), 83–110.
[11] *Ibid.*

that proceeding without consent represents an infringement of an individual's rights, is a wrong to that individual. In other words, if acting without consent is a wrong – and there will be occasions when acting without consent is a wrong – then *consent should be sought*. However, *even on those occasions when acting without consent is a wrong*, that wrong may, sometimes, be justified. In such circumstances, it can *only* be justified when it is both *necessary* and *proportionate* to do that wrong in the broader context: 'it is the lesser of two evils'.

The second important point is that, even if consent is obtained, this itself is not sufficient to discharge all responsibilities. An individual might still do wrong to a third party. We note that it is not only the recipient of the consent who might do such wrong (by failing to respect the rights of a third party); the consenting agent might offer consent to processing without due regard for the interests of others. These points reflect two fallacies proposed by Beyleveld and Brownsword in earlier work: the Fallacy of Necessity (where there is no consent, there must be a wrong), and the Fallacy of Sufficiency (where there is consent, there cannot be wrong).[12]

Both fallacies would be present in any claim that consent alone can provide comprehensive privacy protection to research use of genetic data. An insistence upon informed consent as an absolute requirement would, at times, frustrate research without any judgment of proportionality. One must consider, even on these occasions when acting without consent does represent a wrong to a person, whether that wrong can be justified – including *within* the context of privacy protection – by reference to a public-interest decision-making process that takes into account the broadest range of (privacy) interests engaged by the research use in question. There certainly are circumstances in which it would be impossible, or entirely impracticable, to gain consent before using genetic data for particular research purposes. This is true *even if* one imagines there to be only a single data subject associable with a particular record of information. Examples would include the research use of previously collected data where the opportunities for contact with data subjects have been lost or very large-scale (e.g. whole population) datasets for which the administrative burden of seeking and recording consent prospectively would be overwhelming. They would also include research uses where dissent could be anticipated and that dissent would frustrate the research (e.g. by leaving research underpowered or by introducing unacceptable levels of bias).

---

[12] D. Beyleveld and R. Brownsword, *Consent in the Law* (Oxford: Hart Publishing, 2007).

There are deficiencies in the current regulatory framework when it comes to clarifying when the harm done by proceeding without consent can be justified. For example, the Directive does not provide any indication of when *research* use of genetic data in the absence of consent, or in the face of active dissent, might constitute 'the lesser of two evils': it does not even require consideration of the possibility that transactions involving research uses of genetic data might be protected as part of the protection of particular privacy norms.

Failing to *require* expressly that Member States ensure that domestic law accommodates the possibility of non-consented research use of genetic data being justified, when both necessary and proportionate, may be said to have encouraged the fallacy of necessity. This cannot represent proper privacy protection, because privacy is about norms of access as well as separation. Again, it must be emphasised that this is not to undermine the importance of consent. If an individual's right to privacy is engaged, then to fail to obtain consent may be to do her a wrong. In such cases, it is only appropriate when it is both a *necessary* and a *proportionate* response to protect a more significant (privacy) interest. In this context, it is, however, important to remember that both the (primary) data subject and the researcher may themselves have particular responsibilities to protect the interests of third parties. The obtaining of consent from a (primary) data subject by a researcher does not discharge these responsibilities to third parties.

In this respect, as well as the fallacy of necessity, the Directive may also encourage the fallacy of sufficiency. It suggests that explicit consent may legitimise the processing of personal genetic data with insufficient additional requirement for the interests of third parties, or the interests of the (primary) data subject (beyond their interest in consent), to be taken into account. In the context of research uses of genetic data, relevant third parties include other individuals to whom the data relates, but it also includes the interests of researchers and those who may be affected by the results of the research. The interests of the primary data subject extend to those engaged by possible future associations with the data. These responsibilities cannot be fully discharged by consent but nor can they be discharged through the anonymisation of data.

Anonymisation

Just as consent cannot provide a magic bullet to prevent privacy infringements, neither can the anonymisation of data. The limits of anonymisation as a method of protecting privacy are particularly clear if one understands privacy to be defined by norms of exclusivity, and then one considers the preferences regarding access that have been, and might be, applied to research use of genetic data. If protecting privacy is about preserving the exclusivity that particular norms imply, then such exclusivity cannot be maintained if significant information flows are not even acknowledged by the gateway regulatory concept: states of separation cannot be moderated if particular types of relevant information transaction remain unaccounted for within the regulatory scheme.

Data currently held in a context that associates it with *only* a particular identifiable individual is not the only data to which preferences might apply. In fact, if data is already held in a context that associates it with a particular individual, then – within that context – the identifying information is not itself disclosive and may be of relatively little concern. It is only as data is shifted across interpretive contexts, and identifiers enable fresh associations, that *new* data is disclosed and associated with particular individuals. Crucially, in such circumstances, the data that enables the linkage need not apply to *only one particular* individual. Through joining together pieces of information that might relate to more than one person, a unique portfolio of data may be created. It is extremely difficult to anticipate which data will enable such linkage and it is certainly not just the common identifiers that might enable it.

While individual identifiability (or association) with specific *recorded* information can, in certain circumstances, be extremely important, and the significance of the type of transaction that *is* regulated by the concept of personal data is not to be underestimated, preferences for exclusivity are not limited to data currently associated with particular identifiable individuals. As the *future* association of even anonymous data with particular individuals or groups can be anticipated, those individuals or groups might also have their own particular preferences regarding who has access to what data under what circumstances. As we move towards the automatic extraction of anonymous data from massive datasets on an industrial scale, any failure even to register this type of process within a regulatory framework is particularly worrying.

Implications for reform: short term

What follows is a number of suggestions for regulatory reform. They do not represent a complete regulatory agenda. That would require a different book. The purpose of this one has simply been to try and demonstrate the incompatibility of the concept of personal information with a comprehensive protection of informational privacy. This analysis does, however, prompt some thoughts on how current protections might be extended or amended and a few of these thoughts are contained below. They are loosely organised according to the time frame within which they might conceivably be achieved. In the short term, there are at least three things that could be done within the context of the existing European regulatory framework that would improve the protection of informational privacy. They might require action at the national level, but such action is within the current competence of Member States of the European Union.

1   Extend the class of data subjects

Data with significance for others, in terms of patterns and preferences regarding the exclusivity of that data, should be used in ways that acknowledge and respect that significance. Certainly, the possibility of multiple data subjects should be recognised. The lack of clarity within the Directive about the relationship between 'data in common' and 'personal data' is lamentable. Family members have been previously recognised to have a legal interest in the processing of genetic data that is held in common[13] but the nature of any right that they might enjoy in the context of data protection is unclear. The Article 29 Working Party recognises it as an 'alternative' that they might be recognised as data subjects in their own right, but a controversial and difficult one. I have argued that difficulties are, in part, currently due to the failure of Member States to meet their responsibilities (under Article 13 of the Directive) and to restrict clearly the scope of the responsibilities of data controllers and the rights of (primary) data subjects provided for by the Directive in order to protect the fundamental rights and freedoms of others. If they did so, then they might create national frameworks capable of providing appropriate protection for all.

Harmonisation would require countries to co-ordinate national activity and, admittedly, this seems unlikely. The possibility of undesirable inconsistency remaining (or even increasing) across different Member States is just one of the significant problems associated with recognising multiple data subjects (at least in the short term). However, these are the problems that follow from recognising that multiple individuals have interests at stake, and may have preferences regarding the operative norms of exclusivity, which are capable of conflicting. This is an inevitable, and at times even desirable, consequence of a legal regime recognising that fundamental rights and freedoms are to be enjoyed by all. It would

---

[13] *Ragnhildur Guðmundsdóttir* v. *The State of Iceland.* Thursday 27 November 2003. No.151/2003. See also Chapter 4, note 50.

be an understatement to describe as unfortunate a response to the problem that simply placed an entire category of persons outside of the protective regime established by the Directive, and denied that they have any interests in data, *even where* to recognise it would introduce no conflict. The existence of an unprotected class of persons is undesirable and inconsistent with the Directive's stated aim of protecting fundamental rights and freedoms, in particular privacy.

However, if the rights of secondary data subjects were to be recognised, then they must also be qualified by appropriate respect for the rights of others. Such others include not only other (primary and secondary) data subjects, but also additional third parties, including researchers and data controllers where their interests and preferences would be impacted. With such qualification they should, however, be able to exercise appropriate rights of access to genetic data, and also to object to data being processed, where a failure to exercise such rights would have the effect of unjustifiably infringing their fundamental rights and freedoms. The responsibility to notify persons of such processing, again appropriately qualified, should also be recognised in order to permit meaningful exercise of the rights to access and to object to processing where it is justified. The fact that such circumstances may be limited by legitimate considerations of impracticability is no reason not to account for their possibility.

2   *Anonymisation as a process*

The Data Protection Directive provides a long list of actions and activities that constitute the 'processing' of 'personal data'. 'Anonymisation' of data does not occur in that list. Even if there is a clear intention to anonymise data for research purposes *and that intention is in the mind of the person at the time they obtain the data* (whether obtained directly from the data subject or via a third party), there is no express requirement that the intention to anonymise the data, or the purposes of the processing intended for the anonymised data, needs to be notified to the data subject. This omission is unjustifiable.

While an argument can be constructed that such an intention would need to be notified as part of 'fair and lawful processing'[14] there is English case law to oppose such an argument. In *R* v. *Department of*

---

[14] That is, if there is an intention to anonymise data and use it for a research purpose, then a failure to notify of this may deceive or mislead persons of the purposes for which their data will be used (contrary to the first data protection principle).

Health ex parte *Source Informatics* Simon Brown LJ supported the 'common-sense' he perceived in counsel's argument that

> Council Directive (95/46/EC) can have no more application to the operation of anonymising data than to the use or disclosure of anonymous data (which, of course, by definition is not 'personal data' and to which, therefore, it is conceded that the Directive has no application).[15]

The reasoning appeared to be that a process of anonymisation could not be said to jeopardise an individual's interest in privacy. That claim is inconsistent with the concept of privacy advanced here as norms of exclusivity.[16] Even if this notion of privacy were to be rejected, and one that reduced privacy to the simple protection of identity were to be embraced, then a failure to notify people that there was an intention to anonymise their data, and to use that data for specific purposes, would still undermine the *expectation* that people will be asked before their data are used for research purposes.[17] This is an expectation that extends, for some people at least, to include uses of anonymised data.[18] If this is their preference regarding access, then failing to account for it within the regulatory framework undermines that framework's claims to legitimacy.

This responsibility to notify individuals of research uses of anonymised data might also, of course, be trumped if it should represent a disproportionate interference with a more significant interest – as might the responsibility to continue to notify of research uses of data (which

---

[15] [2001] QB 424, [44].

[16] See also D. Townend, M. J. Taylor, J. Wright and D. Wickins-Drazilova, 'Privacy interests in biobanking: a preliminary view on a European perspective', in J. Kaye and M. Stranger, *Principles and Practice in Biobank Governance* (Aldershot: Ashgate, 2009).

[17] If data is not collected expressly for research purposes, such as where it is collected in the healthcare context, there is some debate about what would constitute a 'reasonable expectation', but there is evidence that patients do not in fact currently expect their personal health information to be shared for research purposes without consultation. See, for example, The Bolton Research Group, 'Patients' knowledge and expectations of confidentiality in primary health care: a quantitative study' *British Journal of General Practice* 50 (2000), 901–2; Research Capability Programme Consultation Team, 'Summary of responses to the consultation on the additional uses of patient data', NHS Connecting for Health (27 November 2009) www.dh.gov.uk/prod_consum_dh/groups/dh_digitalassets/documents/digitalasset/dh_110715.pdf.; V. Armstrong, J. Barnett, H. Cooper, M. Monkman, J. Moran-Ellis and R. Shepherd, *Public Perspectives on the Governance of Biomedical Research: A Qualitative Study in a Deliberative Context* (London: Wellcome Trust, 2007); IpSOS MORI/MRC, *The Use of Personal Health Information in Medical Research* (Medical Research Council, 2007). But see also K. Hoeyer, B. O. Olofsson, T. Mjorndal and N. Lynoe, 'The ethics of research using biobanks: reasons to question the importance attributed to informed consent', *Archived of Internal Medicine* 165 (2005), 97–100.

[18] Research Capability Programme Consultation Team, 'Summary of responses to the consultation on the additional uses of patient data', 6.

should also be recognised), if there are changes to previously notified purposes, whether data are anonymised or not. Such arguments of necessity, and proportionality, should, however, be run in the context of a public-interest argument capable of offering reasonable justification for not acceding to particular preferences in case of challenge. To oppose any such responsibility, on the grounds of a wish to avoid burdening researchers, is to ignore the fact that, at present, we have a situation that fails expressly to place *any* responsibility upon researchers to provide relevant information to data subjects about the processing of anonymised data, even where there would be only a trivial cost or inconvenience involved. Although hopefully unlikely, this does theoretically allow for the possibility that researchers, intending to extract de-identified data from a research record obtained in identifiable form, and suspecting that consent for such processing would be withheld, can deliberately conceal this intended use of de-identified data at the time it is collected.

3   *Identifiability is context dependent*

There should be greater recognition of the context-dependent nature of identifiability. Recognising this would have a number of advantages. Not least of these is that, if appropriate structural, organisational, technical and/or contractual measures are taken effectively to prevent such contextualisation, then data should be considered to be effectively anonymised (i.e. treated as non-identifiable in those contexts).[19] This would allow researchers, when the processing of effectively anonymised data was compatible with proper privacy protection, to retain potentially identifiable data within research datasets, if the relevant contexts were effectively controlled to prevent data being associated with a particular individual. At the same time, it would make clear that, if control were to be lost over context (either intentionally, e.g. through publication, or unintentionally, e.g. through security breach), then even data considered to be anonymous by the researcher might in some cases be identifiable by others in other contexts. This should encourage a precautionary approach towards the collection of data that might enable identification in other contexts, but one that was proportionate to the possibility of control over context being lost. It would remove the imperative to strip certain identifiers from records, even though they might be useful in research terms and their retention might also be

[19] M. Chapman, T. Cresswell, C. Dezateux, N. Khan, D. Neal and M. Taylor, *Report of the Research Database Working Group of the NIGB* (London: NIGB, 2010), 6.

consistent with the privacy preferences of the contributors, simply because they enabled (non-disclosive) identification in the contexts in which they are held. Controlling the *contexts* within which more valuable research data resides (to prevent unwanted future associations) is preferable to stripping data of particular (common) identifiers and then losing control over the contexts entirely. There are ways of establishing such control (e.g. through holding potential identifiers – of any kind – in separate databases and only bringing them together temporarily as necessary for particular processing), and access agreements with other researchers should provide for such precautionary approaches to the processing of any genetic data. It is important to remember when data is allowed to move between different interpretive contexts that future (unwanted) associations can be made – and privacy can be compromised – even through the processing of data that is currently understood to be anonymous.

Implications for reform: medium term

The medium-term ambition must be to develop mechanisms to account for the full range of privacy interests engaged by research using genetic data in a transparent way. There are at least four things that might help to achieve this ambition:

1   Extend the class of data subjects

If the class of data subjects were to be extended in the short term through individual action by Member States (as suggested above), then the medium-term ambition must be for such extension to be recognised within the context of the Directive itself. A more comprehensive consideration of secondary data subjects might also create standing for their recognition even where there is no primary data subject. One of the ways that individuals could be legally empowered to challenge the processing of genetic data perceived by them to be capable of affecting their privacy is through data protection law. Any short-term change would have to be made within the context of the current law, with its requirement that data relates to *an identifiable* individual. In the medium term it is possible to imagine how the regulatory framework could be extended to apply when data does *not* apply to *an identifiable individual*. In cases where data relates to individuals *as members of an identifiable group*, then the data may be considered to be anonymous at the individual level, but the capacity for future association with individuals as members of those groups might still be demonstrated. Extending the concept of data subject in this direction, with all the caveats mentioned above regarding proportionality and practicability, would recognise the significance of data for members of a group, even though they may not be identifiable as individuals. It would recognise that anonymisation at the individual level does not offer complete protection for an individual's privacy.

2   *Clarify the relationship between consent and research*

The lack of clarity regarding when researchers need, and do not need, to obtain consent to use genetic data for research purposes could be most usefully addressed through reform of the Directive. At the very least, clarification is needed on how those responsible for interpreting the Directive understand the relationship between consent and research use of genetic data, and this would ideally be co-ordinated so as to be consistent across Europe. As the processing of genetic data without consent engages an individual's right to a private life, as established by Article 8(1) of the European Convention, then processing without consent must be both necessary and proportionate given the level of interference and the significance of the legitimate aim pursued. If, however, it is both *necessary* and *proportionate* – owing to the impossibility of gaining consent, gaining consent requiring a disproportionate effort, or consent undermining the validity of the research itself – then it should be made clear that non-consented research use of genetic data *can* be justified *if* the research itself is sufficiently valuable (to justify that judgment of proportionality). It would be useful for these requirements to be unpacked within the context of the Directive with the process expressly described through which both necessity and proportionality might be judged. Such a process might involve approval by Research Ethics Committees. Alternatively, the provisions made within the Directive for prior checking of particular processing when it poses specific risks to the rights and freedoms of data subjects might be amended so as to expressly apply to research uses.[20] Currently, it is not easy to see how these two alternatives might be joined within a single process of research approval. The authority responsible for supervising the application of data protection law within a particular territory[21] is not necessarily integrated into the national systems for research governance. This may be an unfortunate disconnect for a researcher seeking clarity on when she might process personal genetic data without a particular research participant's consent. Those responsible for administering the national

---

[20] Recital 54; Article 20.   [21] See Article 28(1).

research governance process might at least ensure that they provide useful examples, both of when genetic data will be considered to be personal data and also when, and how, it might be processed without consent, that are consistent with the positions taken by both relevant Research Ethics Committees and also supervisory authorities for data protection.

3   Improved research infrastructure

In a field already characterised by high levels of uncertainty and frustration, some of my suggestions might sound alarming. If we are to recognise a broader range of privacy interests engaged by research using genetic data, then we need to devise practicable, and therefore appropriately resourced, means of doing so. It should not fall to researchers alone to devise or supply the research infrastructure that enables proper protection of privacy. Shifts in the regulatory environment might actually work to the advantage of both data subjects and researchers. For example, at the moment, the bright-line distinction that the law seeks to draw between 'identifiable' and 'anonymised' data not only is artificial, but also discourages any move towards identifiability (which might be desirable from a research perspective). Recognising more consistent obligations in relation to all genetic data may remove some of the barriers to contextual shifts (e.g. through data linkage) towards more identifiable contexts that would be advantageous from a research perspective.[22]

4   Samples

Biological samples should be recognised to be personal data in appropriate circumstances. Such circumstances would include, as a minimum, that a sample had already been removed from the human body. Until, and unless, a sample has been removed there are good reasons for recognising biological material to fall under a separate, and often more restrictive, regulatory regime. However, if a sample has been (lawfully) removed from a human body, and there is an intention to subject that sample to analysis yielding information that might be related to an identifiable person or group, then there is every reason to regard that sample as constituting *personal data*. It does not, until subject to analysis, yield any information, but to rest a regulatory distinction on that

---

[22] For more see Taylor, 'Health research, data protection, and the public interest in notification'.

difference alone would be to ascribe interpretive pedigree with undue significance. What should, wherever practicable, be taken into account are the possibilities of interpretive potential and the resulting conse-quences, in terms of the preferred norms of exclusivity, for the manage-ment of the association between data and persons in the future.

Implications for reform: long term

Even if the term 'personal data' is extended in the ways suggested above in the short and medium term, this does not address the fundamental incompatibility between the idea of personal information and informa-tional privacy. In the long term, the ambition must be to move beyond the idea that a regulatory framework dependent entirely upon the idea of 'personal information' is capable of maintaining the norms of exclusivity associated with genetic data. As an organising idea, it has the benefit that, intuitively, it appears to have the virtue of being both relatively contained as a concept but also sufficiently flexible to capture any data associated with an individual in a relevant way. This is a fiction. The illusion of containment can only be provided by an emphasis upon interpretive pedigree. The possibility to associate data with an individual in a relevant way is provided by interpretive potential. While 'interpretive pedigree' can tie data to a particular individual, 'interpretive potential' cannot.

There may be much to be gained from recognising the limits of the concept of 'personal data' and *at the same time* putting in place mechan-isms capable of *accounting* for a broader range of interests in a more transparent way. An important step towards such a system might be achieved by a relatively simple acceptance. If one adopted the idea of 'personal data' and actually embraced the idea of *data* rather than infor-mation, and understood the appellation 'personal' to indicate potential rather than pedigree, then one would have an organising idea that *was* capable, in principle at least, of applying to the full range of circum-stances in which individuals (as individuals and as members of groups) were associated with data. Personal data, rather than personal information, might actually provide a way forward after all.

Recognising the limits of the currently regulatory framework is cer-tainly not to suggest that protection for particular *norms* of exclusivity would be better achieved by better *preventing* access to data. Exclusivity is maintained by ensuring *appropriate* access is protected. Research use of genetic data is valuable and the unjustified frustration of valuable research activity cannot be consistent with the normative standards underlying privacy protection. The aspiration must be for research to be subject only to proportionate protection in a transparent way. This does, however, require research itself to be more transparent with regard to its uses of de-identified and aggregate data. Unless decision-making processes can transparently take into account the interests that people have in data that might be associated with them, we cannot expect people to trust that the decisions taken are justifiable in the light of such interests: we cannot expect any reliance that their interests have been accounted for within the system. In this case, we risk the legitimacy of the decision-making process itself as well as the research that it approves.

The necessity and proportionality of any interference with particular preferences can only be assessed if *all* relevant interests are taken into account when determining appropriate uses of genetic data in the context of 'proper' privacy protection. The regulatory challenges faced by an attempt to achieve appropriate protection for the norms of exclusivity associated with genetic data are, undoubtedly, considerable. Meaning and reason are to be attached to information flows with significance to many different individuals who may have many conflicting, and at times conflicted, priorities. Some of these individuals are likely to remain ignorant of the existence of the information and may be in no position themselves to participate actively in any decision-making process. This does not mean, however, that their preferences can be safely ignored.

There is a public interest in maintaining a legitimate regulatory structure and this will only be achieved if relevant interests are transparently accounted for within relevant decision-making processes. As David Townend puts it:

Public interest can, and I would argue must, be conceived as a part of the protection of fundamental rights and freedoms, and very much as an essential part of that regime of protection, rather than as a necessary departure from it.[23]

The public interest in privacy protection requires that one *ought* to protect privacy – and respect preferences for access or non-access to genetic data – wherever possible. If we are to secure a protection of privacy capable of sustaining public trust and confidence, through to the realisation of the benefits of research use of genetic data in the long term, then the regulatory process must be capable of both accounting for the preferences that people value and adjudicating between them in a way that they can accept as defensible. This involves ensuring that mechanisms are in place to allow people to challenge decisions on processing to

---

[23] D. M. R. Townend, 'Overriding data subjects' rights in the public interest', in D. Beyleveld, D. Townend, S. Rouillé-Mirza and J. Wright (eds.), *The Data Protection Directive and Medical Research Across Europe* (Aldershot: Ashgate, 2004), 89–101.

ensure that it is consistent with the public interest in proper privacy protection. The concept of personal data, at least as currently defined and operationalised, does not provide scope for mechanisms accessible by all those who may consider the processing of genetic data to infringe their privacy.

Index

Wherever possible in the case of topics with many references, these have either been divided into sub-topics or only the most significant discussions of the topic are listed. Because the entire work is about 'genetic data' the use of this term (and certain others which occur constantly throughout the book) as an entry point has been minimised. Information will be found under the corresponding detailed topics.